IMAGES
of America

PULASKI COUNTY

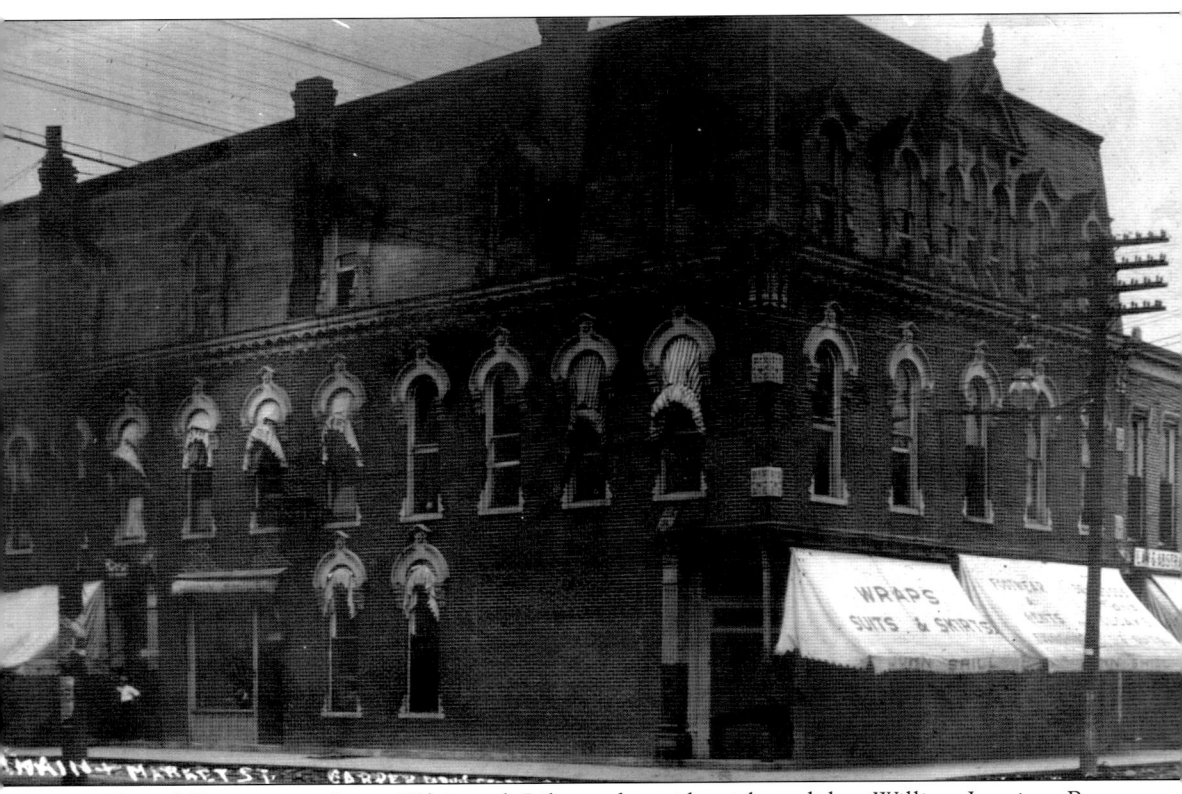

Famed Hoosier poet James Whitcomb Riley and presidential candidate William Jennings Bryan once appeared at the Vurpillat Opera House in Winamac. Constructed in 1882, the building was designed by James Rhodes in a late-Victorian architectural style called Second Empire mansard. In May 1883, the local newspaper reported the "large and brilliantly lighted hall [was] partly filled with the beauty and chivalry of Winamac," who attended the opera house's opening to see a performance of the *Spectre Bridegroom*. "Our people all take pride in the possession of so fine an opera house," the newspaper account boasted. Indeed for the next 30 years, the Vurpillat Opera House literally took center stage in the social life of Winamac-area citizens. It was seldom closed. In August 1999, the Pulaski County Historical Society took possession of the opera house and began the painstaking process of restoring the old building, shown here in about 1910. (Sara Slaven.)

On the cover: The heart of Pulaski County has always been its farmland, which is not just a source of income but also a way of life. This vintage farm scene dates to about 1894 and was taken at the Joseph P. Gilsinger farm south of the village of Pulaski in Indian Creek Township. Although the people in the photograph are not identified, the picture appears to have been set up to display the farm horses and equipment—no doubt prophetic as Gilsinger went into partnership to open a general mercantile business in 1899, which eventually evolved into a John Deere dealership. Over 100 years later, the business continues under family management. (Paul and Brenda Gilsinger.)

IMAGES of America
PULASKI COUNTY

Karen Clem Fritz

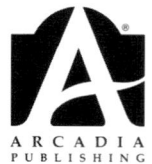

Copyright © 2009 by Karen Clem Fritz
ISBN 978-0-7385-6118-9

Published by Arcadia Publishing
Charleston SC, Chicago IL, Portsmouth NH, San Francisco CA

Printed in the United States of America

Library of Congress Catalog Card Number: 2008935191

For all general information contact Arcadia Publishing at:
Telephone 843-853-2070
Fax 843-853-0044
E-mail sales@arcadiapublishing.com
For customer service and orders:
Toll-Free 1-888-313-2665

Visit us on the Internet at www.arcadiapublishing.com

To my husband, Scott, and children Kacie, Andrew, and Elizabeth, who fill my life with love and laughter, and to my parents, Wayne and Wilma Clem, for their encouragement every step of the way.

Contents

Foreword   6

Acknowledgments   7

Introduction   8

1.   How It Once Looked   9

2.   People Met along the Way   45

3.   Going about Business   71

4.   Putting Time Off to Good Use   105

Foreword

There is something special about being born and raised in small-town Indiana. We native Hoosiers find it hard to purge from our minds those experiences, the cast of characters, and the images of life here. Yes, there are similar communities across the land, but in 30 years of originating broadcasts from towns in every state in America, I have found nothing quite like rural Indiana. It is home. It sure feels good to be here.

Driving along Route 14 coming into Winamac, it is easy to forget that you are less than two hours from Chicago. I have found that regardless of the season, it looks pretty much like a tourism bureau photograph of rural Indiana. Something about Pulaski County always makes me want to "get lost" here for a few hours . . . or for a few days.

On autumn afternoons here, I have shared the roads with farmers, their trucks loaded with the new crop. I kept the window down to hear them run though the gears. I have been caught in a traffic jam of the crowd leaving the gym on a January night. I had the window up and could still tell someone had won. And I have enjoyed that remarkable feeling on a morning in June when someone actually waved at me here. Yes, they waved. I checked the window, checked the lights, and checked the wipers. Something had to be wrong.

In her collection of Pulaski County photographs, Karen Clem Fritz reminds us of those small-town Indiana experiences. She reminds us that businesses have blossomed, and many have disappeared. She helps us recall that there have been bountiful years for the local growers as well as some tough seasons. She tweaks our memory about the big local news stories and at least one of national scope.

You might want to get a good magnifying glass if you do not already own one. You will, I predict, revisit many of these photographs in the days ahead. Upon further examination, you *will* see something you never saw before. And it is possible—in fact, I think it is likely—that no matter how long you have been around these parts, you will learn something about Pulaski County and its people that you never fully appreciated before now.

Max Armstrong, agriculture broadcaster
Chicago (for now), Hoosier (always)

Acknowledgments

Thanks go to the Pulaski County Historical Society for its determined dedication to the preservation of local history; Alan McPherson who recommended this project; my business partner Brad Conn; my college classmate and pal Max Armstrong; Pulaski County Public Library; Natalie Federer of the Pulaski County Historical Society Museum; Sue Risner of the Medaryville History Museum; Tom Keller and Ruth Zehner of Monterey; the Monterey-Tippecanoe Public Library; the *Francesville Tribune*; the Francesville-Salem Township Public Library; my early mentor, the late Janet Gorrell Meyer; the late William L. Starr; Betty Lou Hughes, editor of the *Pulaski County Sesquicentennial* history; genealogist and historian Janet Onken; and all who generously shared photographs. Thanks especially goes to Pulaski County historian Lynda Irving for her amazing knowledge, wit, and enthusiasm.

The images in this volume that appear courtesy of the Pulaski County Historical Society Museum will be designated as PCHS Museum.

INTRODUCTION

Pulaski County is rarely a destination. It is seldom on anyone's way to somewhere. It has pretty much always been that way.

Many consider it a nostalgic destination—adults who left after high school for more exciting places return with their children to visit grandma. They reminisce around the dinner table, recalling old tractors, prize pigs at the county fair, going to town on Saturday nights, and, of course, the basketball teams that *almost* won coveted championships.

Pulaski County is not only a place for fond memories. Families who carve out their lives here face challenges unknown to their city cousins, but they also enjoy a wholesome lifestyle envied by those stuck in the urban traffic jams.

The land that now forms Pulaski County was ceded by the Potawatomi Indians to the United States on October 26, 1832, in a treaty signed in Rochester in neighboring Fulton County. It was another 10 years before the Native Americans relocated, but before the ink dried on the treaty, white trappers, hunters, and squatters moved into the new territory from settlements along the Wabash River. Crude cabins appeared along the area waterways. The state legislature approved an 18-by-24-mile area to be known as Pulaski County in 1835, but four years passed before the county was formally organized on May 6, 1839, when a group of men met in a log cabin and designated "Winnemack" as the county seat. Winamac was named after a Potawatomi Indian chief who lived in the area in the early 1800s. The county was named after Gen. Casimir Pulaski, a Polish-born hero who fought in the American Revolution. The county has four incorporated towns, Winamac, Francesville, Medaryville, and Monterey, and several villages, including Star City, Pulaski, Denham, Ripley, Beardstown, and Thornhope.

Pulaski County is northern Indiana's most rural and isolated county. The population today numbers almost exactly what it did 100 years ago. Pulaski's children are reared to practice morals and manners, responsibility and respect. Pulaski history and culture revolve around agriculture and small-town life. School and church events provide entertainment. Simple pleasures are found in social and service clubs, street fairs, ball games, and picnics on the riverbank. A pioneer spirit continues to thrive here—a rich and increasingly rare lifestyle that produces solid citizens who credit their success to their roots.

This is by no means a complete historical work. It is, rather, a sampling of the people, places, and events that have shaped Pulaski County—a place where residents today are familiar with the latest electronics, national politics, and international commerce but live in an American rural treasure land where elements of yesterday remain as much a lifestyle as a memory.

One
How It Once Looked

In the spring of 1881, a small notice appeared in the local paper announcing that the barns on the old Carper house property, located at the main intersection of the county seat, Winamac, had been rented to Henry Baker for a livery and feed stable. Across the street on the public square, county business was quietly conducted in the modest Civil War–era brick courthouse. Another 14 years would pass before the present ornate limestone courthouse was built.

Elsewhere downtown, construction was booming. Wood-frame structures were giving way to sturdy brick buildings. On the west side of Market Street, the spectacular brick Keller Block and the Frain Hotel were just completed and opened for business.

A short block away, mercantile businessman Joseph D. Vurpillat, who operated his little store on Pearl Street, was dreaming and developing plans for a three-story brick block, which would house his store plus offices on the second floor and a public hall on the top story.

In January 1882, a much larger notice appeared in the newspaper announcing that Vurpillat planned to construct his building on the site of the "late Carper House." Throughout the next year, county residents followed the chronicles on the progress of the Vurpillat building's construction—from the digging of the foundation by the "shovel brigade" and the work of the brick masons and plasterers to the slating of the roof and the arrival of the plate glass for the windows (at an impressive cost of almost $1,000). In January 1883, Vurpillat moved his store into the new building, while the Citizens' Bank joined him in the adjacent new first-floor space that fronted Market Street. In the meantime, work continued on finishing the office spaces on the second floor and the opera house on the top floor. Eventually, doctors, dentists, chiropractors, lawyers, and photographers used the offices on the second floor.

Similar scenes were playing out across the towns of Pulaski County in the last years of the 19th century and the opening years of the one that followed. Some historians have referred to this age as Indiana's golden years. These are the days that grandpa and grandma remembered.

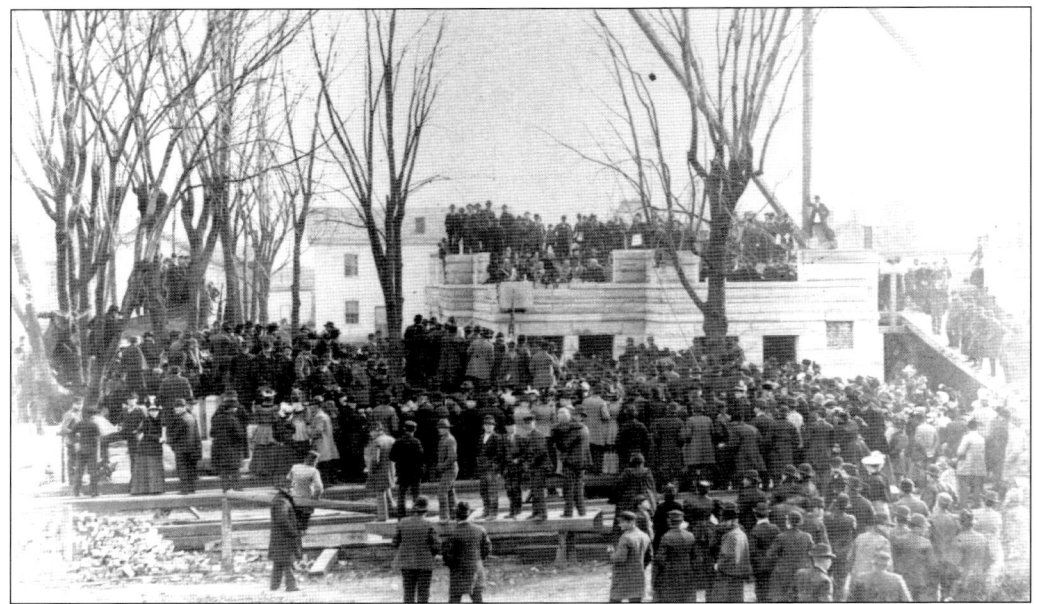

A ceremony to lay the cornerstone of the new courthouse in Winamac drew county residents to the town square on November 27, 1894. Earlier that year, county officials made the decision to replace the brick courthouse completed in 1862 during the Civil War. The county's first courthouse was a wood-frame building constructed in 1849, 10 years after the county was founded. (PCHS Museum.)

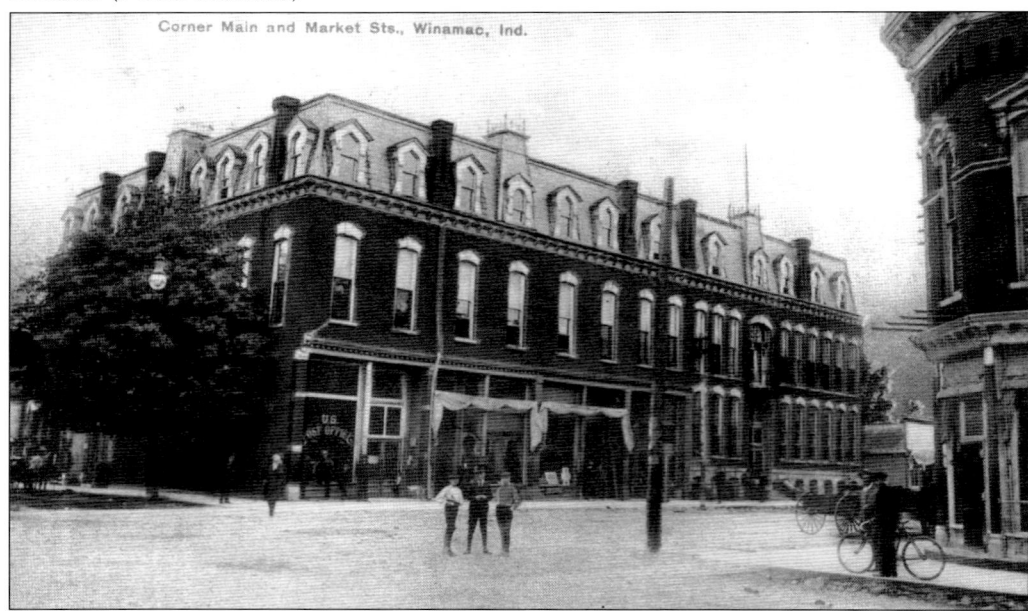

The Frain Hotel, shown here in about 1907, stood proudly across Market Street from the new courthouse. In addition to the hotel accommodations, over the decades the building also housed a barbershop, a drugstore, a post office, an undertaker, and a hardware store. Before demolition of the hotel in 1965, the back bar of the hotel was relocated to the Riverside Inn (better known as Bill and Babe's) in Pulaski. (Sara Slaven.)

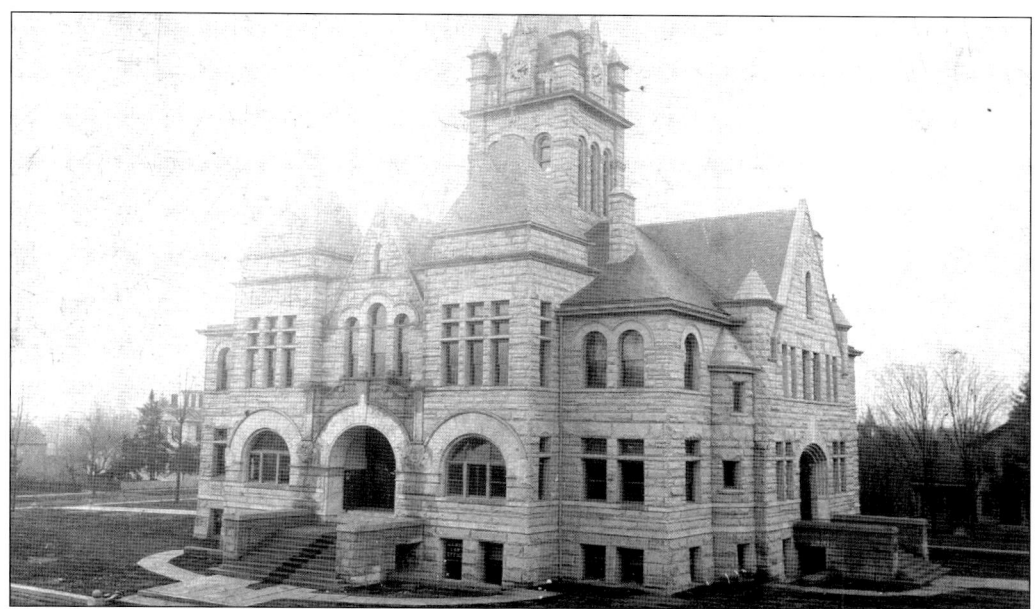

The new Indiana limestone Pulaski County Courthouse, completed in 1895, is seen here in its early years. One report recalls that some of the limestone blocks for the building construction were hauled to Winamac from Logansport by horse and wagon. In 2008, the courthouse was named to the U.S. and Indiana historical registers. This photograph, taken from the opera house across Main Street, may be from October 26, 1904. What appears to be a red carpet rolled down the courthouse steps was perhaps placed to welcome Democratic presidential candidate William Jennings Bryan who spoke in Winamac on that day. (PCHS Museum.)

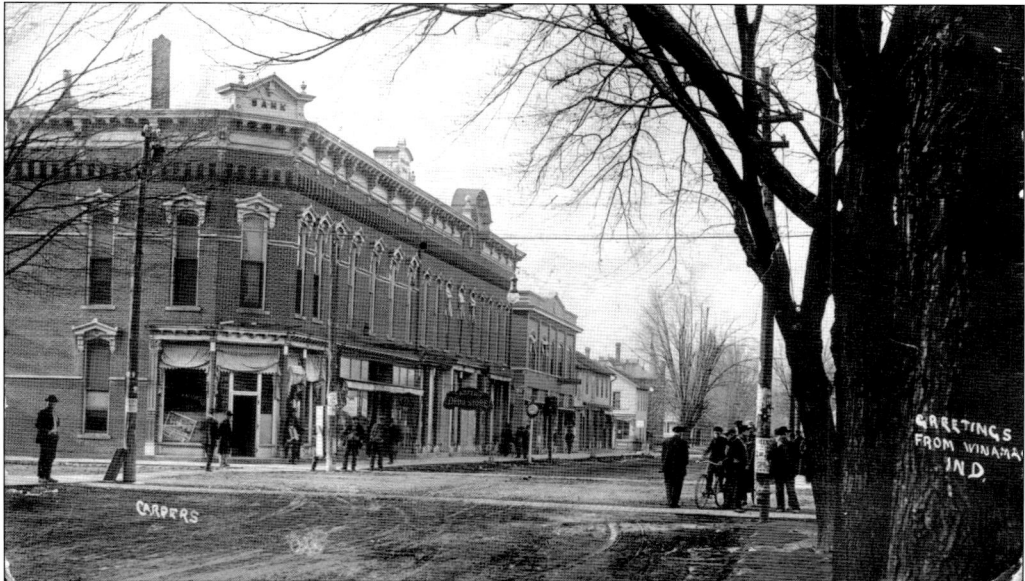

Downtown Winamac is pictured during winter in this postcard dated July 1910. The view looks north on unpaved Market Street at the Main Street intersection. A clock atop a post stands along the sidewalk in front of Carper's Drug Store in the center. Two former frame buildings stand on the west side of Market Street at the Pearl Street intersection. (Dee Galbreath.)

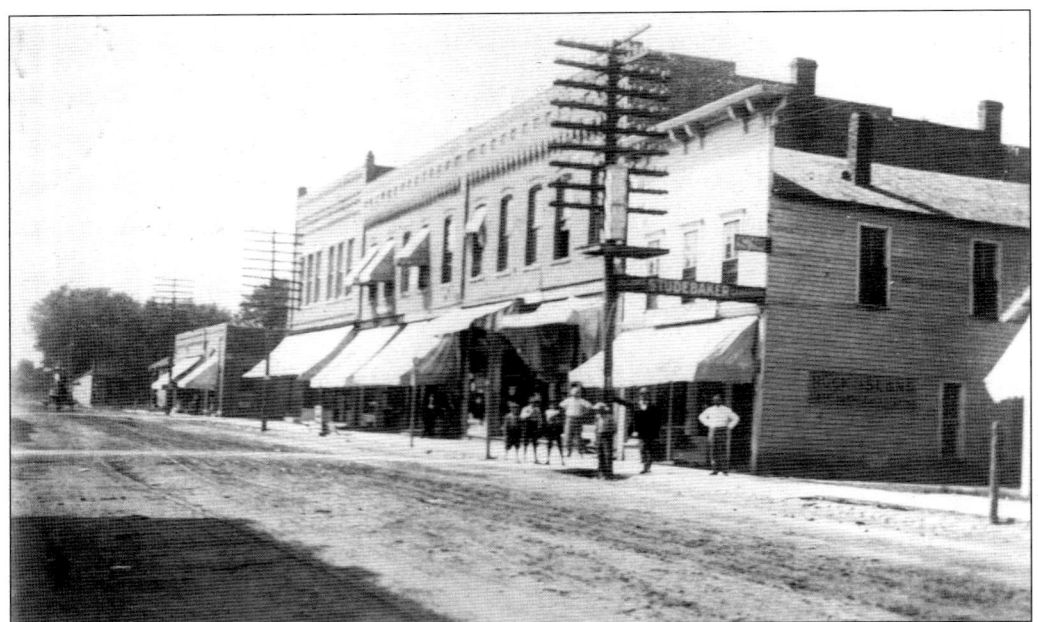

This postcard, dated in 1909, shows the business block on Montgomery Street in Francesville, looking west. The sign on the side of the building advertises "Rock Island Plows and Goods." The business also offers Studebaker carriages. Many of these buildings burned in the fire of December 1944. (PCHS Museum.)

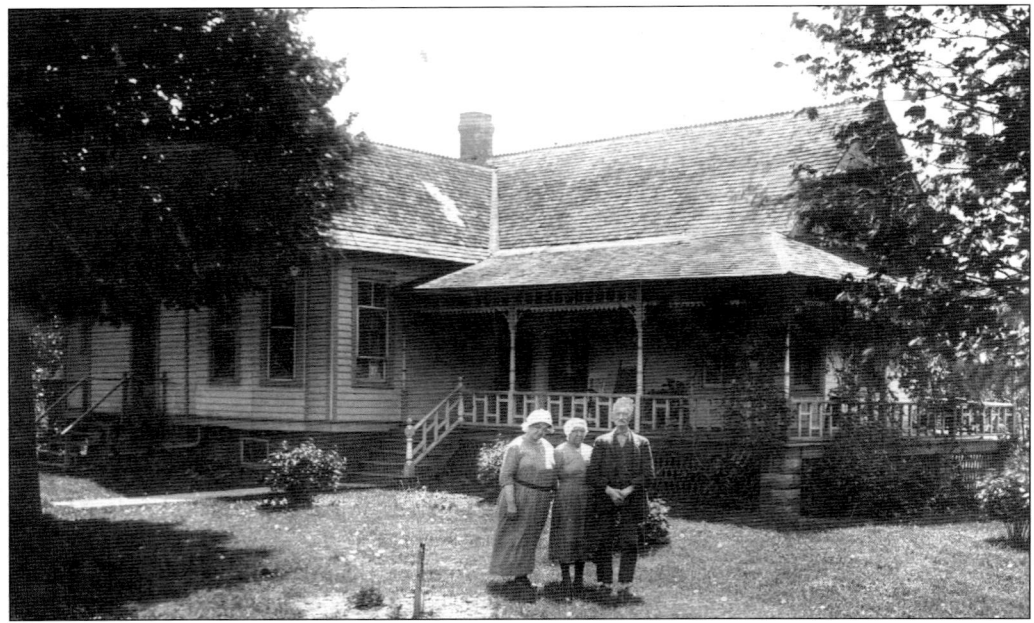

Many modest but charming homes built at the end of the 19th century in Pulaski County communities remained at the dawn of the 21st century, including this Star City home built about 1899 on Wirick Street. Standing in front of their home are J. P. Ambler and two of his daughters, Idella (left) and Maude. Ambler was a butcher and operated a meat market in Star City from about 1895 to 1911. (PCHS Museum.)

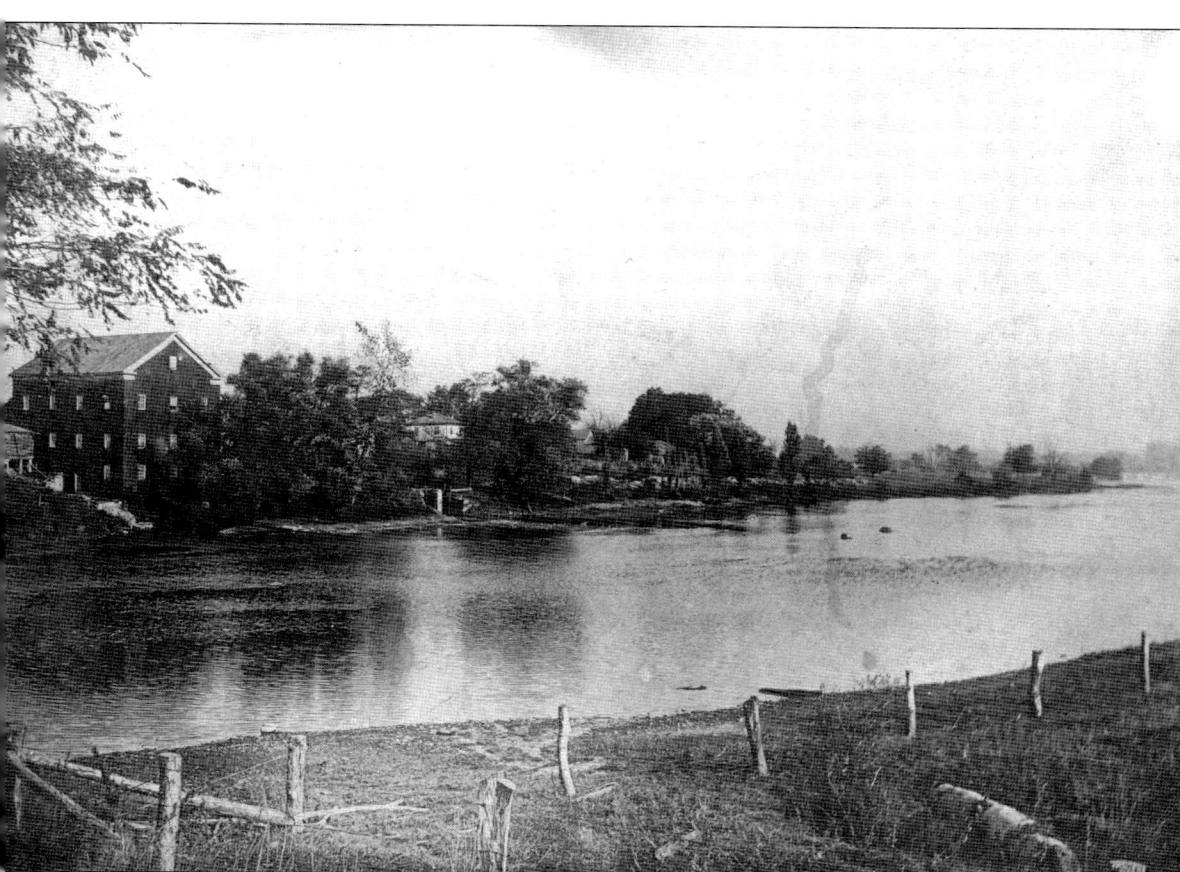

In its early history, Pulaski County had several saw- and gristmills along the Tippecanoe River and its tributaries. Perhaps the best remembered is this gristmill in the village of Pulaski. Six men formed the Pulaski Manufacturing Company in 1853 and obtained permission from the state to construct a dam and millrace just north of the mill site. The mill took about two years two build, with local farmers assisting the contractor in the placement of the huge beams in the three-and-a-half-story structure. The millrace powered three buhrstones, which were later replaced by rollers. The little town of Pulaski was platted with 56 lots around the mill while it was still under construction. Housing and businesses followed to serve the mill workmen. Ownership of the mill changed hands many times over the following decades, but the mill continued as an important business to local farmers and the Pulaski village. By the second decade of the 20th century, however, residents were beginning to consider new uses and modernization of the outdated mill. The property was eventually abandoned, and in July 1920, the mill was destroyed by fire. (PCHS Museum.)

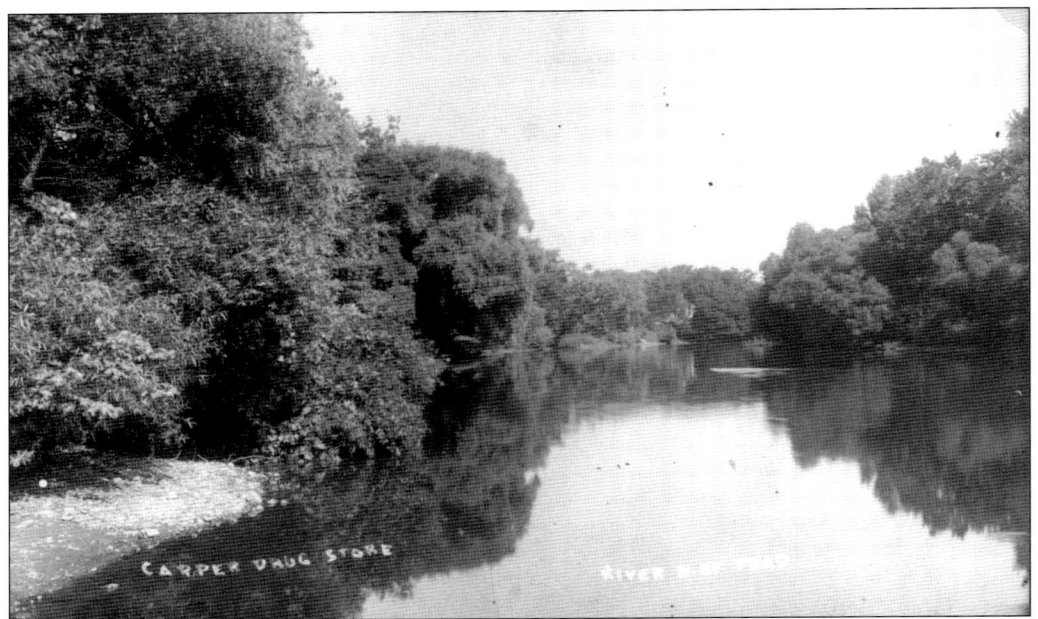

The Tippecanoe River winds around the town park in Winamac, as seen in this 1908 postcard. The view looks north from where the Pearl Street ford was once located. In addition to the fords, there was once a ferry service in Winamac. The toll cost 25¢ for a horse team and wagon. (Sara Slaven.)

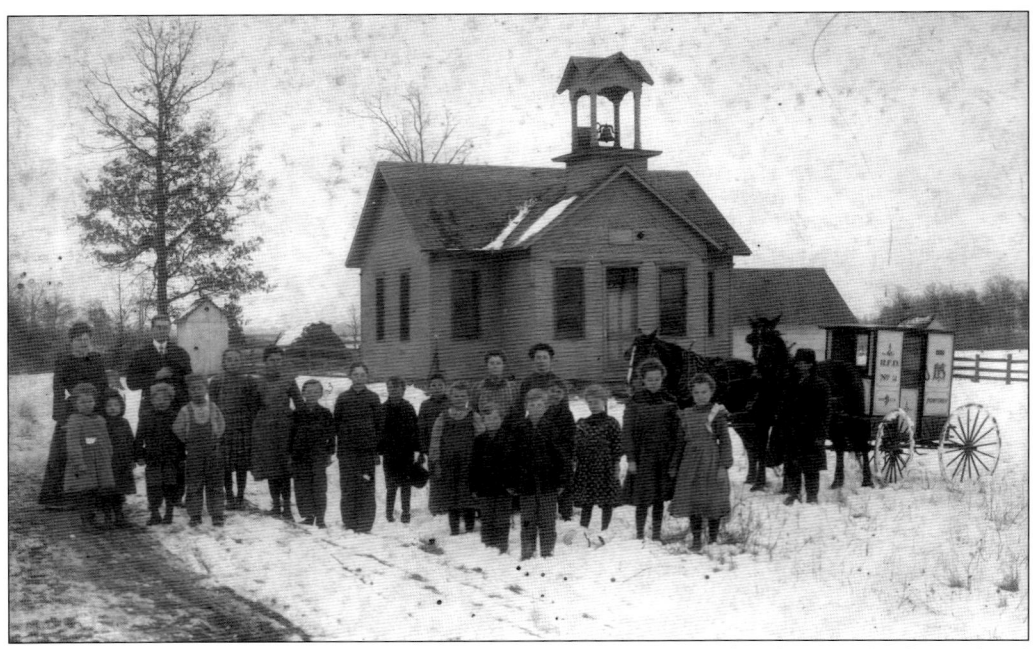

The pupils at Wade School in eastern Tippecanoe Township gathered in the snow for this undated photograph, probably taken about 1905. The teacher was Fannie Davidson. A horse-drawn school hack stands nearby. The average teacher's pay in 1902 was $2.12 per day with 25 percent withheld until the year's end. (Monterey-Tippecanoe Township Library.)

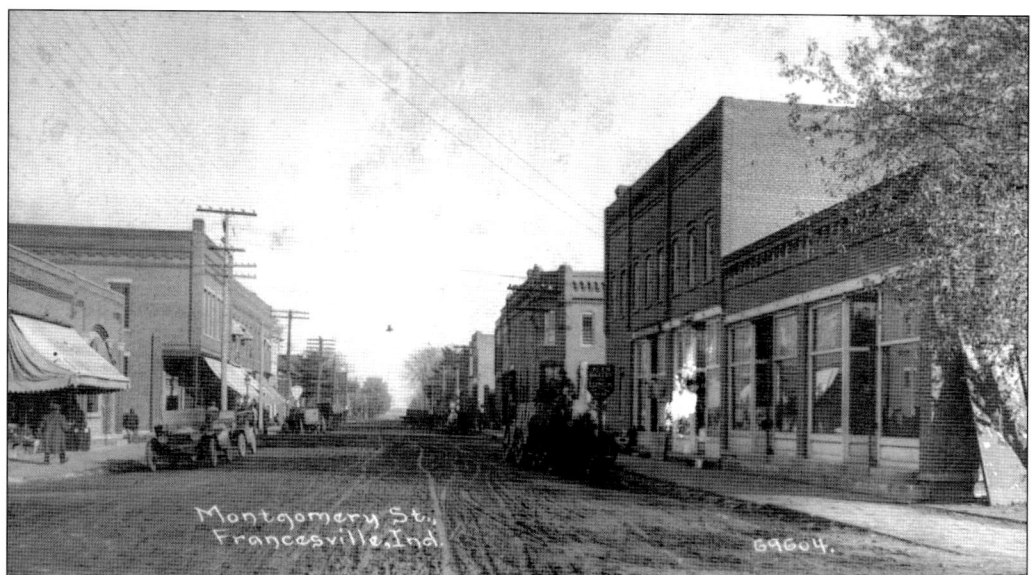

This view of Francesville from the early 1900s looks east on Montgomery Street from the railroad tracks. A walk through the business district then took a visitor past drugstores, a bakery, at least six groceries, a millinery shop for the ladies, and a tailor for the gentlemen. There were a couple of doctors, a barber who also served as a dentist, and a jeweler who performed eye exams. The town also had a bank, a telephone company, a post office, hardware and general merchandise stores, plus lawyers and real estate agents. (Alyce Onken.)

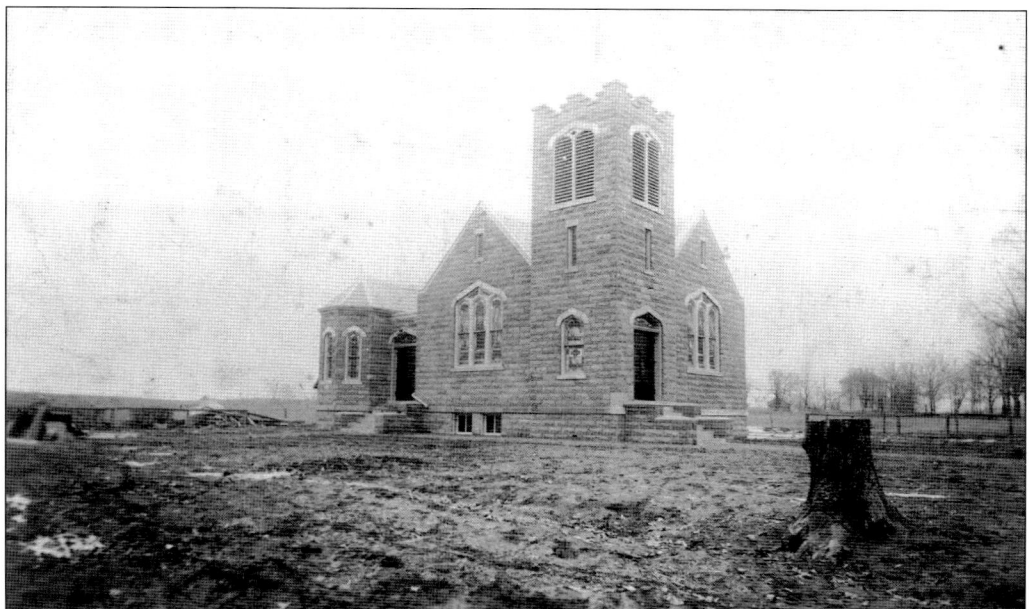

The Pulaski Presbyterian Church congregation was established in October 1890 with 53 charter members. In 1904, Rev. G. W. Simon called a session meeting where it was decided to build this cement block church on the west side of the Tippecanoe River. The cement blocks were made on the church grounds by congregation members. The stained glass for the windows was imported from Italy. (PCHS Museum.)

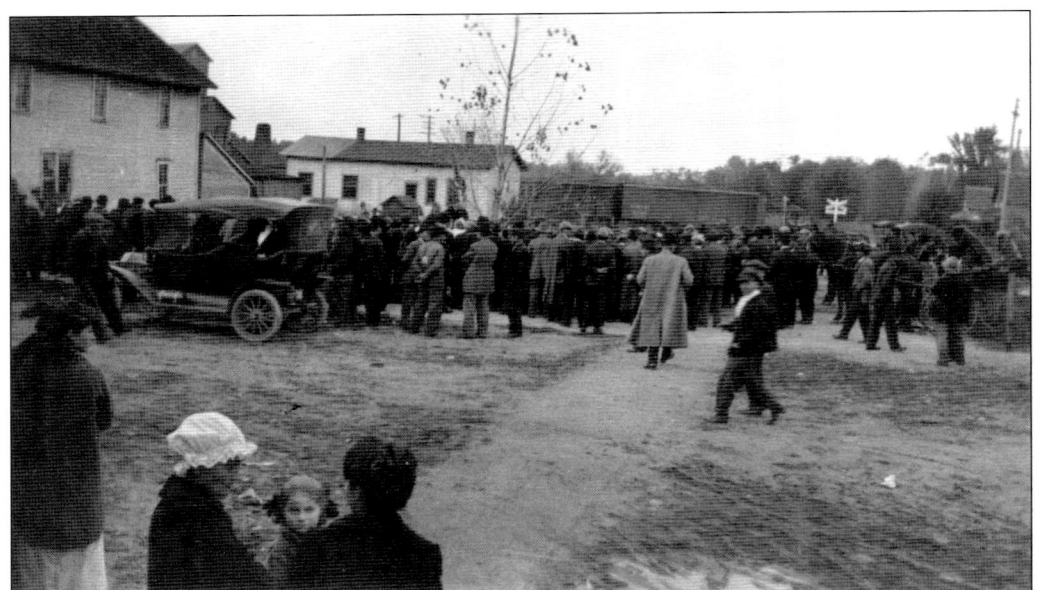

Banker Charles Keitzer took this fascinating photograph in mid-town Monterey in the 1920s. It is not known what event drew the crowd. A row of horse-drawn carriages can be seen parked at the right. A man slightly elevated above the crowd in front of an American flag appears to be speaking to the group; he can be seen in front of the white building at center. (Charles Kelsey.)

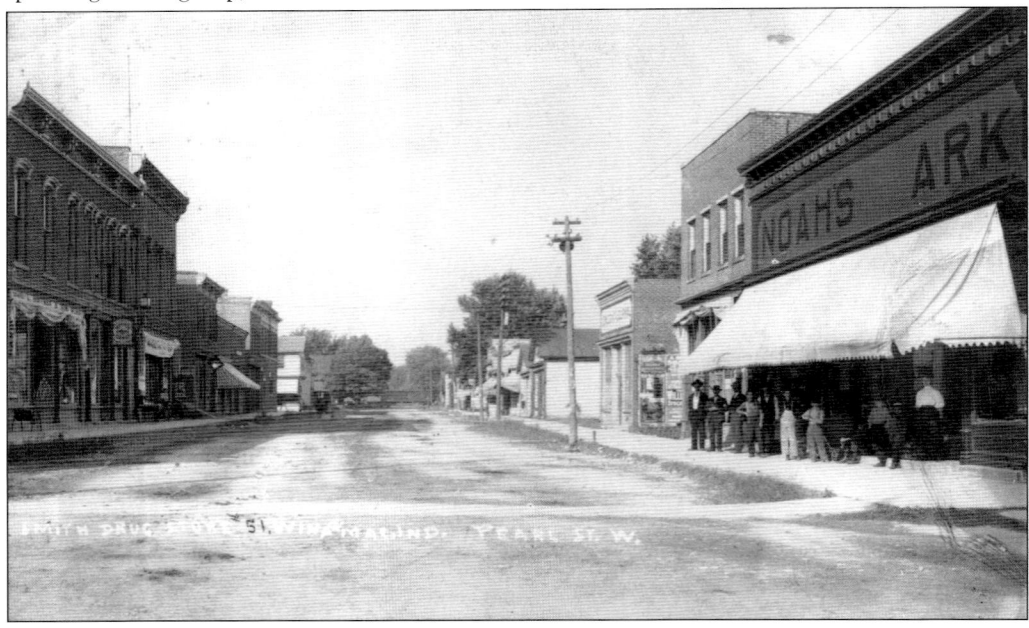

Noah Freeman, a pioneer who came to Winamac in 1854 at age 38, acquired John Gillespie's grocery on Pearl Street in June 1891. Freeman shared the building with Jacob Haas, a clothier, until 1894, when Haas moved to Market Street. Freeman expanded, adding dry goods to his grocery stock. At that time, he advertised as "Winamac's Cheap Cash Store." The name Noah's Ark, as seen in this picture dated about 1909, came from an advertisement run by Freeman in January 1895. (Sara Slaven.)

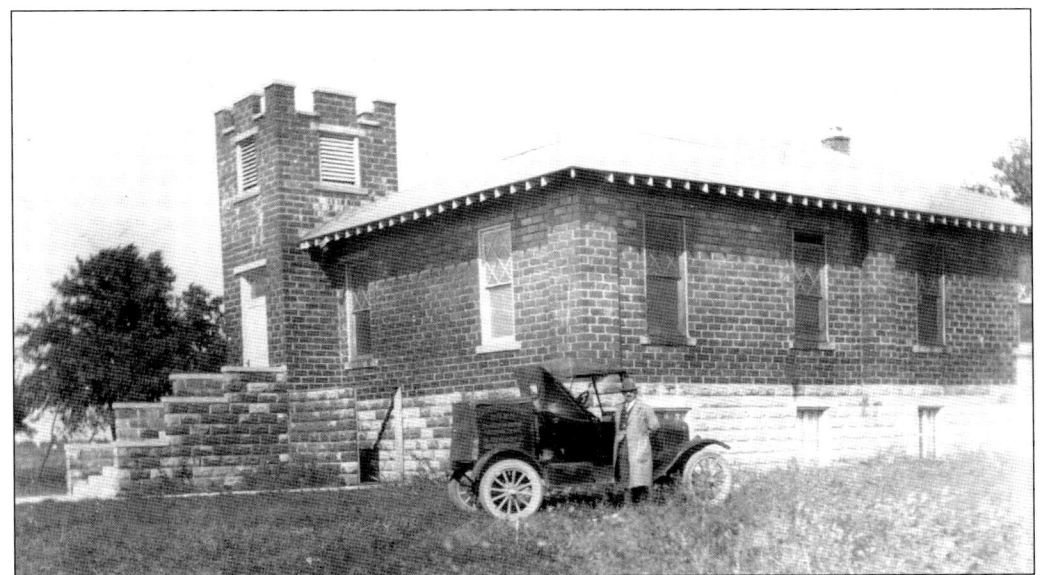

The little town of Denham once included a post office, a grain elevator, a general store, a dance and pool hall, a schoolhouse, and two churches. The Baptist church, shown here, was built in 1920. Babies were baptized in a horse tank outside the church. The sign on the truck reads, "C.A. Porter Missionary; Auto No. 25; The American Baptist Publication Society; The American Baptist Home Mission Society." (Ralph Fritz.)

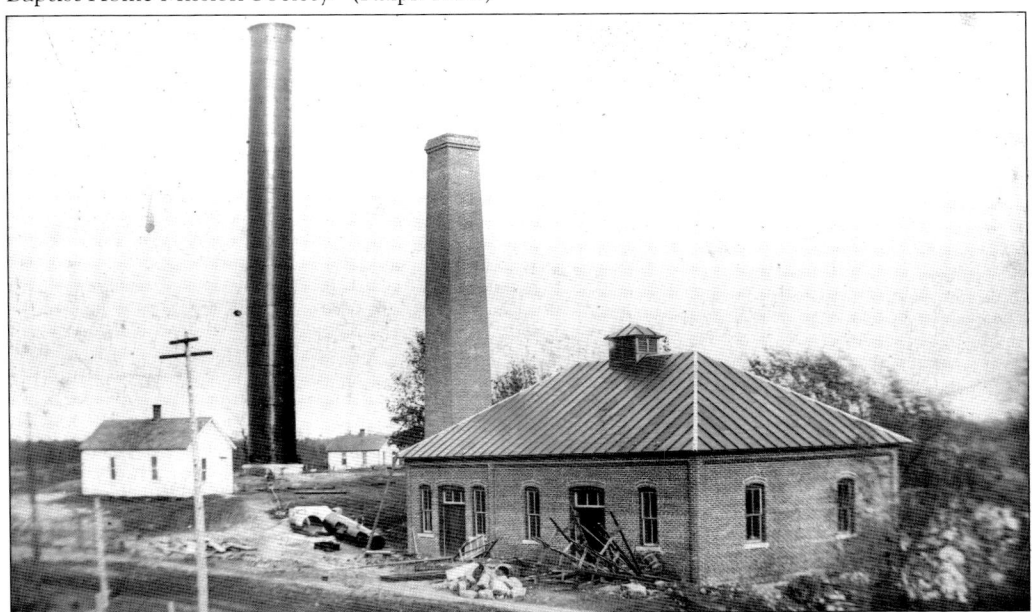

By the late 1880s, residents of Winamac were seeking the modern convenience of having water piped into their homes. Thus, the construction of a public waterworks and electric plant was undertaken. This photograph was taken soon after construction was completed in 1898. The first water mains through town were extended in 1923, and water meters were purchased by the town council for installation in homes in 1926. The landmark standpipe was torn down in June 2004, and a new facility was built soon after. (PCHS Museum, donated by Sarah Wank Morrison.)

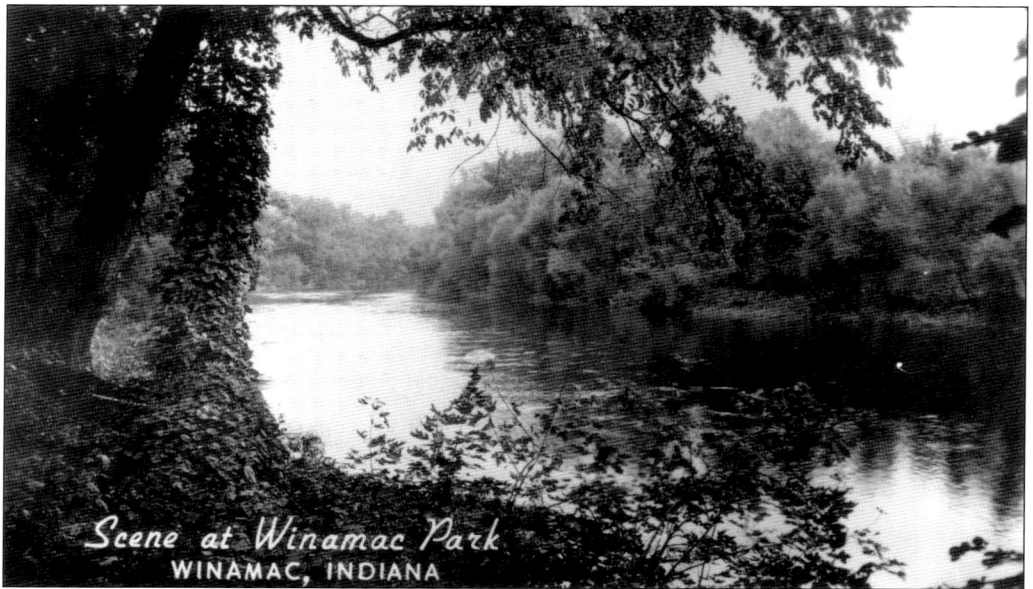

The Winamac Town Park, located in a horseshoe bend of the Tippecanoe River, has always been one of Winamac's greatest assets. This postcard photograph, postmarked in 1948, shows a river scene along the park. (Sara Slaven.)

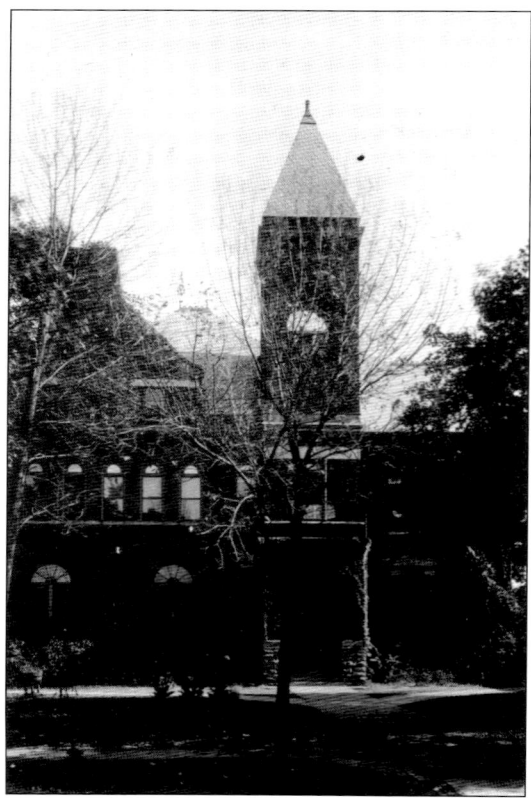

After the brick school in Winamac burned in March 1892, plans were immediately made to replace it. Bids for rebuilding the school were accepted two months later, and the new facility opened in 1893. This postcard photograph of the school was postmarked in 1923. (Sara Slaven.)

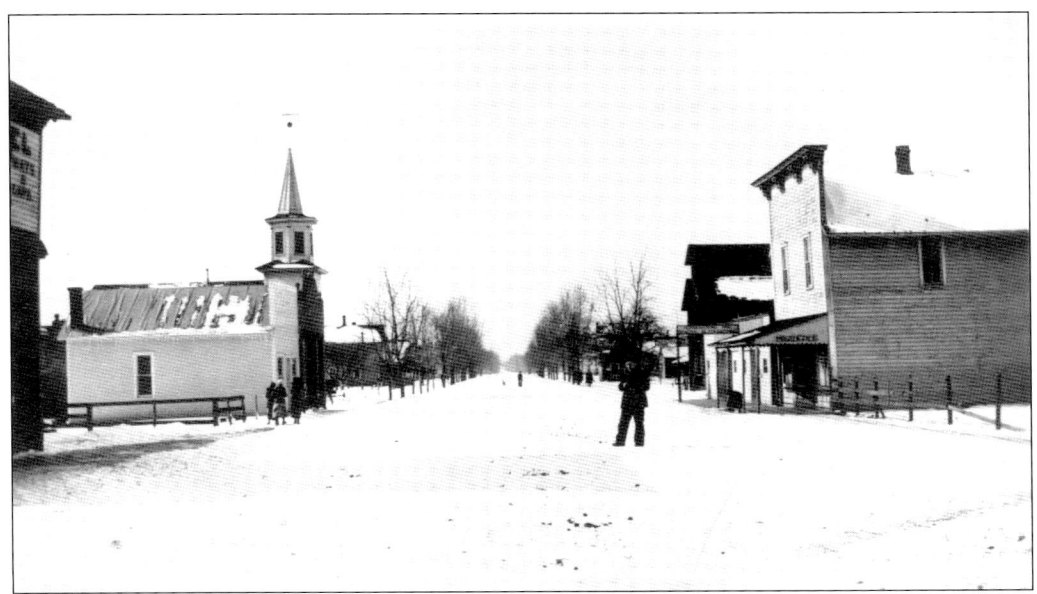

Charlie Keitzer took several photographs of a winter wonderland snowfall in Monterey in 1912. This picture looks west down Main Street. On the left are the grocery store/meat market and Methodist church. On the right are a restaurant and Zehner's Flour Mill. (Charles Kelsey.)

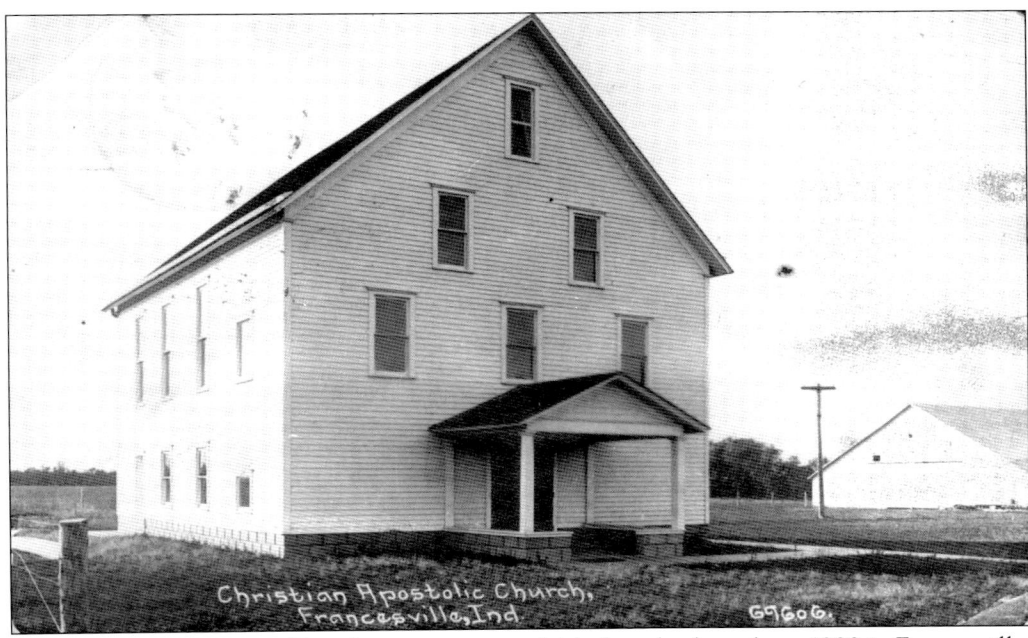

The Apostolic Christian Church congregation, which dates back to about 1900 in Francesville, built this two-story wooden church about 1910 on the Albert Gudeman farm near town. Stables were built near the church to accommodate the horses and buggies of church members. As with many churches in the county, classes and worship were conducted in the German language until the time of World War I. This postcard is postmarked 1910. (Alyce Onken.)

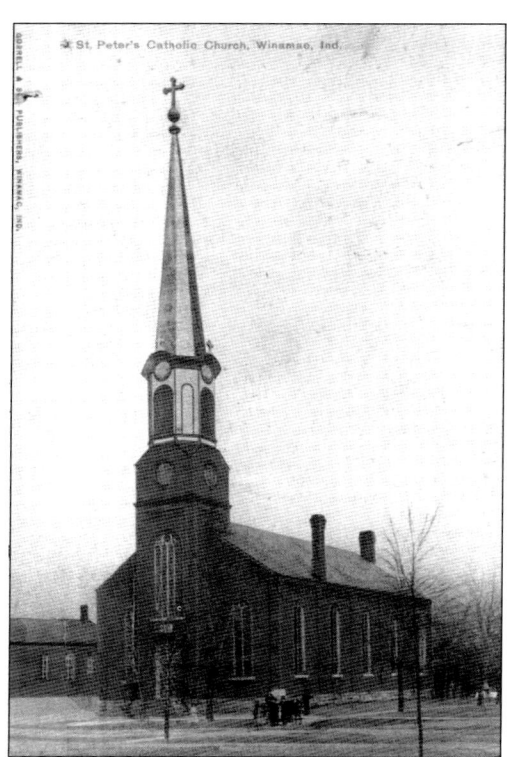

The St. Peter's Catholic Church congregation was organized in Winamac in 1859 and worshiped in a small structure built that year for $700. It was replaced by this church, with its landmark towering steeple, in 1884. The steeple was eventually replaced. A parochial school addition was opened in 1930. (PCHS Museum.)

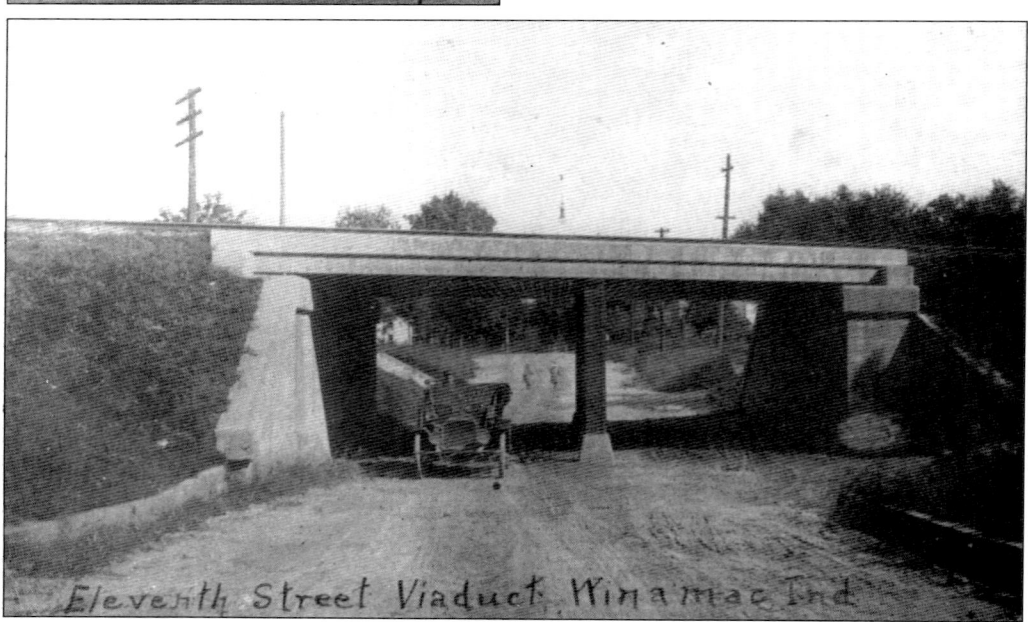

The old railroad viaduct on Eleventh Street in Winamac is pictured in this postcard dated 1915. The viaduct was constructed in 1909 because the railroad crossing proved to be dangerous; a priest was killed at the crossing earlier. For almost 80 years, the narrow viaduct was a local landmark. Railroad service through Winamac ended in 1983, and the viaduct was removed in 1986. (Sara Slaven.)

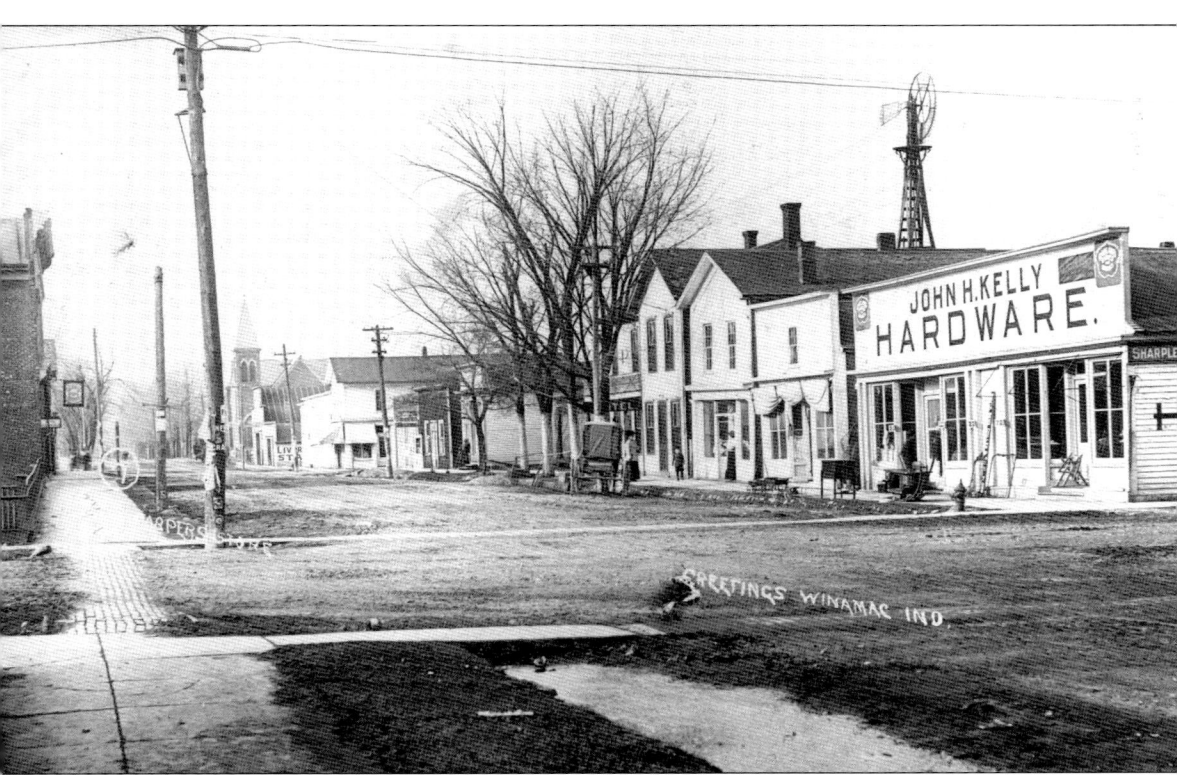

The Kelly Hardware Store was a downtown Winamac landmark for several decades. This photograph from about 1910 looks north on Monticello Street. A sign on the building behind the trees and buggy reads Hotel. The building just before the Methodist church two blocks down the street is a livery stable. John H. Kelley was born in Scotland in 1847. Growing up in Winamac, he learned the tinner's trade as an apprentice to Mr. Hathaway. Soon he was in his own establishment. The business continued in the family until the 1980s with the retirement of the founder's grandson John W. Kelly. (Sara Slaven.)

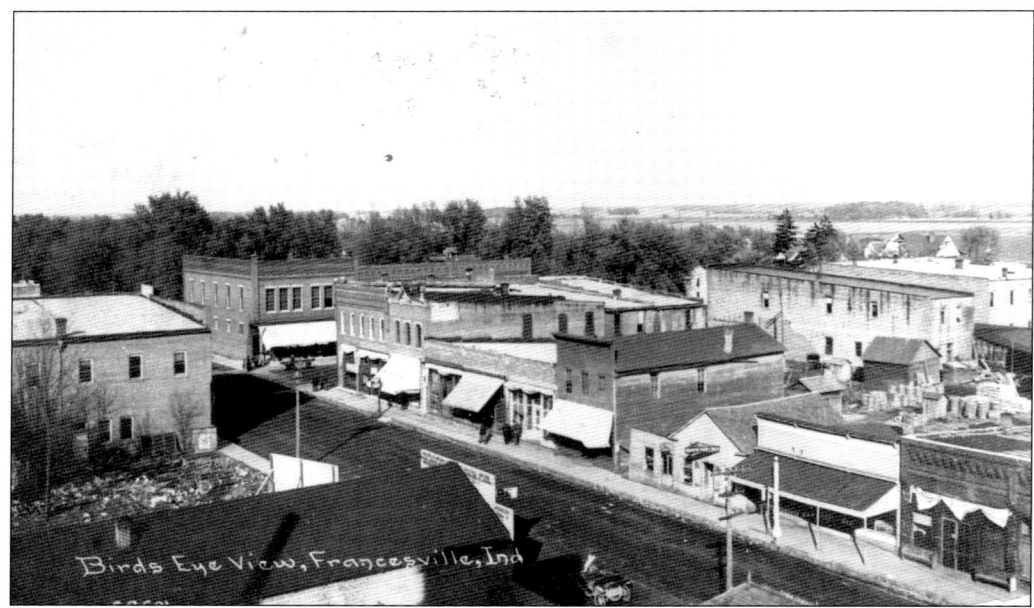

This bird's-eye view of downtown Francesville was taken between 1908 and 1916. Businesses include the Myers Garage, the Fitzpatrick and Hullinger buildings, Hayworth Produce, Daeske Shoe Repair, Brewer's Store, the Busch and Kopka buildings, and Mallon's Store. (Janet Onken.)

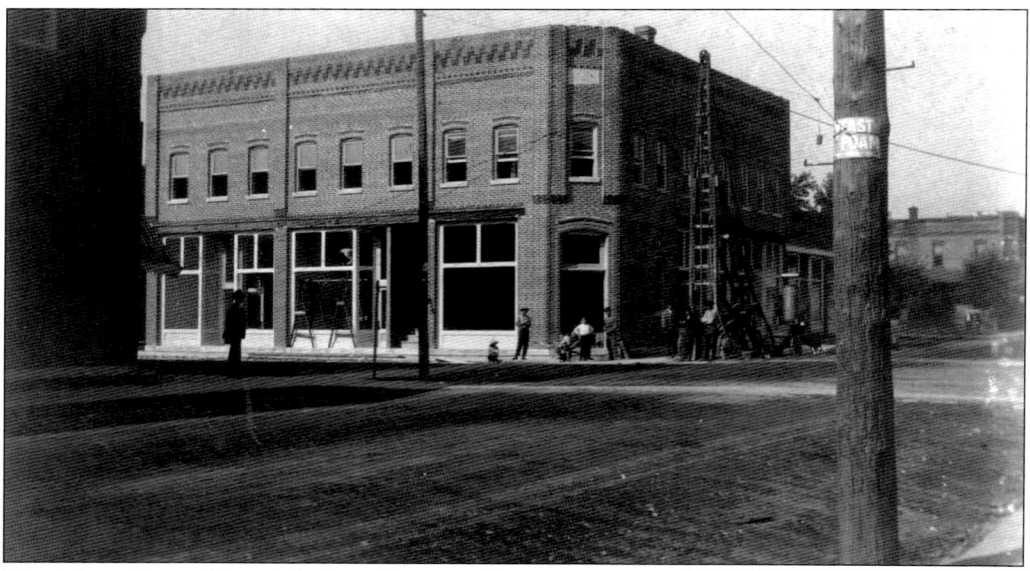

The Myers Opera House block in Francesville was constructed in 1908 by William C. Myers. Many people climbed the stairs to enjoy the silent movies. There was also a theatrical season when stage shows were produced by traveling companies. Fred Gordon's Stock Company was a favorite. In later years, he brought a tent show, known as the Gordon Players. Clyde "Ramblin' Red" Foley was among the popular Chicago WLS Radio artists who appeared at the Myers Theatre. (Alyce Onken.)

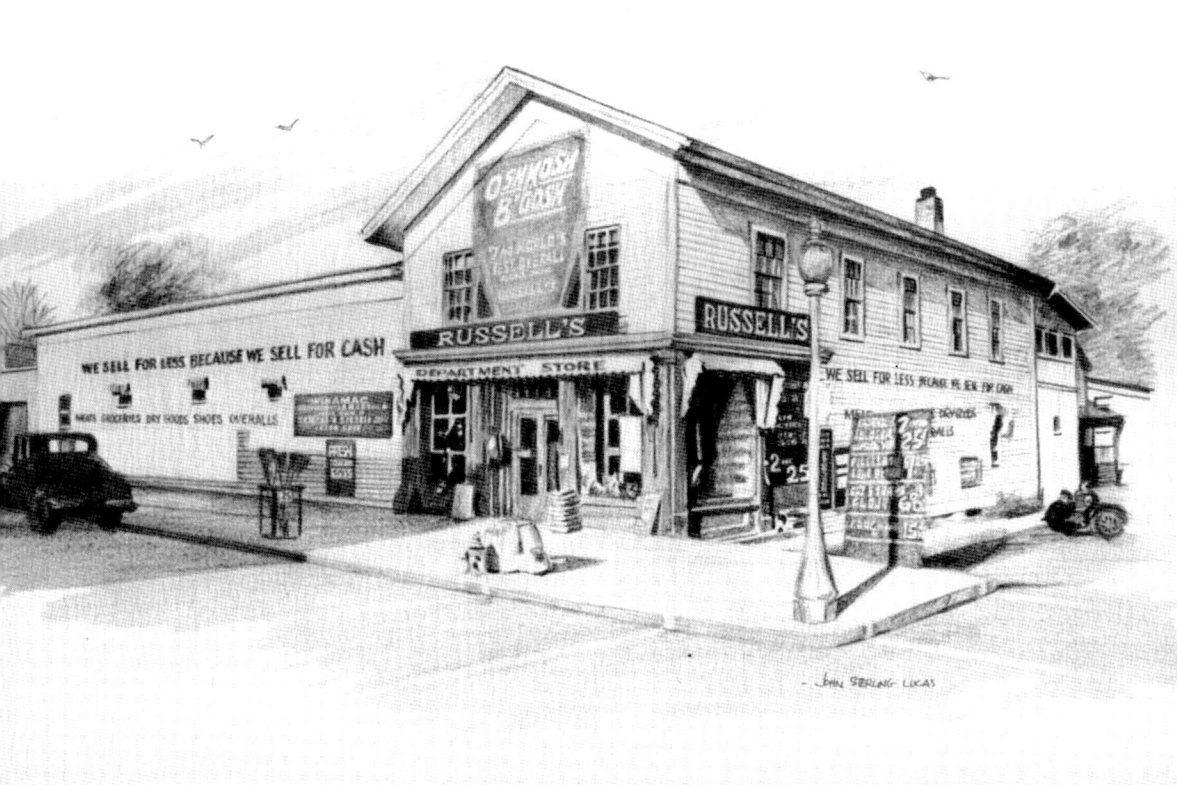

Russell's Old Trading Post was a fixture for over 40 years on the corner of Monticello and Pearl Streets in Winamac, selling groceries and dry goods to customers who were greeted as "old pal" by proprietor E. John Russell. He seldom forgot a name or face. Born in 1888 in nearby Kewanna, Russell began his retail career with a shoe store on Market Street. With a growing family, he purchased the old Falvey store and added clothing and dry goods to the shoe business plus groceries. Soon he added a meat-processing plant, and the "home-killed meats" became a customer favorite. His weekly advertisements seldom quoted prices but instead were titled and told of interesting store happenings. The trading post was destroyed by fire in January 1940 but was quickly rebuilt. Russell died in 1947. The business was operated by his sons Fred, Bill, and Joe for another 32 years. This sketch is by John Sterling Lucas. (Winamac Chamber of Commerce.)

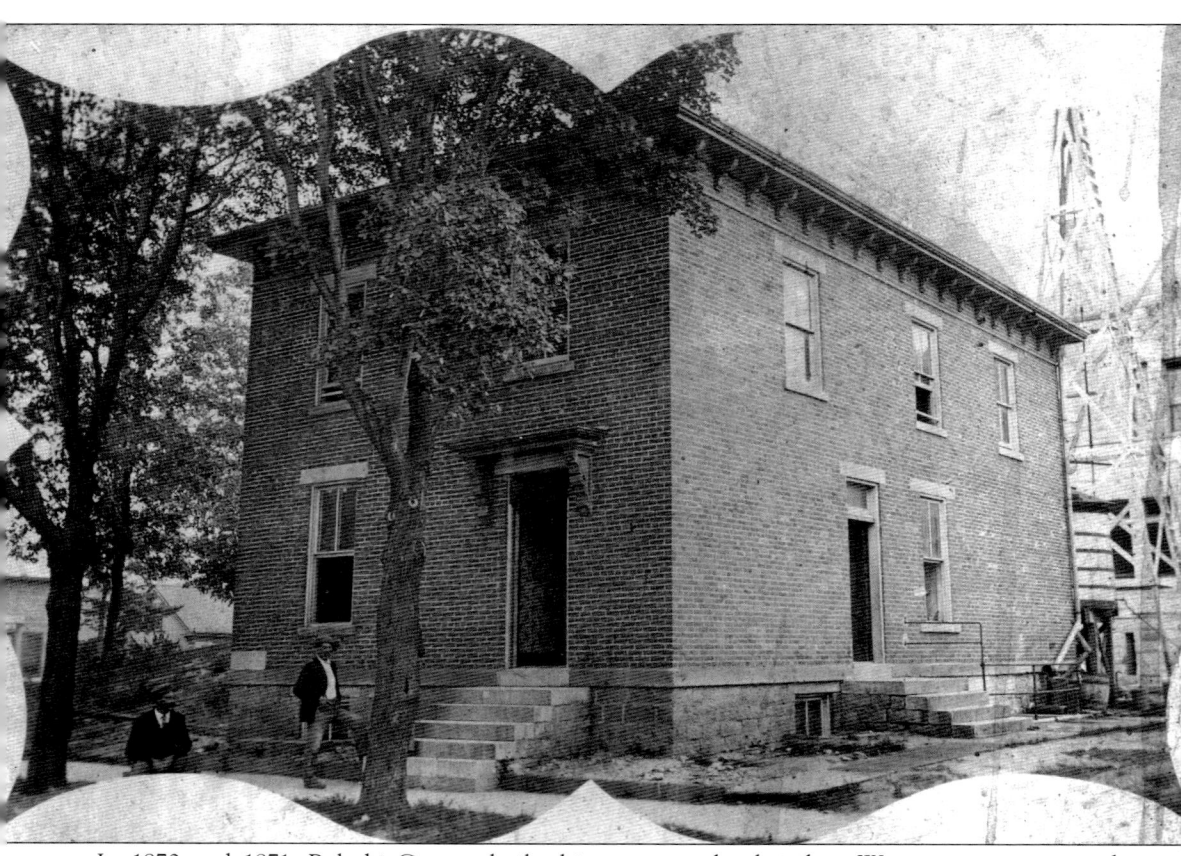

In 1870 and 1871, Pulaski County built this two-story brick jail in Winamac at a reported cost of $7,000. The architect was Edwin May. The photograph was taken in 1895, as the courthouse appears to be under construction in the background. The jail included residential accommodations for the sheriff/jailer. It was torn down later in the year, and the materials were sold for $351 to Jacob Wirick of Star City. (Sara Slaven.)

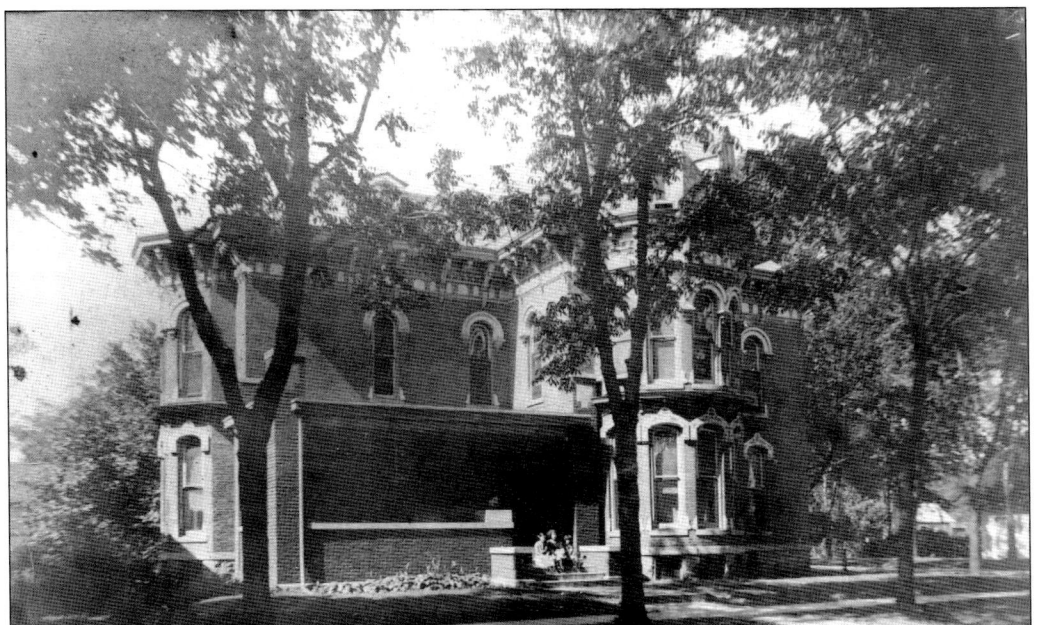

Dr. William Henry Thompson built this home on the 200 block of North Market Street in Winamac in 1884. This photograph is believed to date to the late 1920s, when Judge John G. Reidelbach owned it. In the 1940s, the home was converted into a hotel and was known as the Winamac Hotel. (PCHS Museum.)

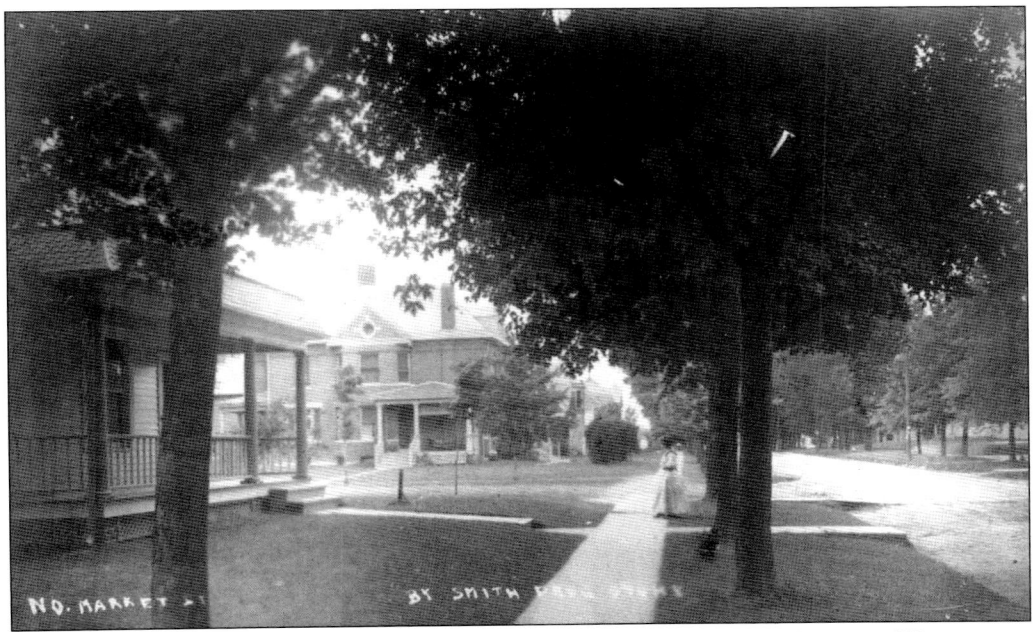

An unidentified woman enjoys a stroll along tree-lined North Market Street in Winamac in this photograph, which dates to about 1915. The brick home in the center of the picture is the historic Dr. George W. Thompson home built in 1897. It was later sold to attorney Louis Reidelbach in 1930. St. Peter's Catholic Church is located across from the home. (Sara Slaven.)

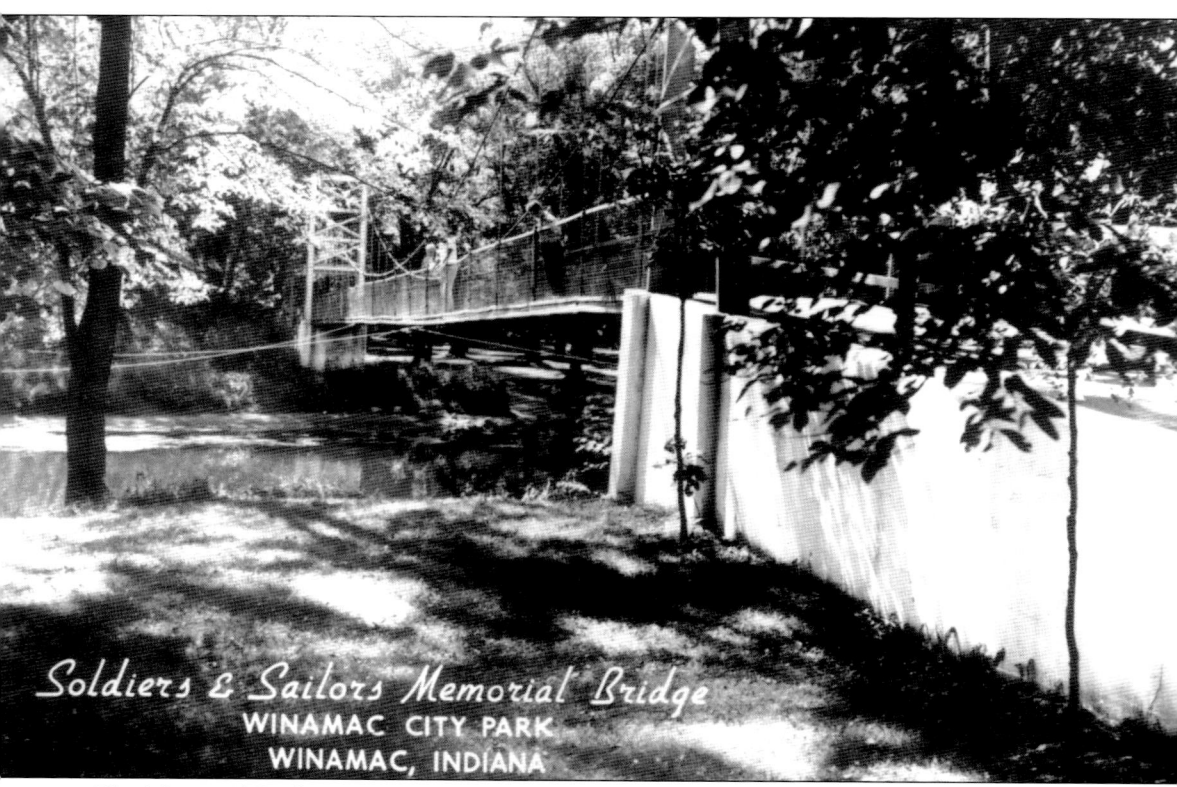

The Memorial Bridge is a unique monument dedicated to all Pulaski County soldiers and sailors who have served the country. More popularly known as the swinging bridge, the suspension footbridge connects downtown Winamac with its town park. It was dedicated on July 4, 1923. (Sara Slaven.)

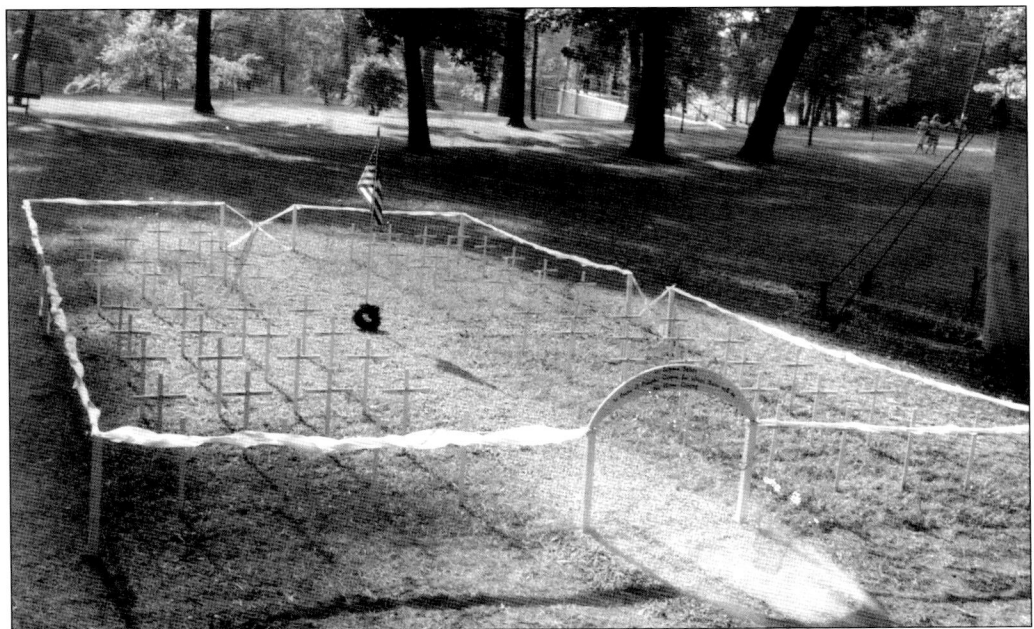

In 1946, a year after the end of World War II, this tribute to the county's war dead was placed at the Winamac park near the Memorial Bridge. The sign over the arch at the mock cemetery reads, "In solemn tribute to those of Pulaski County for whom there will be no homecoming." (PCHS Museum.)

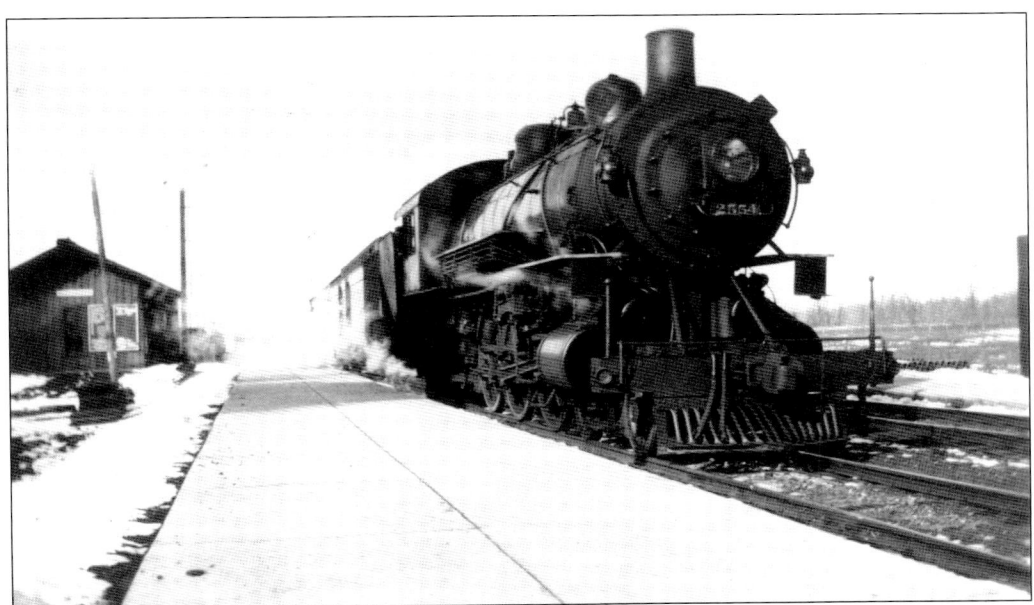

A steam locomotive and train pulls away from the Monterey depot on a snowy winter day in this photograph taken by Charlie Keitzer, dated about 1920. The Erie train station was built by "Old Joe" Keller in 1882. The Erie Lackawanna Railway came through Monterey in 1875. (Charles Kelsey.)

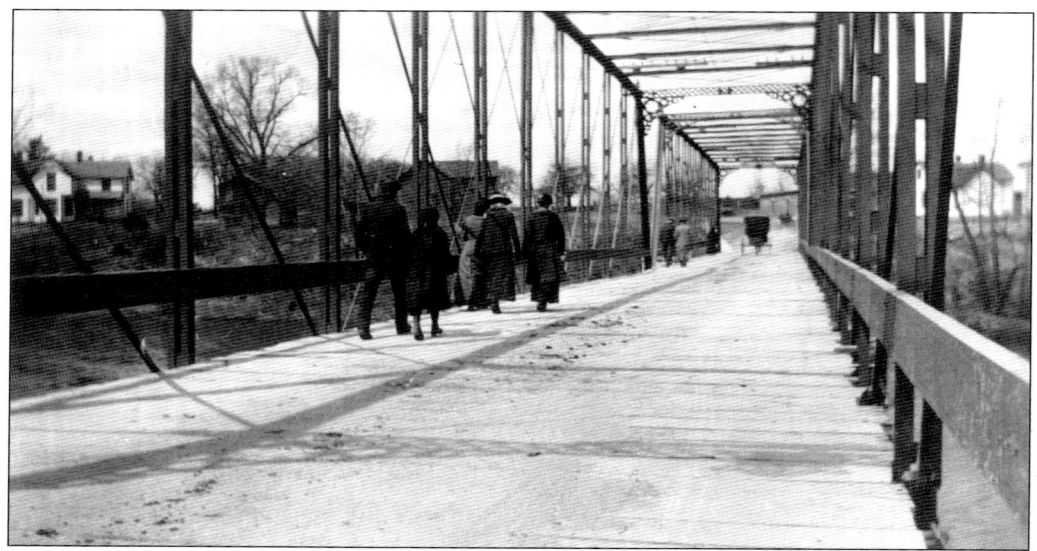

Perhaps on their way home from church, pedestrians and a buggy cross the Tippecanoe River on the wagon bridge in Pulaski in this undated photograph. A stroll across the iron bridge provided a view of the old gristmill and milldam as well as a wide stretch of the river. (Brenda Gilsinger.)

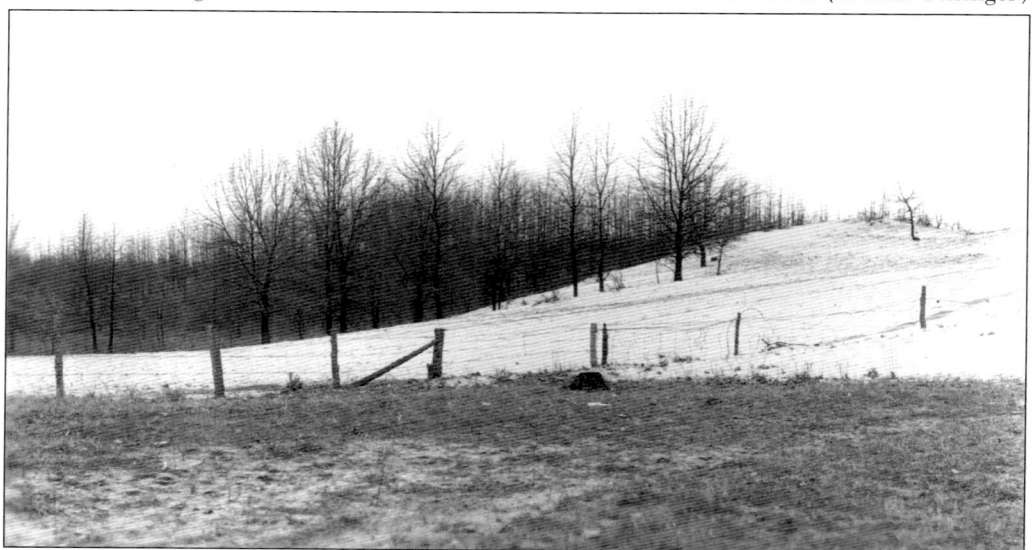

The Tippecanoe River State Park, located about five miles north of Winamac, was developed during the Great Depression in the 1930s as a WPA project—a part of Pres. Franklin Roosevelt's New Deal program. The U.S. Department of the Interior, through its National Park Service, acquired over 7,300 acres of land along the Tippecanoe River for the project, which was first known as the Winamac Recreation Demonstration Area. Most of the land was unsuitable for crops or grazing. The photograph above is typical of how the land looked before the park was developed and planted to a mostly pine and oak forest. This sand hill, now covered with trees, is located near the park entrance. The WPA constructed most of the buildings and other facilities under the direction of the National Park Service. In 1943, the park land was transferred to the Indiana Department of Conservation for operation as a state park. In 1959, nearly 4,600 acres were transferred to create the Winamac Fish and Wildlife Area. (Tippecanoe River State Park.)

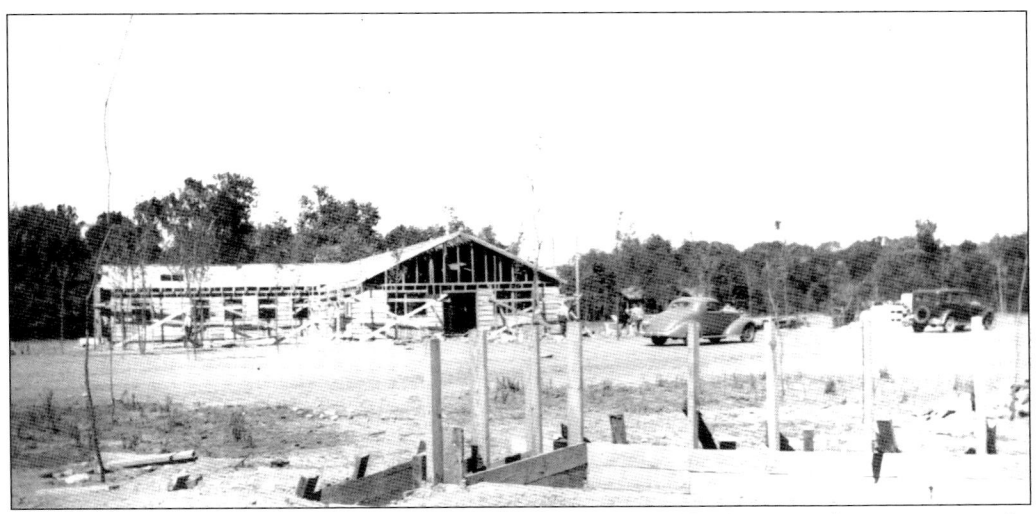

In the spring of 1936, the mess hall and kitchen at group camp No. 1 were under construction by the WPA at the Winamac Recreation Demonstration Area, later to be known as the Tippecanoe River State Park. (Tippecanoe River State Park.)

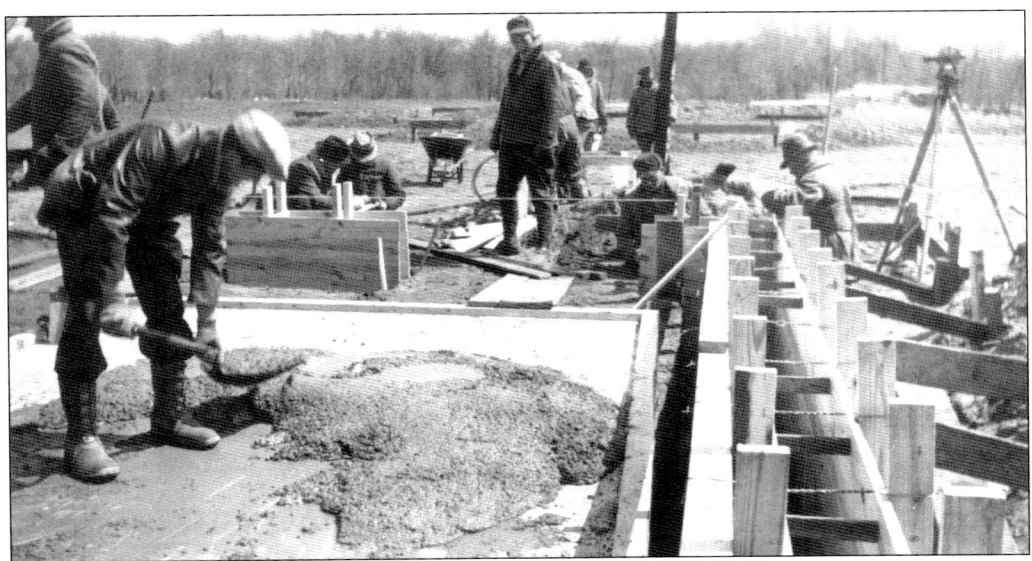

In the dark days of the Great Depression, this WPA project at the Winamac Recreation Demonstration Area provided much-needed jobs for these workers, shown in the spring of 1936. The WPA crews built two camps, complete with cabins, mess hall, kitchen, showers, and restrooms. They also constructed a picnic shelter house, a water system, and a network of trails. (Tippecanoe River State Park.)

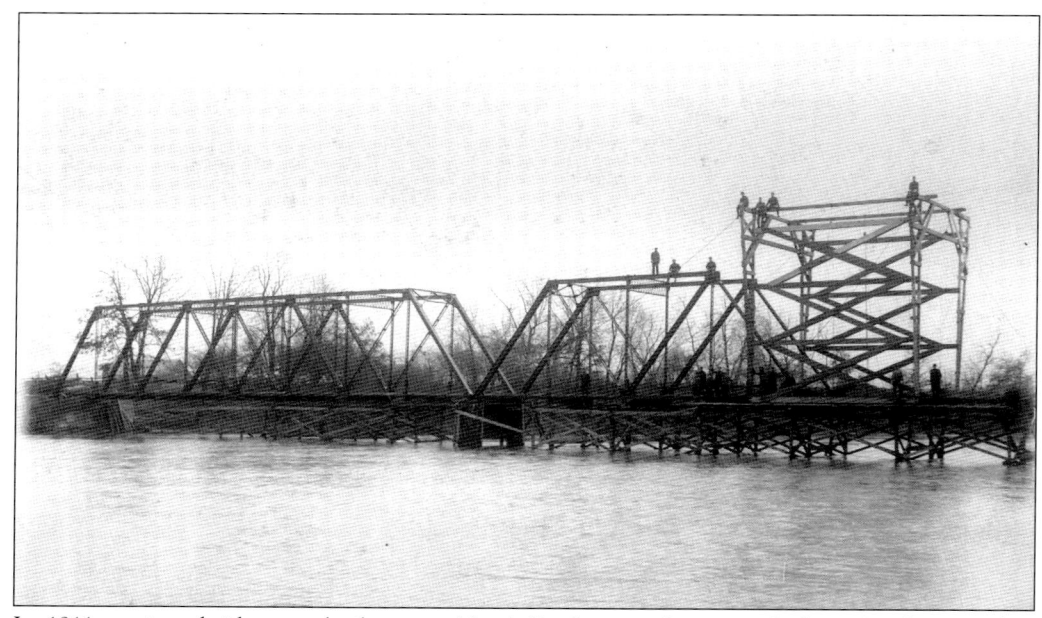

In 1911, an iron bridge was built across Nice's Ford in southwestern Indian Creek Township downstream from the village of Pulaski. The first of the metal bridges in Pulaski County were built in the 1870s, but residents at Nice's Ford had to wait another 40 years for their bridge, which was constructed at a cost of $9,000 by a crew from the Winamac Bridge Company. (PCHS Museum.)

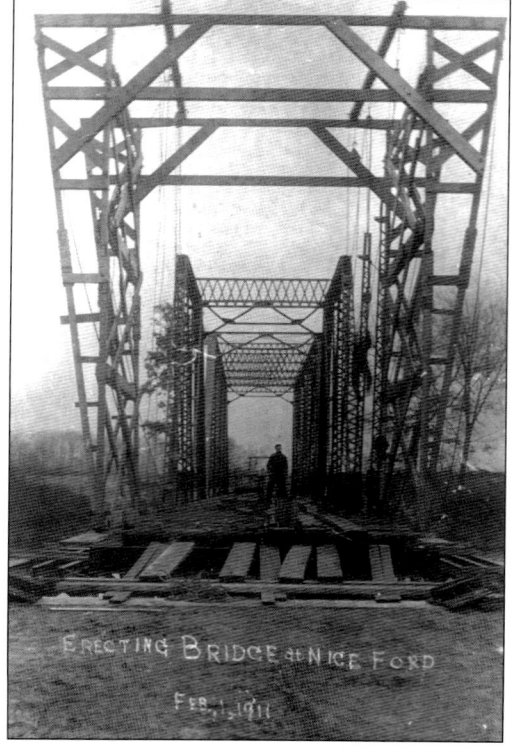

This photograph comes from a postcard that identifies the man standing on the span as Lewis Decker, who helped build Nice's bridge in 1911. (Dee Galbreath.)

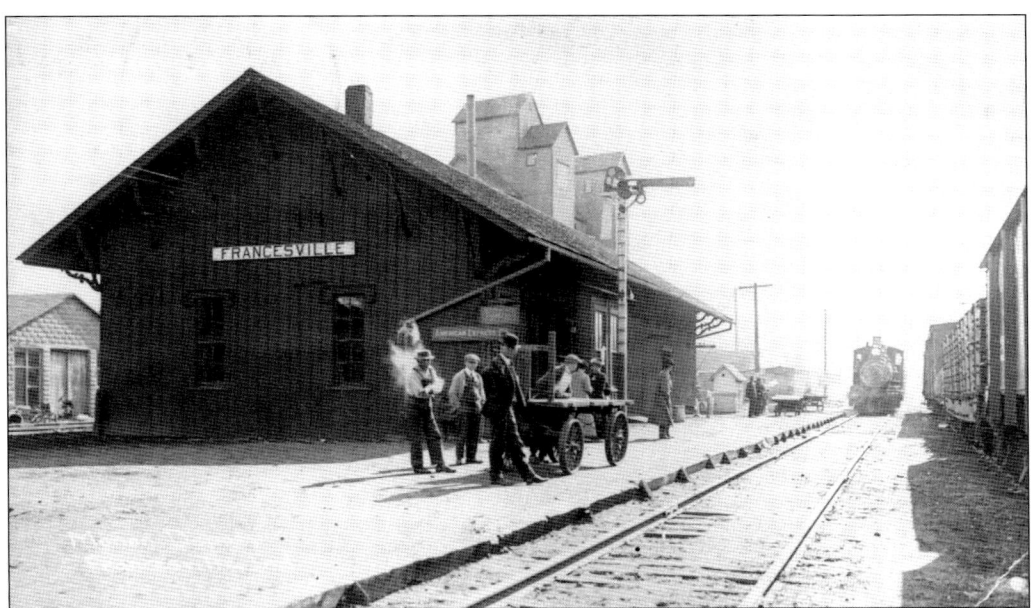

A small crowd of passengers and railway workers awaits the arrival of the next train at the Francesville depot in about 1914. Decades earlier, another modest group gathered at this site to pay respects to the funeral train of Pres. Abraham Lincoln as it passed through the town on its journey to the slain president's final resting place in Illinois. Ironically, Lincoln did not carry Pulaski County in either the 1860 or the 1864 election. (Alyce Onken.)

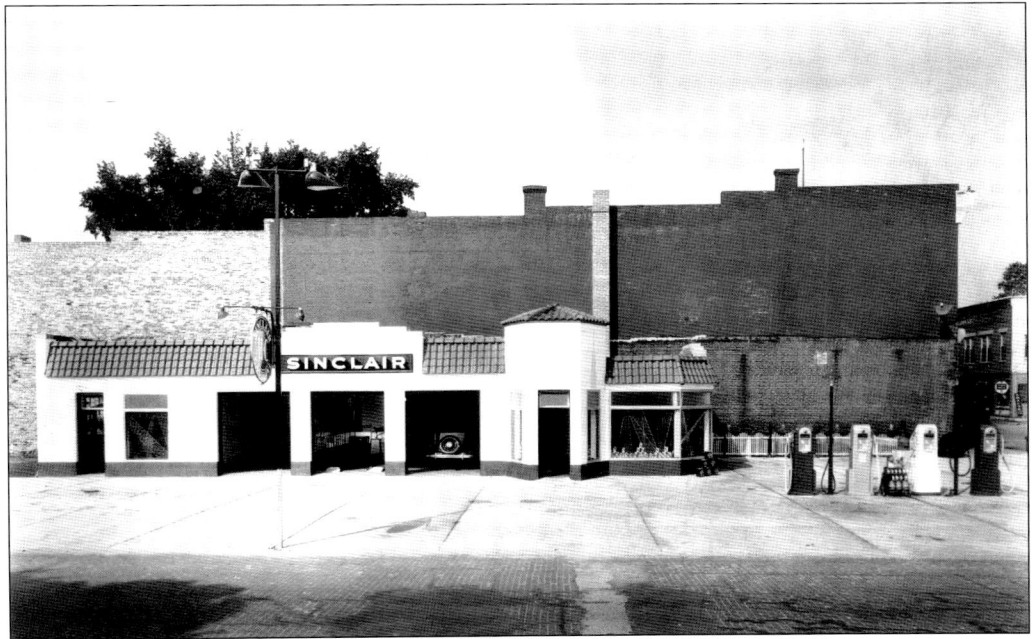

The Sinclair Filling Station, built in 1935, replaced Falvey's Garage, the Ellis Tire Store, and the Judy Beauty Shop on the corner of Monticello and Pearl Streets in Winamac. Owned by George Maddox, the station was built by Robert Gross using a new material known as glass iron. It also had a distinctive red tile roof. (PCHS Museum.)

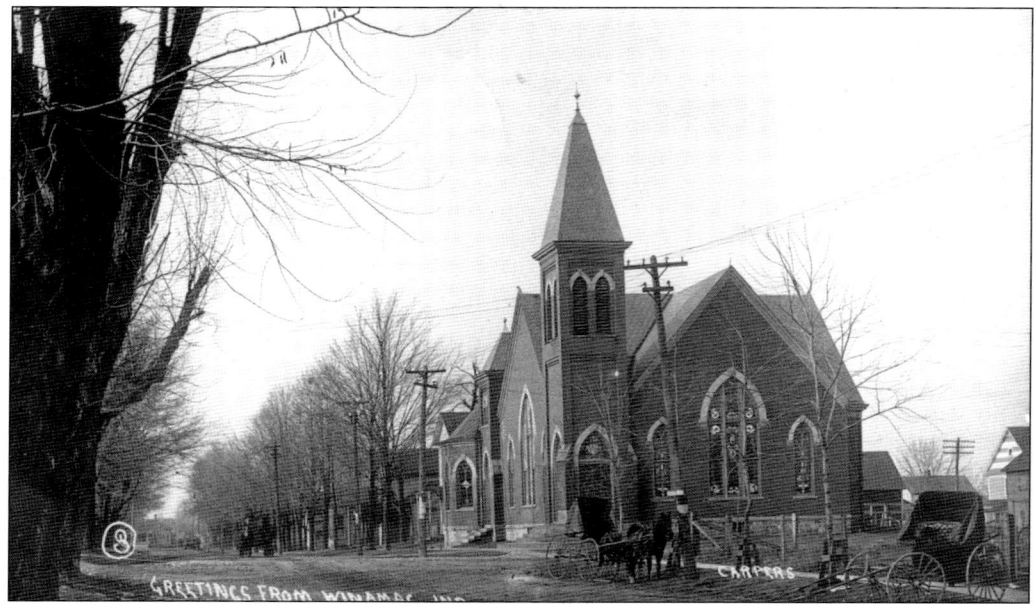

This postcard, dating to August 1911, shows unpaved Monticello Street looking north from Spring Street at the site of the Methodist church. The Winamac Methodist congregation was organized in 1839, the same year that the county was founded. The first church was built in 1868. The church building shown in this picture was constructed in 1901. Legend persists that Chief Winamac is buried under the church. (Sara Slaven.)

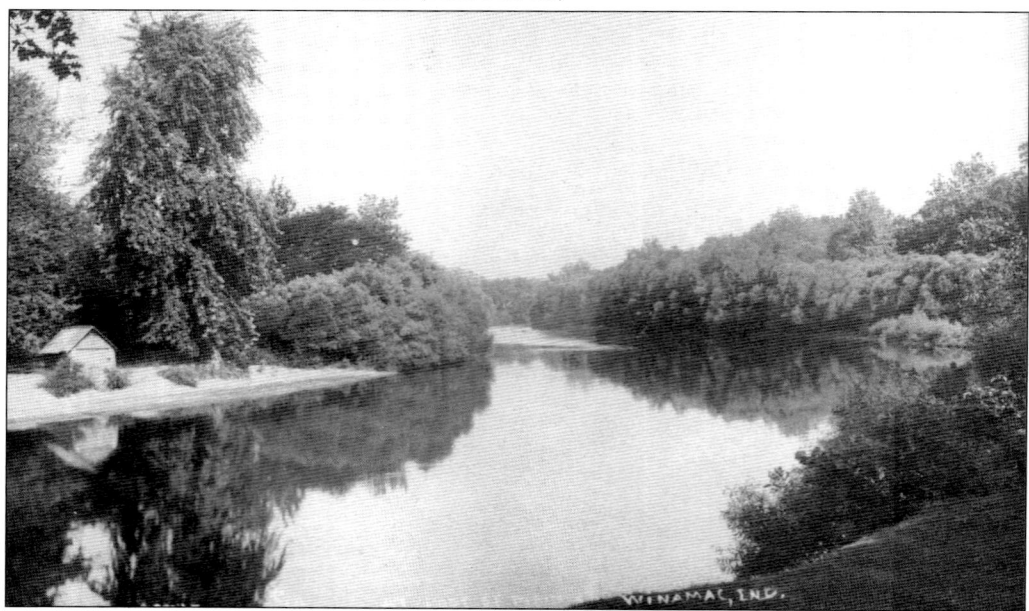

This picture looks downstream on the Tippecanoe River from the foot of Main Street in Winamac. The estimated date is 1905. Although privately owned at that time, the residents of Winamac had already come to view the property within the river peninsula as parkland. The building is believed to be an icehouse or a fishing cabin, of which there were many along both sides of the river. (Sara Slaven.)

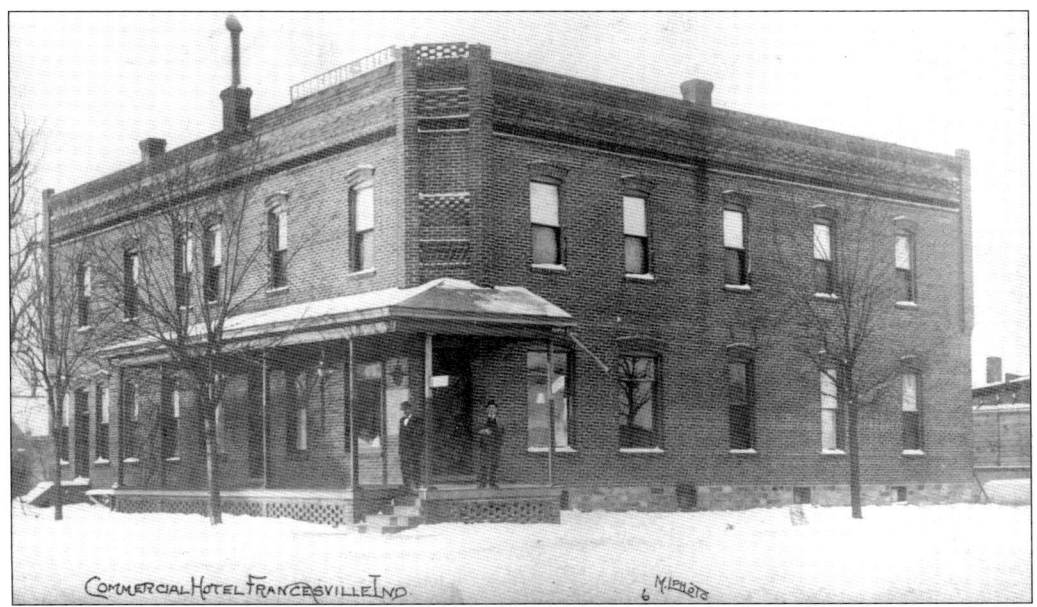

The Commercial Hotel in Francesville, shown here in 1901, was one of two or three hotels in town at the dawn of the 20th century. In the early 1900s, it was owned by John Coy. Over the decades, it had several owners, including Henry Jentz and later C. J. Weldon. Located across from the library on the corner of Monon Avenue and Montgomery Street, the building was later divided into apartments. (Janet Onken.)

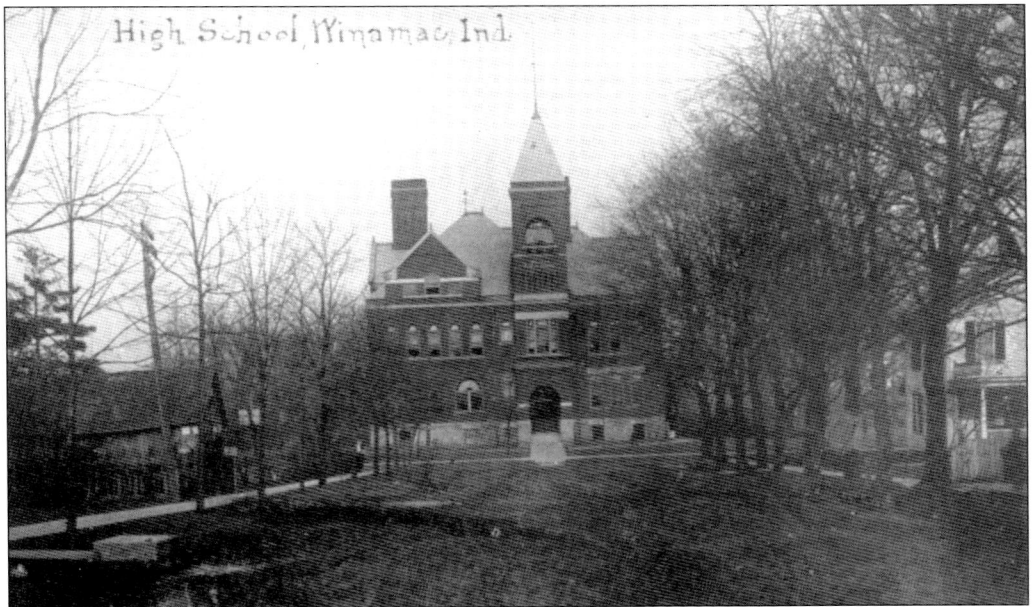

Winamac High School on Front Street (later renamed Riverside Drive) was built in 1893. This picture was taken looking east down Jefferson Street in about 1910. "The fine red-brick public school had electricity and toilets and furnace heat," recalled student Elizabeth Holdermann Frank many decades later. A new brick high school was built next door (to the right) in 1914. The Carnegie library was constructed on the left side of this school in 1916. (Dee Galbreath.)

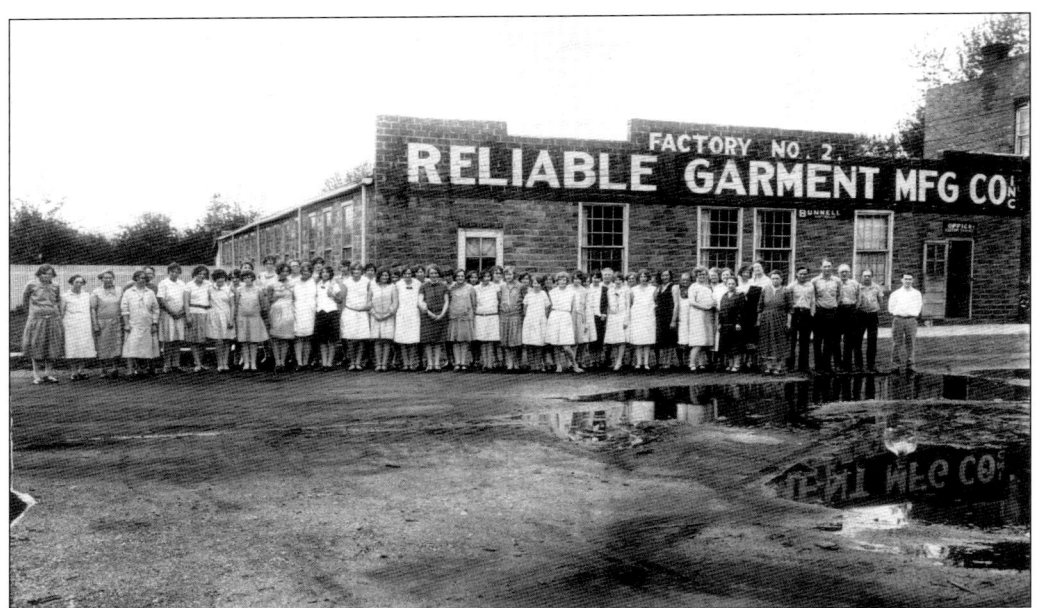

The Reliable Garment Manufacturing Company in Francesville provided jobs for local families for over a decade. In the 1920s, the Francesville Chamber of Commerce and other citizens were instrumental in convincing several enterprises to locate in town. One of these was the garment factory. Money was raised from businessmen and interested individuals to erect a building for the factory on Railroad Street (later Monon Avenue). (Bess Russell.)

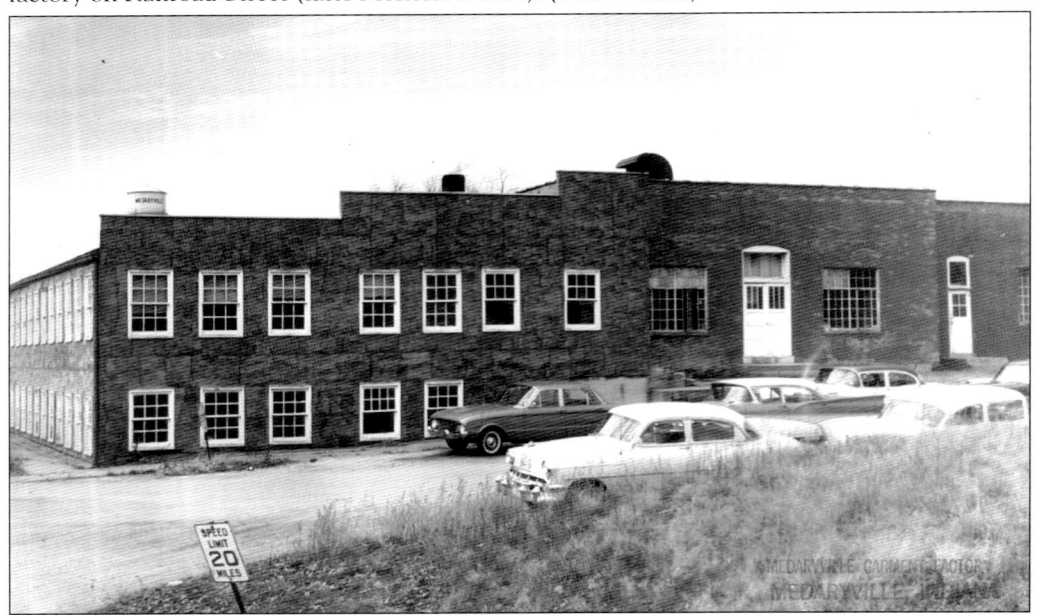

The Medaryville Garment Factory was established in 1922 by Louis Rosenberg, an Austrian immigrant who began his career in the clothing business as a tailor in Chicago. He had opened small clothing factories in several area towns before being offered a good deal by the Medaryville Commercial Club to establish a factory in the recently vacated downtown school building (shown here). After 74 years of operation, the business closed in 1996. (Medaryville History Museum.)

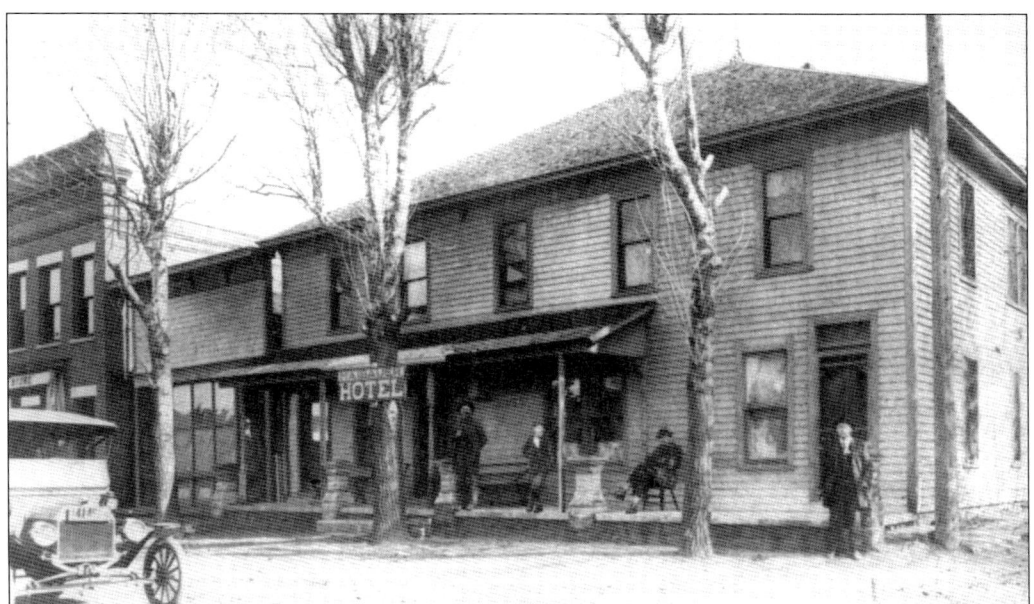

The Maibauer Hotel in Medaryville was located just east of the railroad tracks. At the time of this picture, about 1915, the building at left housed Horner's Store. It later became the bank building. The Maibauers also operated a barbershop and a shoe repair shop. (Medaryville History Museum.)

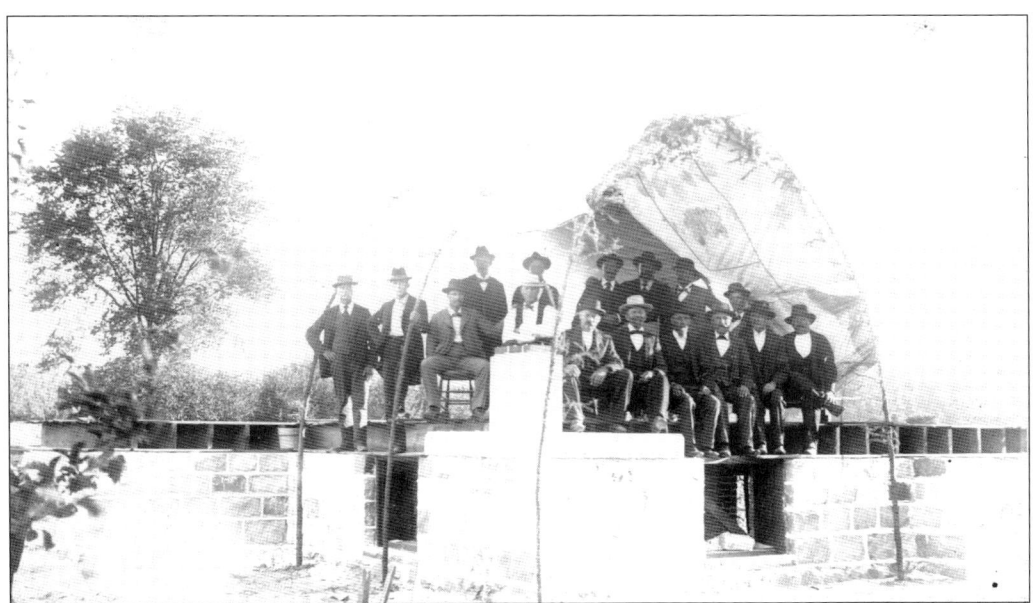

The St. Joseph Catholic Church in Pulaski was built in 1899 and dedicated in May 1900. The new church united two Catholic congregations that were separated by the Tippecanoe River. The contract to build the new church was awarded to Stephan Parcel in August 1898. The cornerstone was laid on the first Sunday in July 1899 before an estimated crowd of 500. (Brenda Gilsinger.)

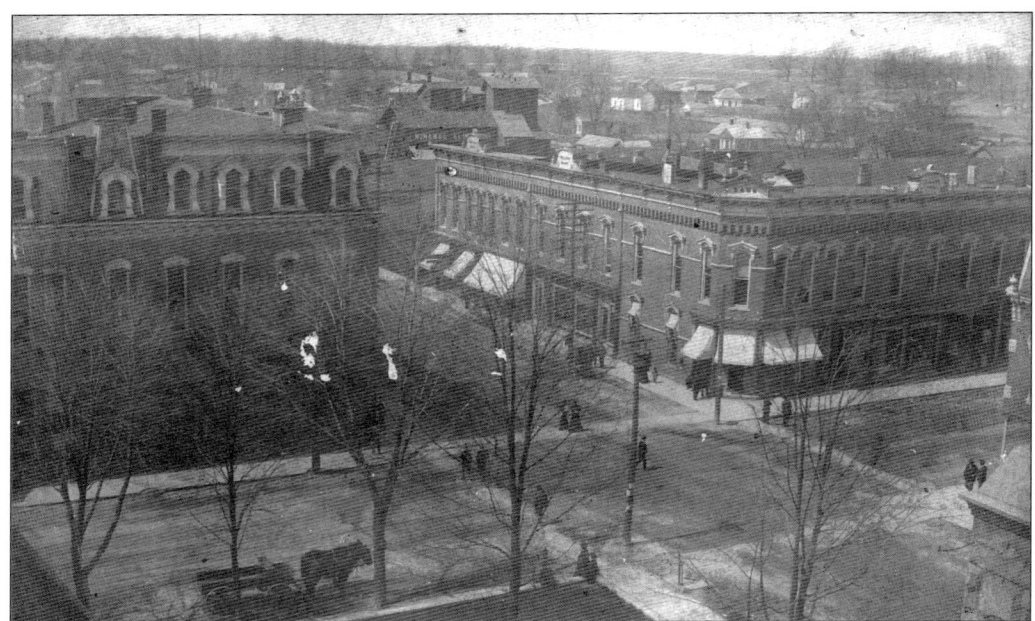

An unidentified photographer climbed into the bell tower of the new courthouse to snap this bird's-eye view of downtown Winamac in about 1896. The Frain Hotel is on the left, and the Keller Block is on the right. From the mid-1890s to the dawn of the 20th century, some street paving began in Winamac along with the replacement of board sidewalks by concrete. By the end of 1897, Winamac had telephones, electric lights, and a water system. (PCHS Museum.)

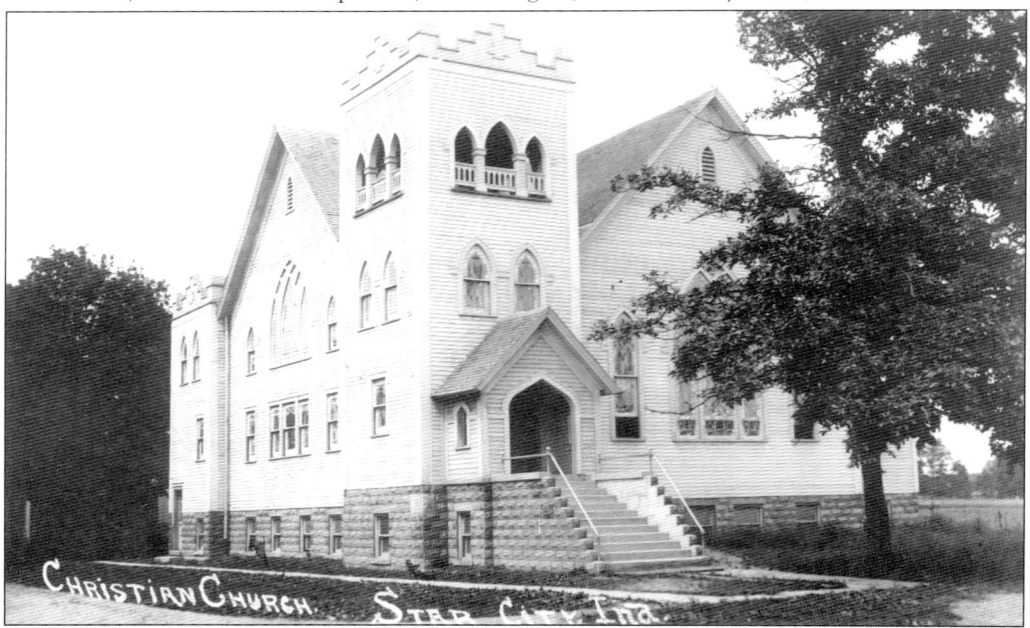

The Star City Church of Christ was organized in 1867. This white frame church was dedicated in February 1914. It replaced the original structure built in 1869 and destroyed by fire in 1913. The total cost of the new church, shown in this postcard dated 1915, was $12,000. The building was demolished in 2003. (PCHS Museum.)

The first iron bridge to cross the Tippecanoe River in the little village of Pulaski was completed in 1876 just south of the gristmill property. The double-span structure was also known as the wagon bridge. The bridge served the town for nearly a century and was then dismantled following replacement by a cement structure a little way upstream. (Brenda Gilsinger.)

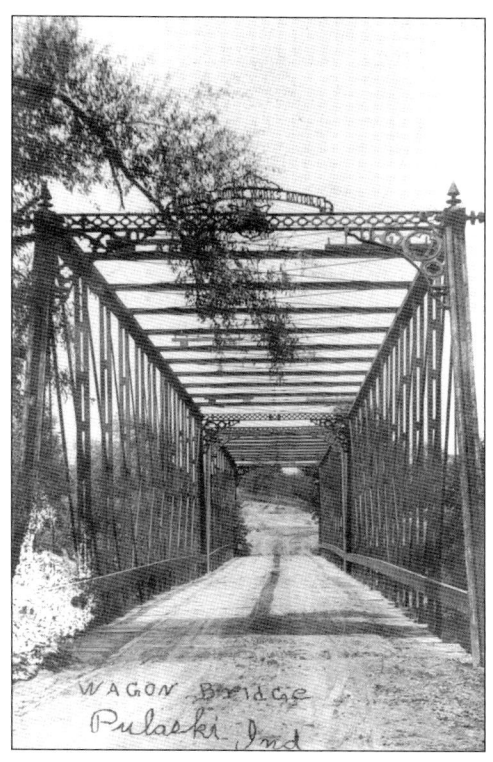

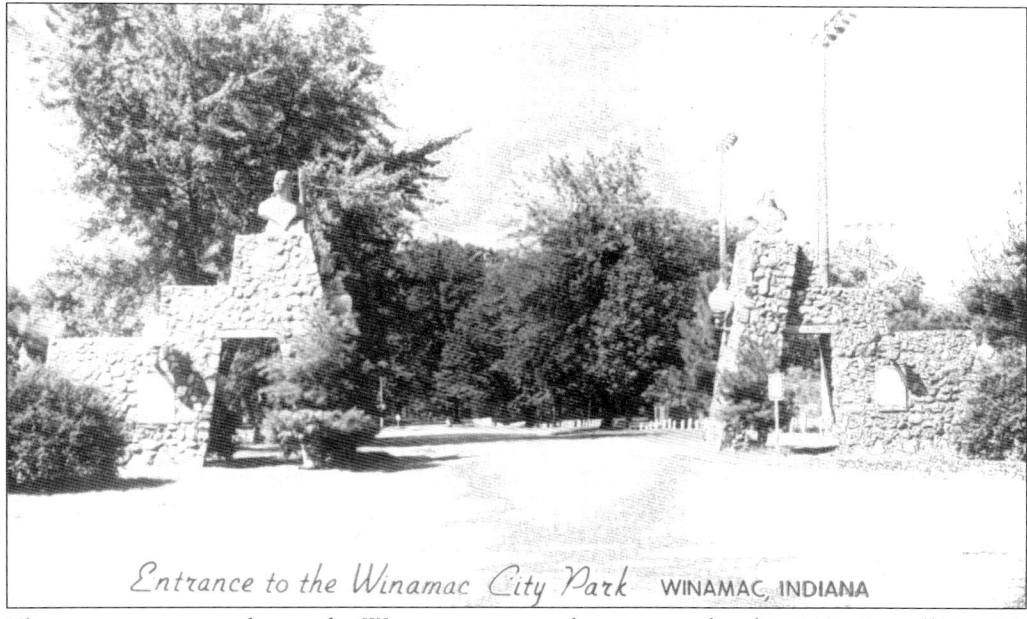

The stone gateway arches at the Winamac town park were completed in 1934. Russell Rearick carved the stone Native American heads that stand sentinel above the arches. In 1933, the park was finally deeded to the Town of Winamac from shareholders of a park association that had purchased the property in 1908. In 1922, the park association made many improvements, including a playground, bathhouses, a bandstand, and a dance pavilion. (Barb Crist.)

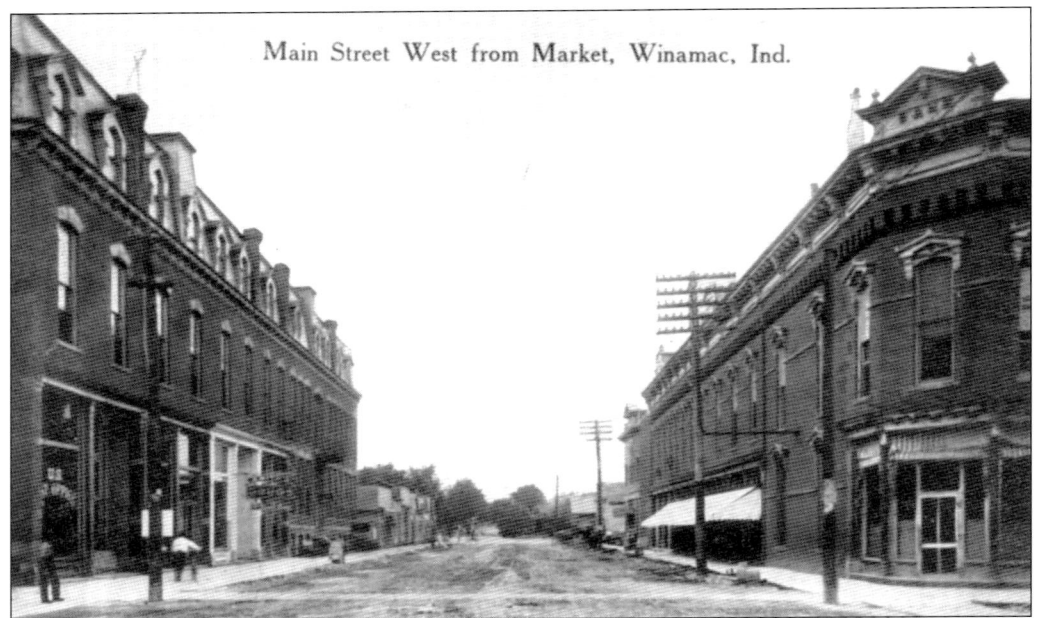

A stroll down Main Street in Winamac looked like this in about 1914, as seen in this postcard that looks west from Market Street. The Frain Hotel is on the left, and among the businesses it housed at that time were the post office and Smith Drug Store, which sold this postcard. On the right is the Keller Block, which housed the First National Bank on the corner. Holdermanns' Grocery was located under the awning. The railroad tracks crossed Main Street at the far end of this picture. (Dee Galbreath.)

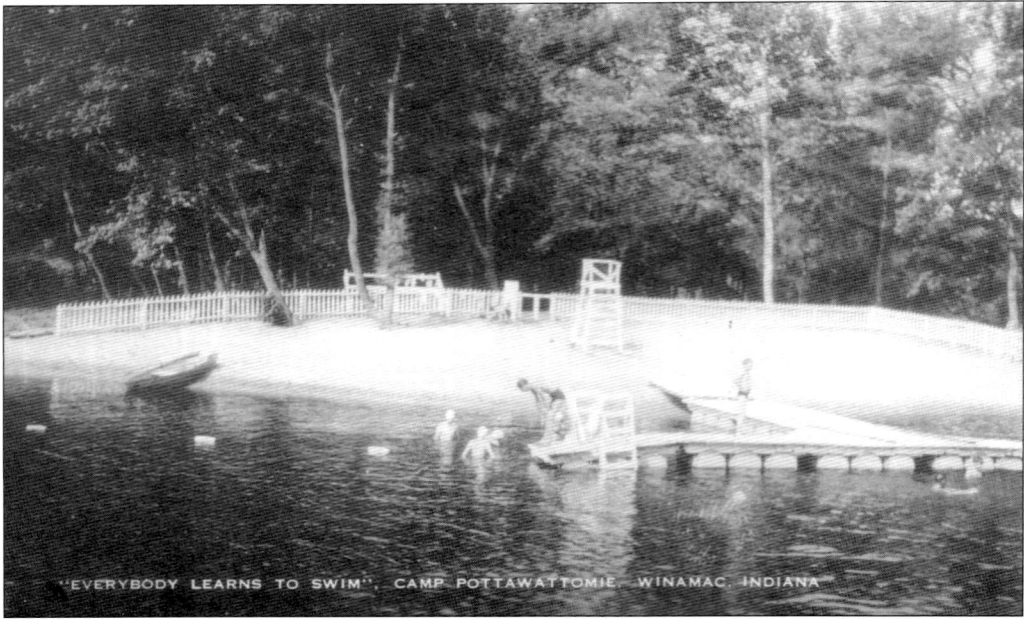

In the days before swimming pools, the Tippecanoe River provided the best means to cool off during the scorching summers. The swim beach at the Winamac town park and the one shown here in 1944 at Camp Potawatomie in the new state park were among the best. (Sara Slaven.)

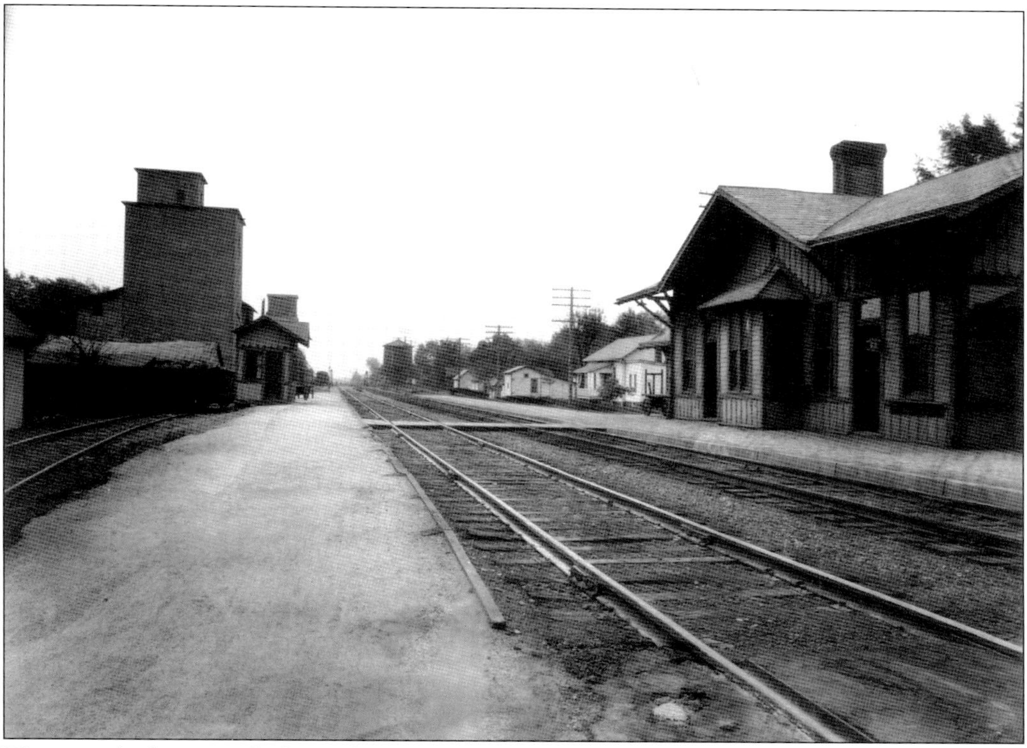

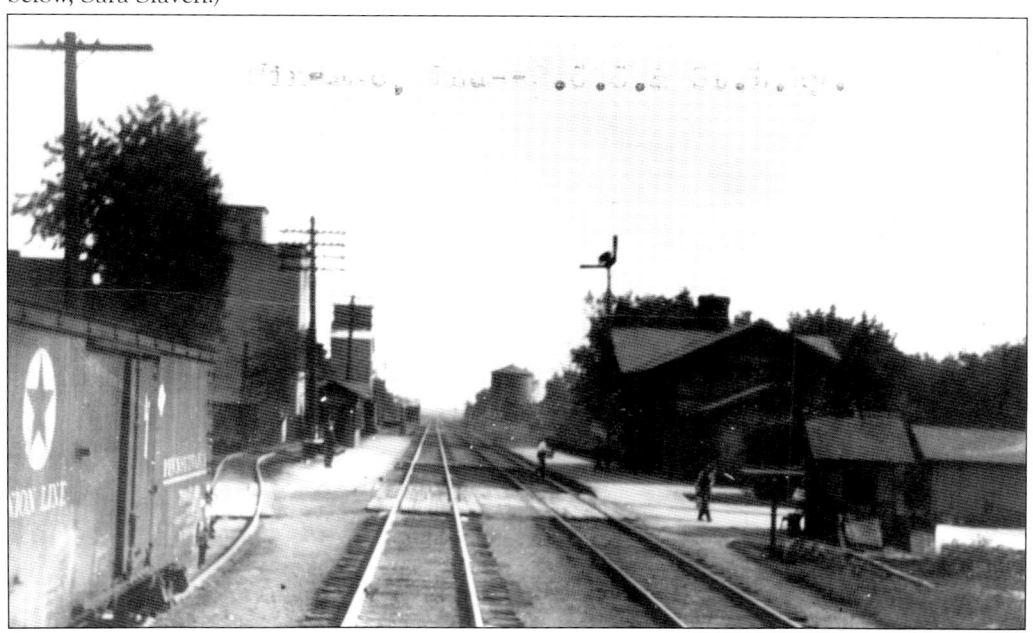

The view looking south down the Pennsylvania Railroad tracks in Winamac can be seen in both of these undated photographs that were taken near the Main Street crossing. They are believed to date to about the 1920s. The depot is at right, and the Starr Elevator can be seen down the tracks on the left. The elevator operated from 1899 to 1928. (Above, PCHS Museum; below, Sara Slaven.)

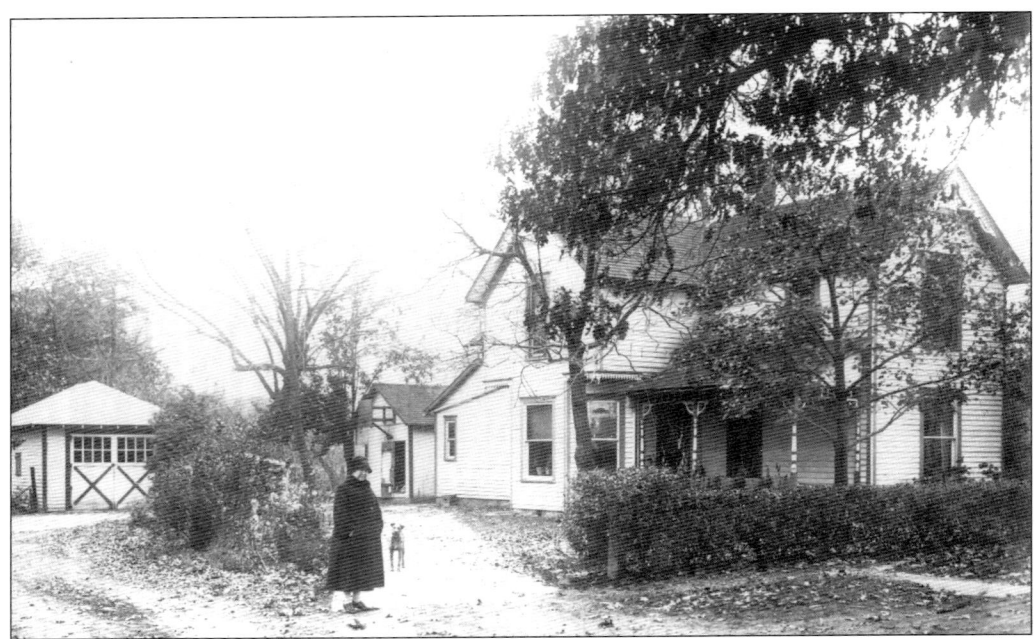

Rosa Shank Gilsinger walks with her dog in front of the family home in Pulaski in this photograph, which dates to the 1930s. Note the basketball goal on the shed behind the house. Gilsinger taught school in Indian Creek Township. She married J. P. Gilsinger in 1903. (Brenda Gilsinger.)

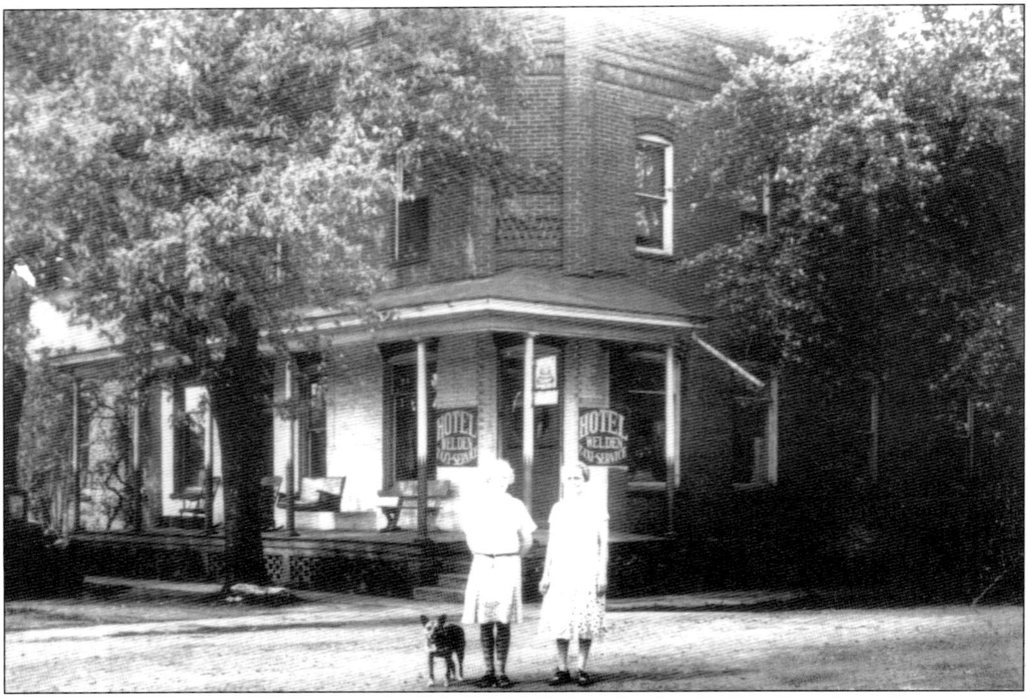

Kathleen Maddox (left) and Minnie Weldon stand outside the Weldon Hotel on the corner of Monon Avenue and Montgomery Street in Francesville. The date is estimated to be in the late 1920s. The Weldons bought the hotel in 1924. (Alyce Onken.)

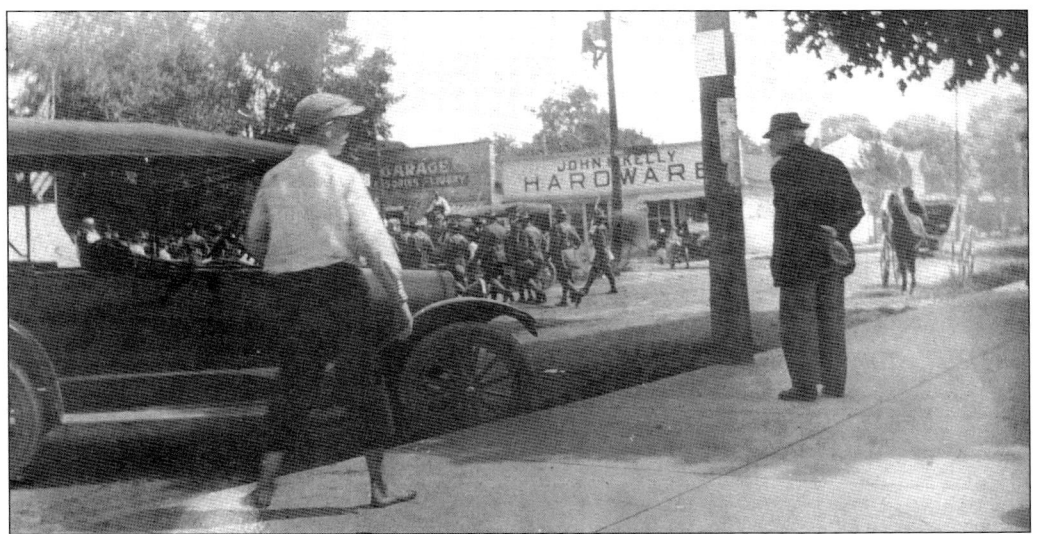

A barefoot youth walks along Main Street while an old man reads a notice on a utility pole in front of the courthouse in Winamac in this 1916 photograph. A local militia group can be seen across the street. It was encamped there for a few days before being sent to Indianapolis and then to Texas during a conflict with Mexico. (PCHS Museum.)

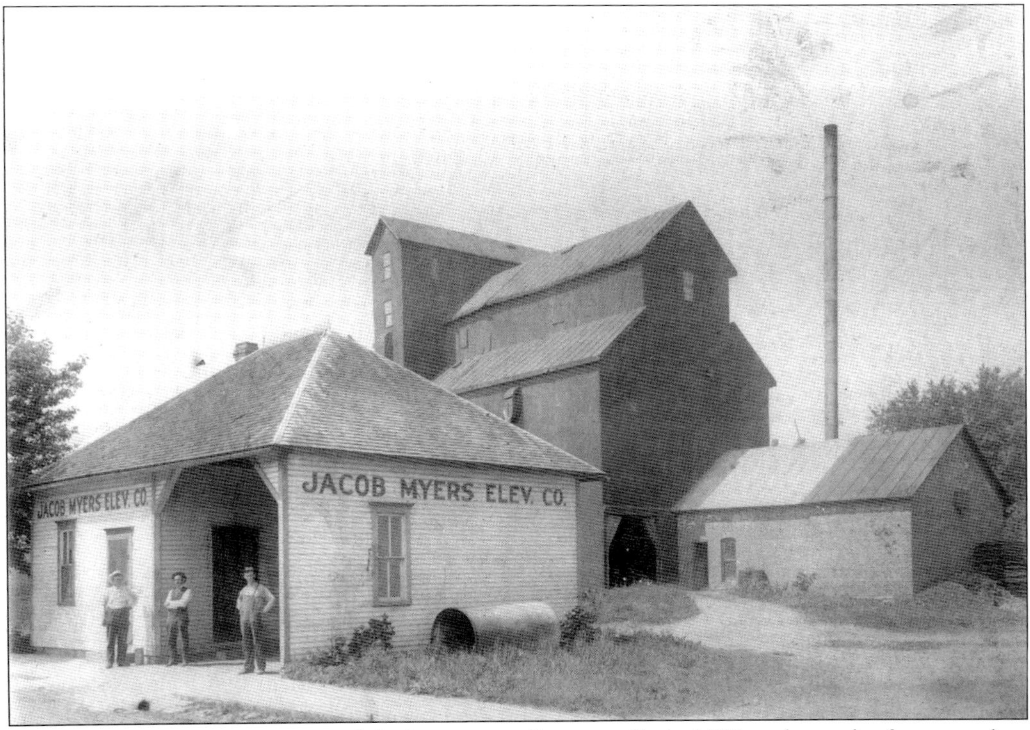

The Jacob Myers elevator opened for business in Francesville in 1896 and was the first complete elevator in the town. In 1914, about the time this picture was taken, the facility became known as Myers Brothers Elevator, operated by Myers's sons Hart (center) and Roy J. (right). The elevator was destroyed by fire in March 1916. (Alyce Onken.)

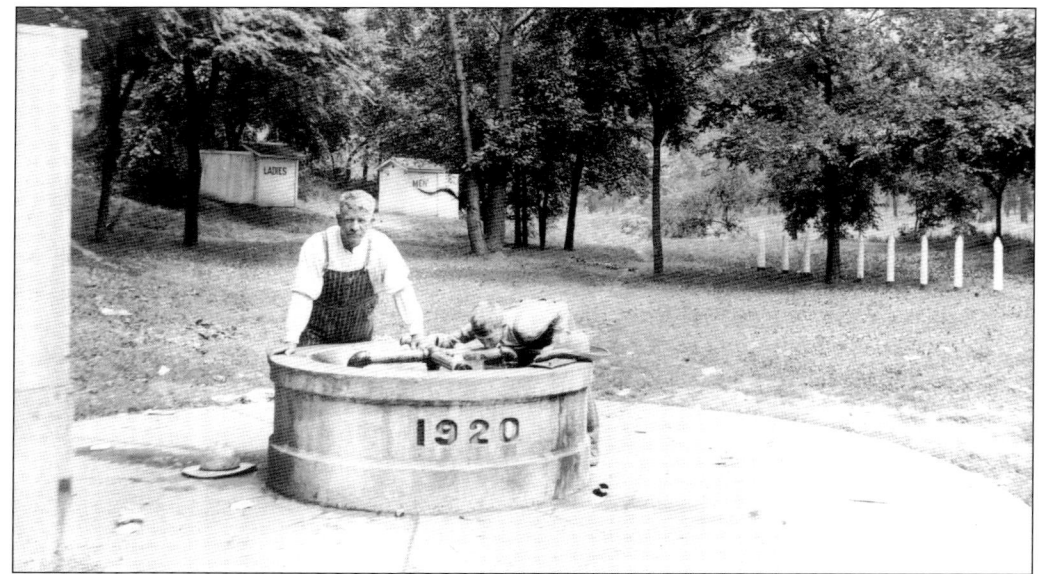

The artesian well in the Winamac town park was drilled in 1887 by the Winamac Gas and Oil Company during Indiana's natural gas boom. Neither gas nor oil was discovered, but a water vein was struck at 264 feet. In this photograph, taken about 1922, young Reuben Olson sips artesian water from the well, while his father, Charles, looks on. By 1920, the well had been damaged through age and vandalism, and it was improved and repaired in that year. (Charlene Olson Fritz.)

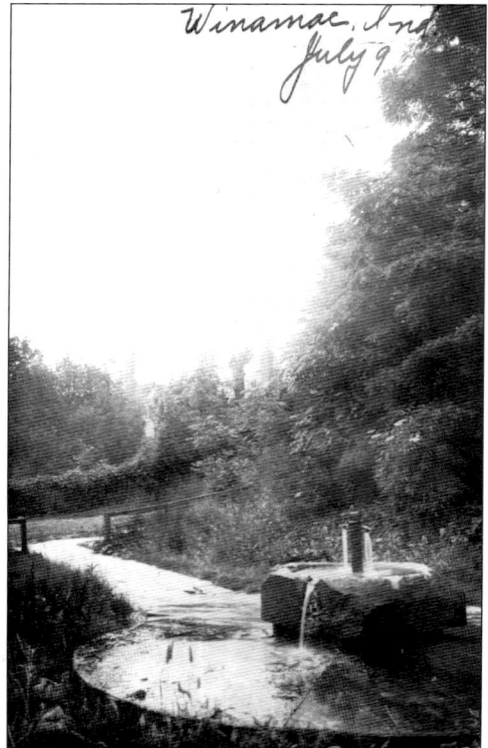

Soon after the artesian well was drilled, an attempt was made to interest town visitors in the "medicinal properties" of the sulfurous-tasting water. The possibility of setting up artesian baths was also considered. Although the idea appealed to many, nothing came of it. This photograph dates to 1905. On the 100th anniversary of the well, the Pulaski County Historical Society placed a historical marker at its site. (Dee Galbreath.)

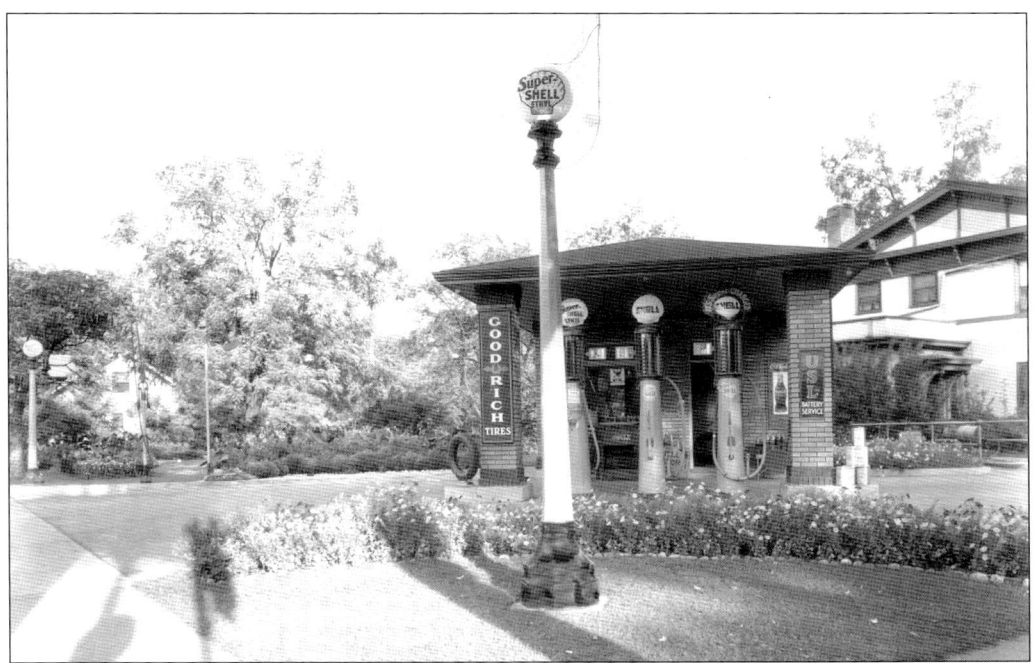

This vintage Shell gas station once stood at the southeast corner of Monticello and Main Streets in Winamac. Edward Haag and Johnny Benbow purchased the station in 1927. A few years later, Haag bought out his partner and continued to run the business until 1943. The station was well known in the community for the extensive flower gardens Haag planted behind it. This photograph was taken in June 1934. (PCHS Museum, donated by Beulah Haag Roller.)

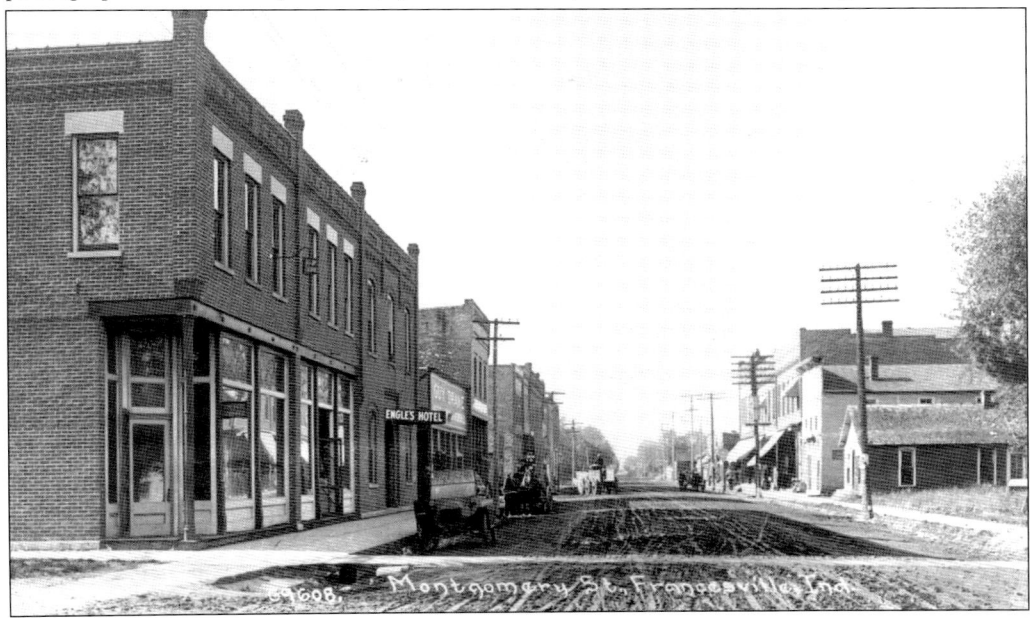

This view of Montgomery Street in Francesville looks west from Brooks Street. The postcard was postmarked in August 1914. A doctor's office was located in the corner building at left. The Engle Hotel is two doors down. (Sara Slaven.)

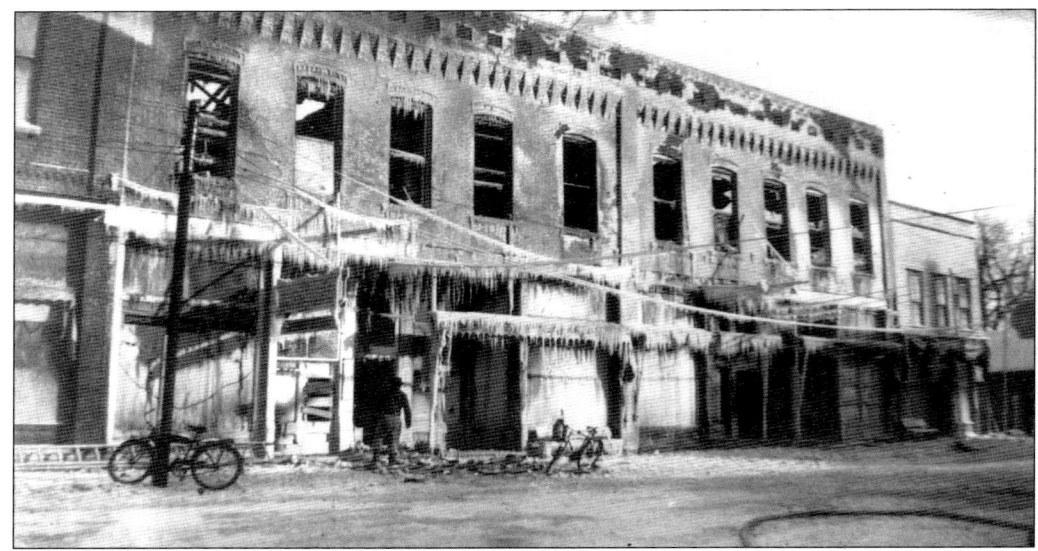

A devastating Christmas Eve 1944 fire consumed almost an entire business block of Francesville. This Christmas morning photograph shows the destruction to Sullivan's Drugs, Nolan's Clothing, Ellis's Grocery, Nolan's Grocery, plus offices and apartments above the stores. Although the losses were heavy, Sullivan's reopened across the street within a few months. Within the year, Weaver Brothers rebuilt the east section of the block and opened a spacious grocery store. Soon after, Getz Plumbing and Heating occupied the rebuilt middle section of the block. (Janet Onken.)

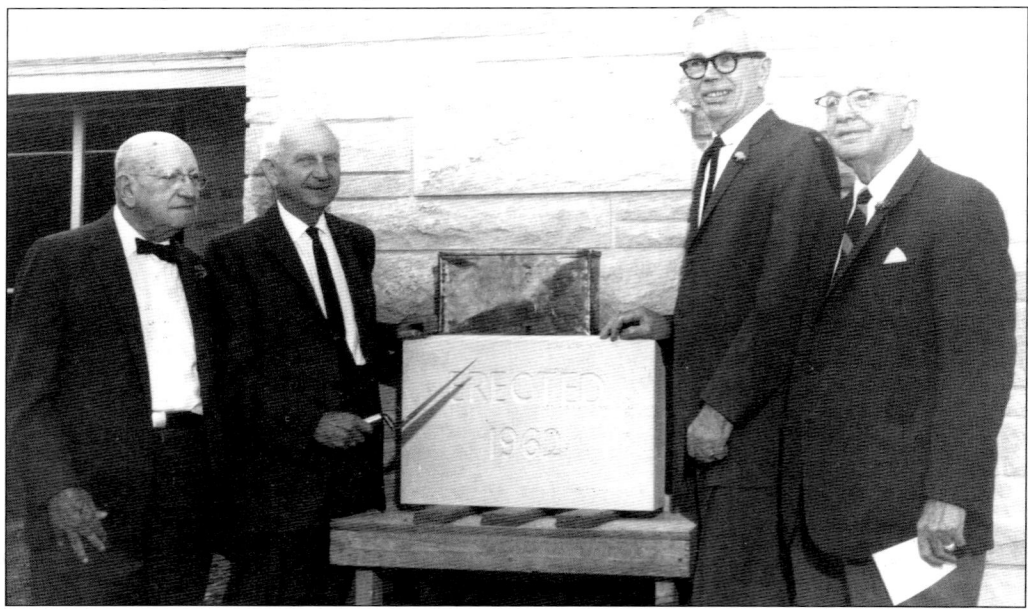

The cornerstone of Pulaski Memorial Hospital was set in place during a ceremony in September 1962. Former Indiana governor Henry Schricker of Knox (second from left) was the guest speaker. With him, from left to right, are Edmund (Ned) Gorrell, Charles Arens, and Ralph Horner. The $700,000 hospital was dedicated on March 3, 1963. During the first week at the hospital, 25 patients were admitted, three babies were born, and several surgeries were performed. (R. Marshall Fritz family.)

Two

PEOPLE MET ALONG THE WAY

"Nobody in town is rich," weekly newspaper editor Ned Gorrell once told a historian in 1946, speaking of the people of Winamac and Pulaski County. "Everybody made it a dime here, a dime there."

To the casual observer, Pulaski County people are just ordinary folks in an out-of-the-way location. Nobody fabulously famous ever came from Pulaski County. But its citizens are special and important to each other in this close-knit and self-reliant county community. They include doctors, farmers, pioneers, soldiers, church congregations, businessmen and women, adventurers, politicians, firemen, and best friends—young and old. They are people who steadfastly go about their business day by day but who will gladly take a minute to chat about family news, listen with real sympathy to a concern, or simply share a companionable observation about the changeable Indiana weather.

Pulaski County residents have often contributed their efforts for the good of the country or made an impact on the outside world. Gorrell told the same historian about a local soldier who landed on a Pacific beach during World War II and found two copies of the *Pulaski County Democrat* in the sand. Agriculture products and manufactured goods have crossed the county lines to enrich the lives of people around the world. Many of those who grew up here have left to teach, preach, heal, build, and serve across the country and beyond the oceans.

Thanks largely to Gorrell, Winamac became the smallest town in the United States in 1921 to have a Kiwanis Club. Because of the solid efforts of men and women like him, this internationally connected club continues with its world and community projects more than 85 years later. They represent the big-hearted people found everywhere across small-town Pulaski County throughout its history, a few of who will be met in this chapter.

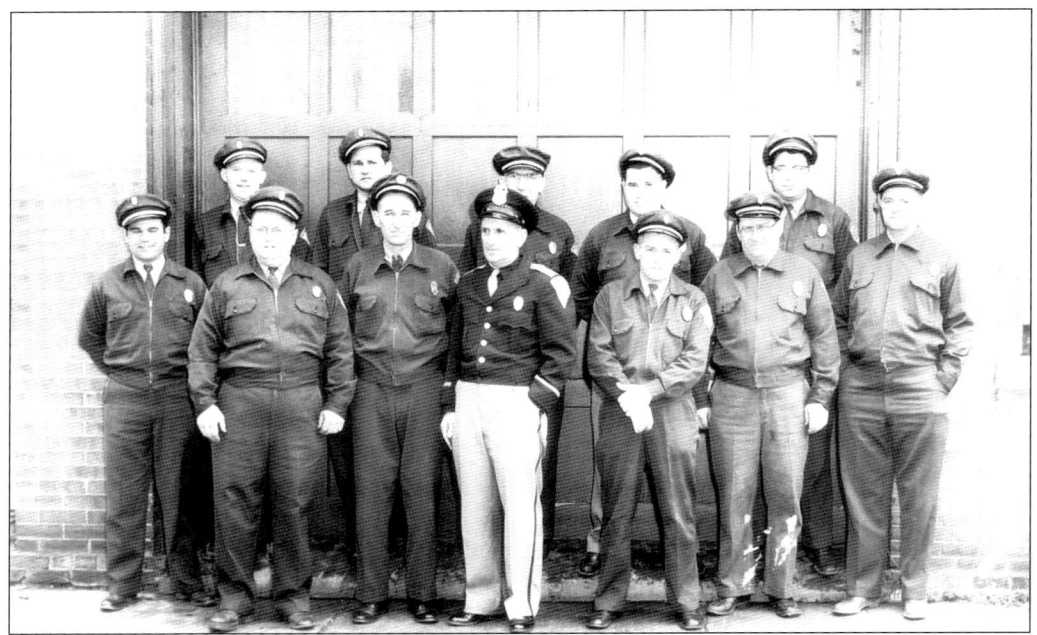

Members of the Medaryville Volunteer Fire Department gathered for this picture in 1958. From left to right are (first row) Tom Howe, Herman Ahler, Bill Schultz, town marshal Ogle "Ring" Lowry, George Schultz, Bill Brick, and Chester Coburn; (second row) Jim Stoll, Bob Clark, Omer Turner, Paul Schultz, and Joe Clark. (Medaryville History Museum.)

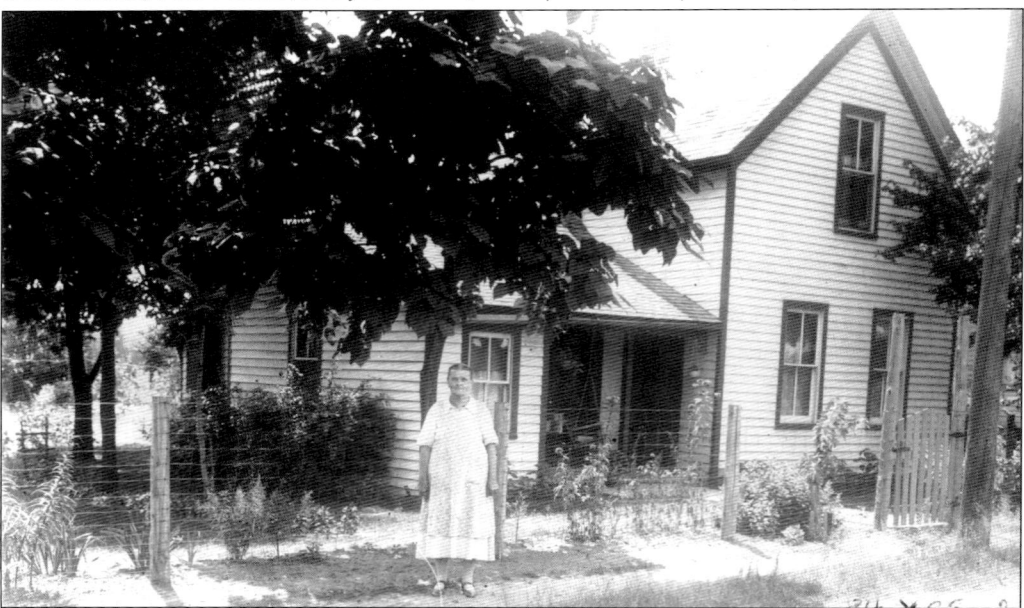

Trasie Nitzschke Schuttrow, at age 74, stands outside her home in Denham in this Great Depression–era photograph taken about 1934. Denham grew up around the railroad station that was established there in 1860. In its heyday, the tiny town had grocery and general stores, a grain elevator, a hat shop, two churches, a school, a saloon, and a pickle factory, among other businesses. (Patrick Schuttrow.)

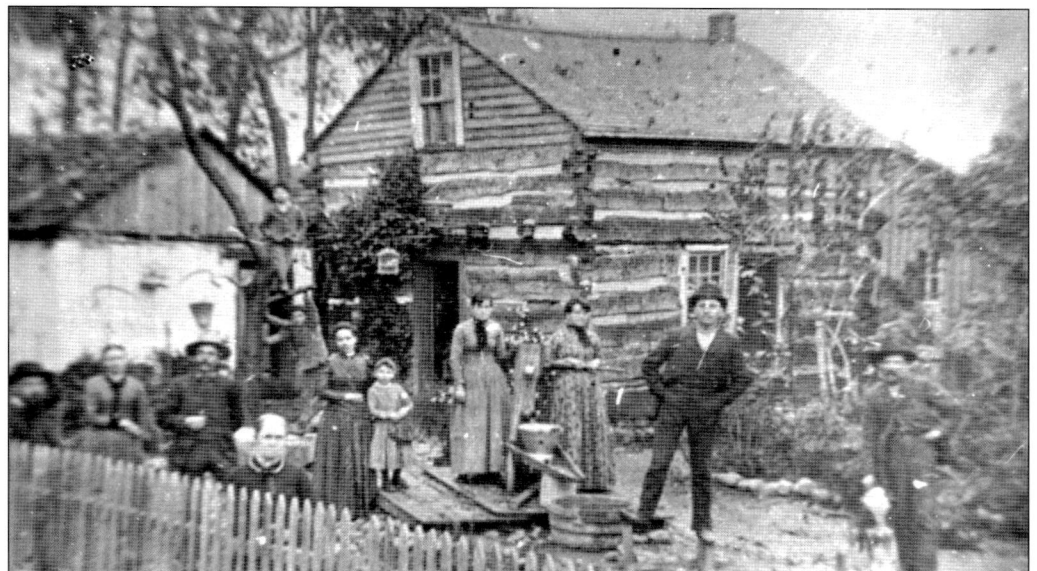

Gawin Sutton Ward and his wife, Love Jane Doud Ward, were married in February 1850 and built this hewed-log house on 40 acres of land purchased in Harrison Township. His father, Samuel, was a pioneer in Harrison Township, moving there in 1840. Samuel's father, John Ward, served in the Revolutionary War. Gawin Ward was a farmer who also hauled freight, mostly salt, from Michigan City to Kewanna. The only person identified in this photograph is Gawin's son Oliver Thomas Ward (born in 1861), second from right. (Carl Williams.)

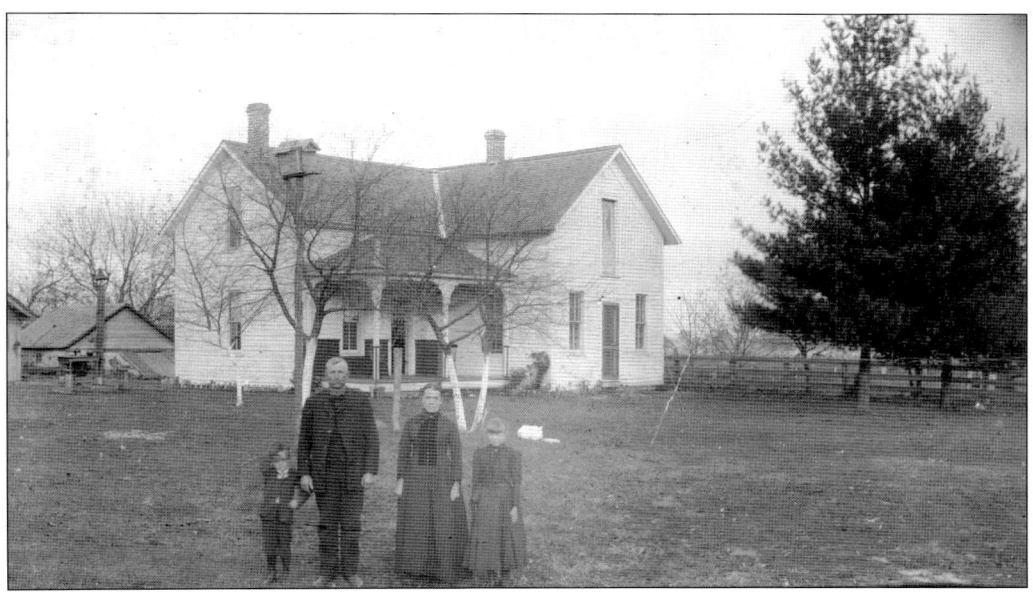

The Moyer family, German immigrants, moved into Indian Creek Township in 1846, making their way from Pennsylvania and then Ohio, a typical migration pattern. Andrew Martin Moyer married Anna Mohart Thompson in 1877. The couple is shown at their farm near Pulaski in about 1892 with daughter Cassie and son Josiah. They were members of the Pepper Church, a German Reformed Church in the neighborhood. (Lois Bishop Heater.)

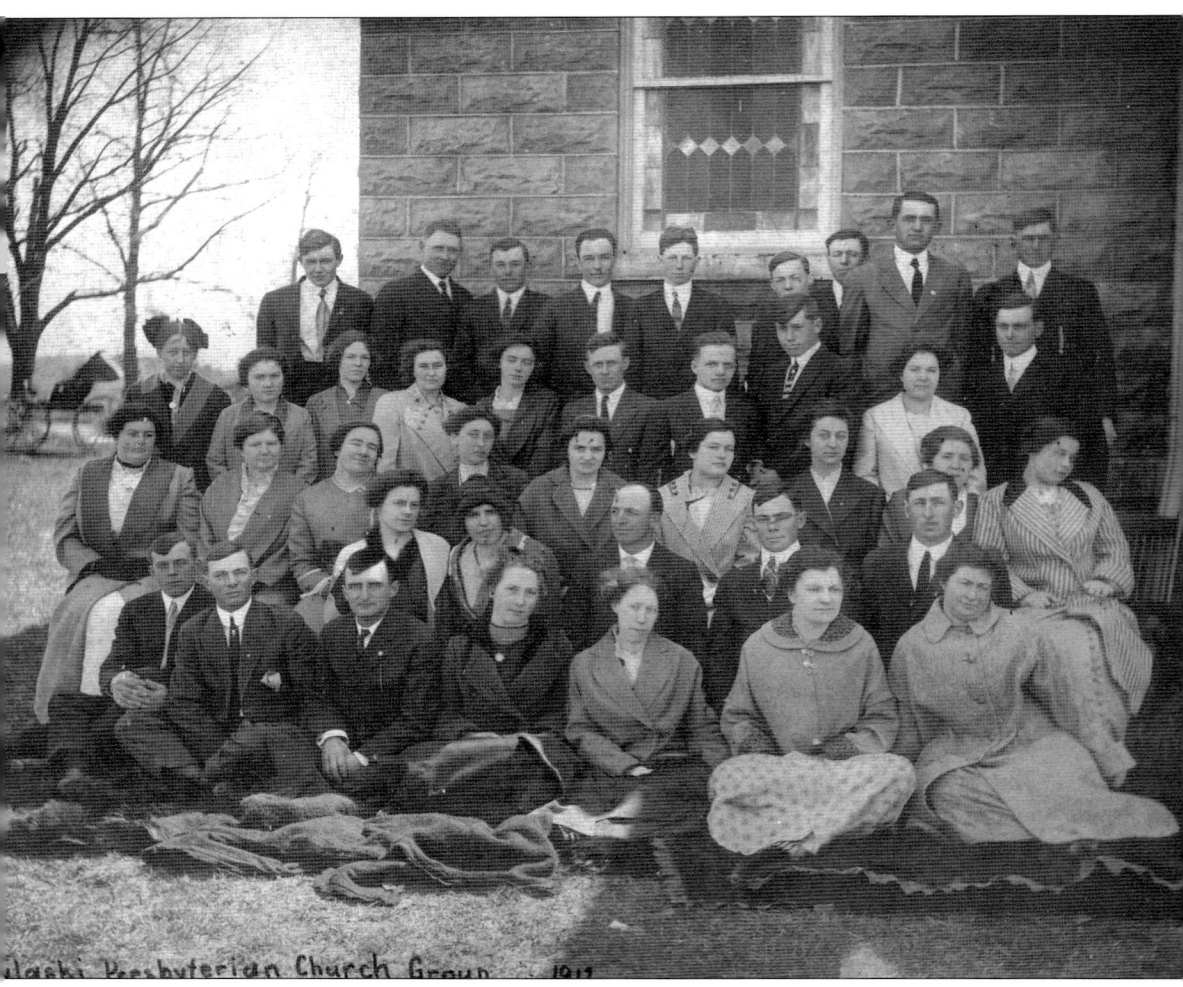

All across Pulaski County, residents, such as these 1912 members of the Pulaski Presbyterian Church, turned to their neighborhood parishes through the decades to nourish their souls and nurture each other. Pictured from left to right are (first row) Carl March, Merle Bowers, Newton Brown, Irene Harpster Nice, Angie Key, Maude Trapp, and Anna Long; (second row) Nellie Paul, Ethel Lowery, Henry "Banty" Wolfe, Harry Bowers, and Schuyler Budd; (third row) Ilo Hoover Stolp, ? Lamb, Gladys Kestle Wolfe, Rose Brucker Hedges, Jeanetta Brown, Sylvia Lowry, Mable Hare, Dora Wolfe Berg, and Ocie Lowry Blinn; (fourth row) Ruth Hare Cotner, Rose Collins Warner, Lestia Lowry, unidentified, Gladys Shaw Harpster, Cloyd "Pete" Long, Charles Brown, Ray Harpster, Gertha Plotner Phillips, and Earl Phillips; (fifth row) Carl Felker, Joe Felker, Oscar Lowery, Ronald Shaw, Albert Kestle, William Shaw, Marion Lamb, Chauncey Felker, and Grover Hedges. (PCHS Museum.)

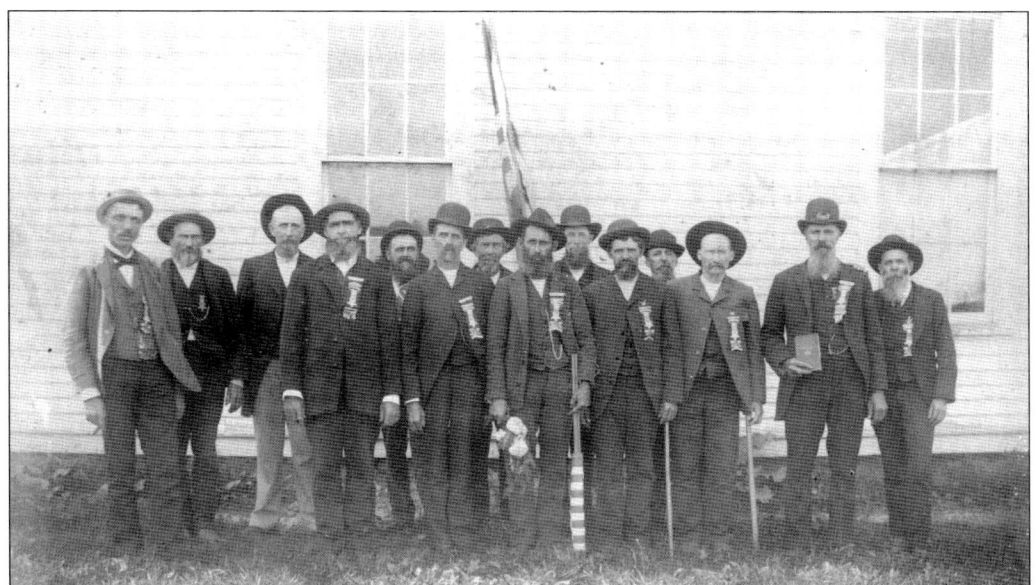

A notice circulated through Winamac within days of the fall of Fort Sumter and the call of Pres. Abraham Lincoln for 75,000 militia. Hundreds of Pulaski County men enlisted. Among them were these men from Francesville. For decades after the Civil War, county veterans gathered on occasion to share their experiences. This picture is believed to date to the early 1900s. The only man identified is Stephen Thrasher who is holding the flag and flowers. (Alyce Onken.)

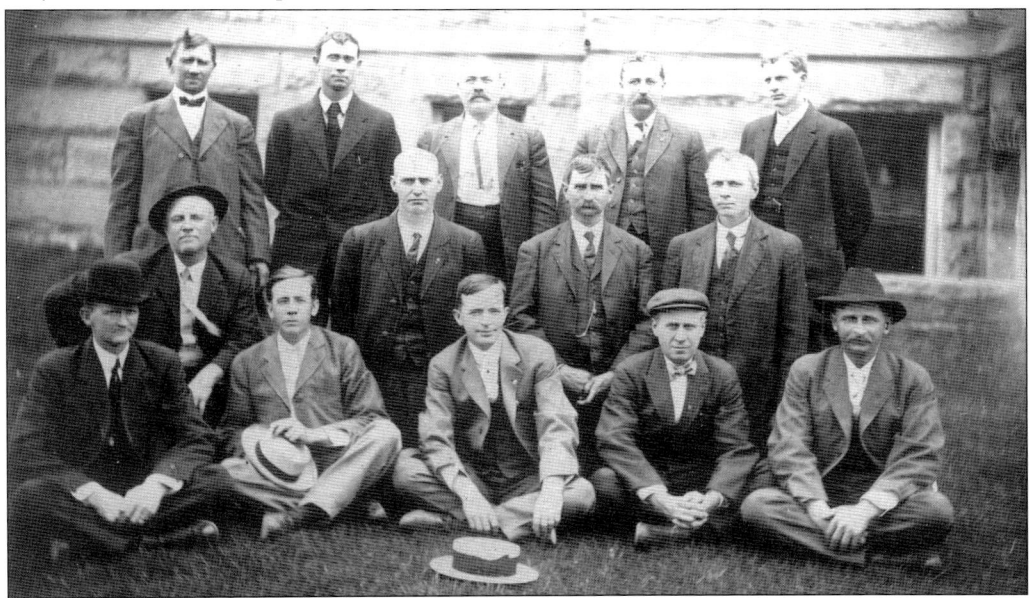

Trustees who served Pulaski County townships from 1908 to 1914 are pictured, including Charles Korner of Van Buren, Ralph Horner, Fred Senn of Indian Creek, George Stipp of Monroe, and county school superintendent Homer Rogers; identifications are not specified to figures in the photograph. Other trustees serving at the time were Jacob Hoffman, John Capouch, John Deckman, Charles Miller, Frank White, Adam James, Fred Westphal, Henry Reinhold, and Dave Bowman. (PCHS Museum, donated by Mrs. Harry Korner.)

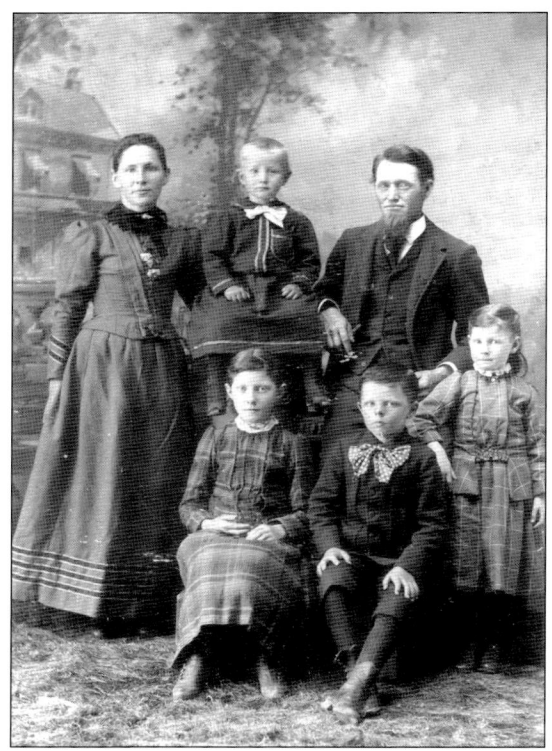

Rudolph and Mary Jane Wiesjahn and their children pose for this formal family portrait, taken by the Wharton Studio in Winamac in about 1892. They lived in Harrison Township. The oldest son (seated in the first row) is Charles, born in 1882. He operated a dairy in Star City in the 1920s and 1930s. The youngest son, Henry, is at top center. (R. Marshall Fritz family.)

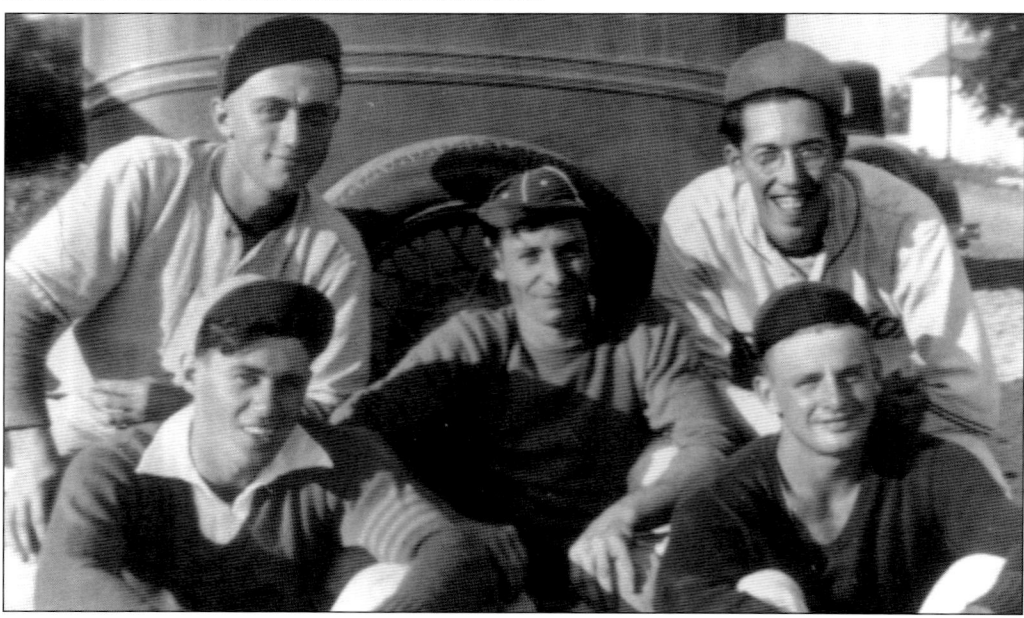

Money may have been scarce in 1938, but tough times never prevented good buddies from enjoying each other's company. There were always ball games in the park, talkie movies at the new Isis Theatre for about 25¢, school plays and operettas, or summer chautauquas. Sharing time together in this picture are, from left to right, (first row) Bob Harpster and Darl Good; (second row) Bob Raderstorf, Gerald Crist, and Suie Shank. (PCHS Museum, donated by June Kestle.)

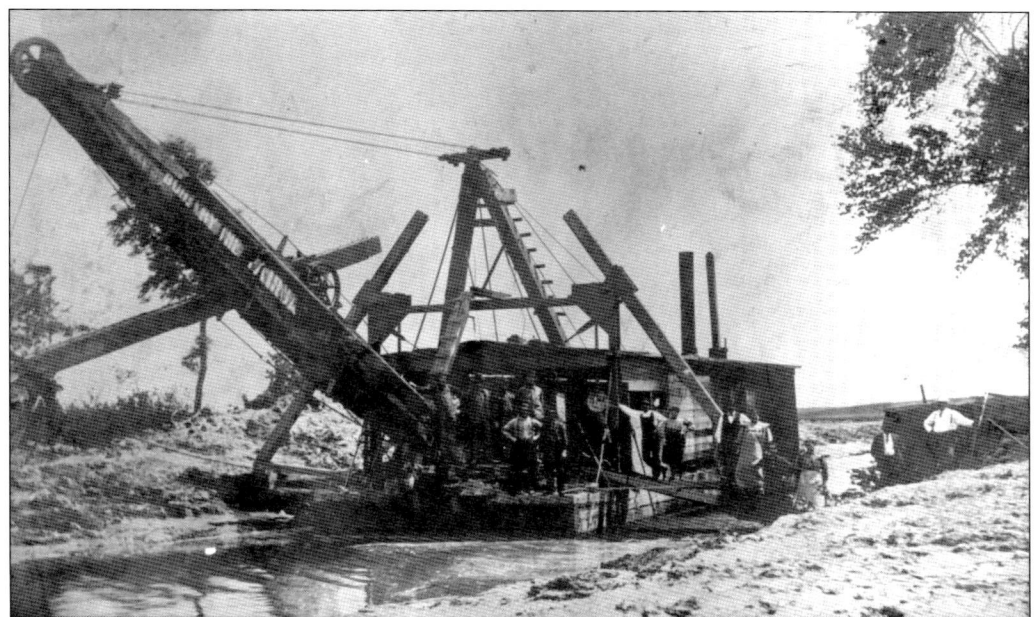

Pulaski County has nearly 1,000 miles of drainage ditches, which are important for ensuring productive cropland. Petitions to the surveyor's office for digging ditches date back to at least 1877. This dredge boat may be among those that operated in Tippecanoe Township in the early 1900s. The crew included some women who did the cooking and laundry on the boat. (Neal Hiatt.)

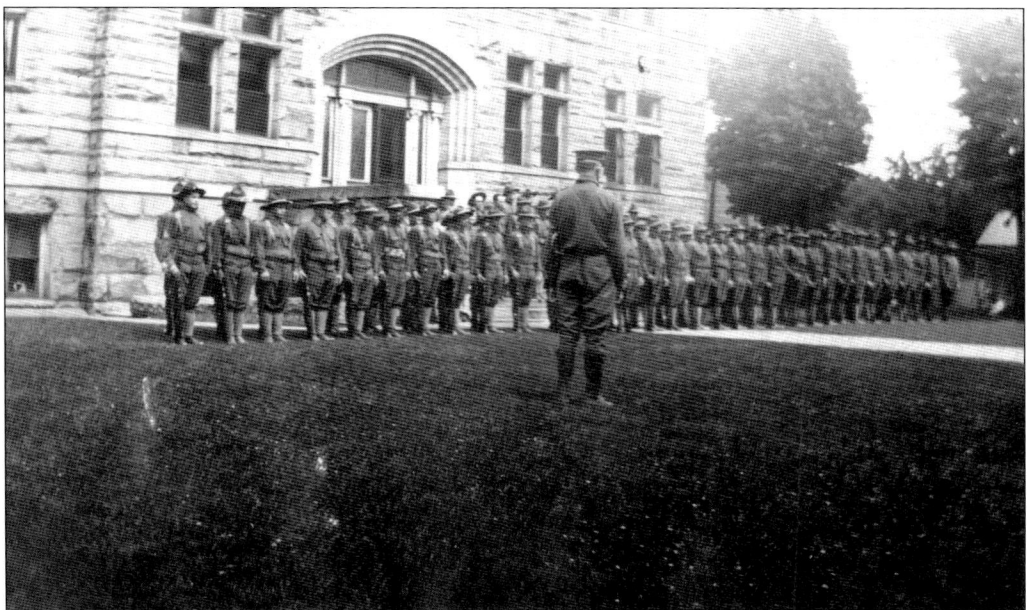

The Winamac Militia, part of the Indiana National Guard, stands for inspection in 1916 before leaving to help settle a border conflict with Mexico. The men camped in tents opposite the courthouse in Winamac for several days and then departed for Fort Harrison in Indianapolis. By mid-July, they were in Texas, and they were home in another five months. (PCHS Museum.)

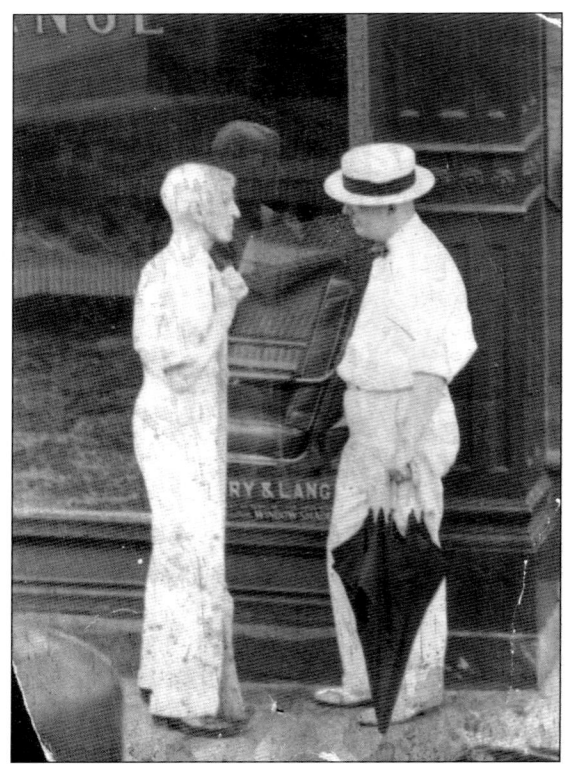

Businessman Marshall "Mac" Carper (left) visits with lawyer Ralph Horner in this undated photograph taken in front of the Fry and Lange furniture store on Market Street in Winamac. Born in 1858, Carper was first a telegrapher, employed at different stations along the Panhandle Railroad. He became better known as proprietor of Carper's Drug Store in Winamac, which he opened in 1879 and continued in business for 59 years. When Carper died in 1936, it was revealed that a $25,000 scholarship for high school graduating seniors had been set up in his name and that of his wife, Lola. (Charles McKinley.)

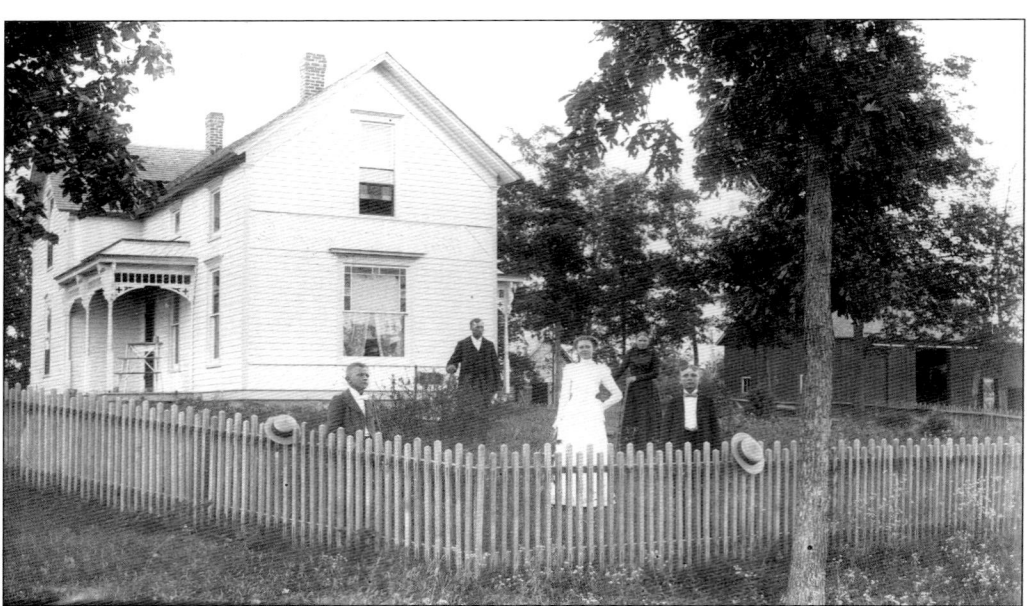

The John F. Kopka family gathered for this photograph on the lawn of their rural farm home in Salem Township about 1900. Pictured from left to right are son Silas; John F.; daughter Theresa; wife, Minnie Westphal Kopka; and son Robert. John F. was elected county commissioner in 1900 and served two terms. (PCHS Museum.)

Frank Kopkey was one of Winamac's more colorful personalities. He served as sheriff for eight years during the 1920s, a vigilant enforcer of prohibition laws. He chased bootleggers crossing through the county between Indianapolis and Chicago. Even so, son Jay recalls, "I never did see Dad put a pair of handcuffs on anybody." Perhaps that had something to do with Kopkey's reputation as a skillful boxer. At age 17, the farm boy went west with his four brothers and settled in Tacoma, Washington, where he worked in a fire station. He took up boxing and soon earned the name "Tacoma Bear Cat." For eight years, Kopkey fought in matches up and down the West Coast as a light heavyweight boxer. After returning to Winamac and becoming sheriff, Kopkey participated in a few more boxing matches in the early 1920s. He later became a Winamac insurance and real estate agent. (Jay Kopkey.)

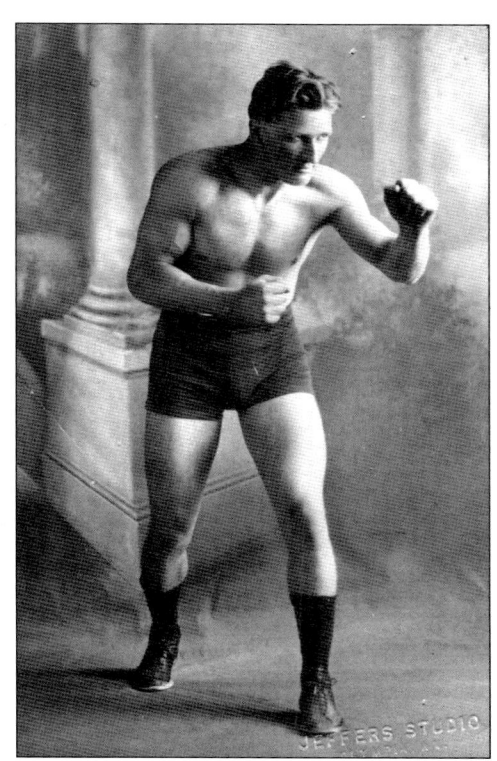

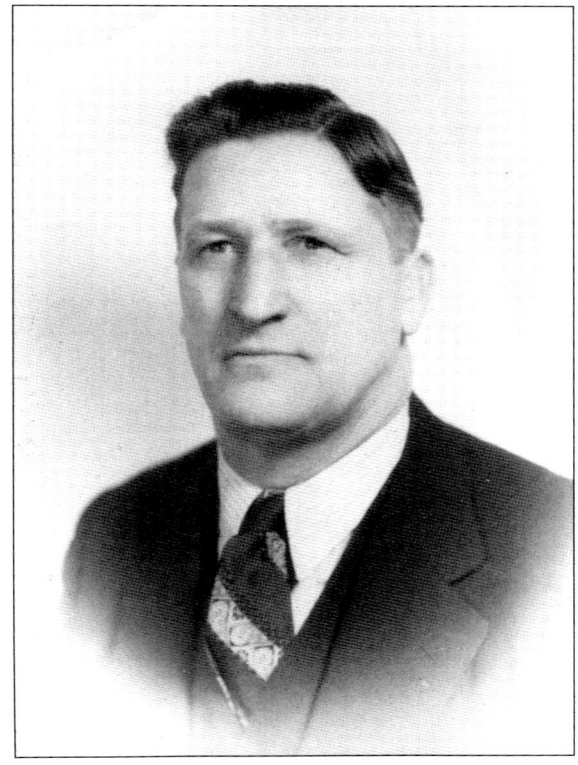

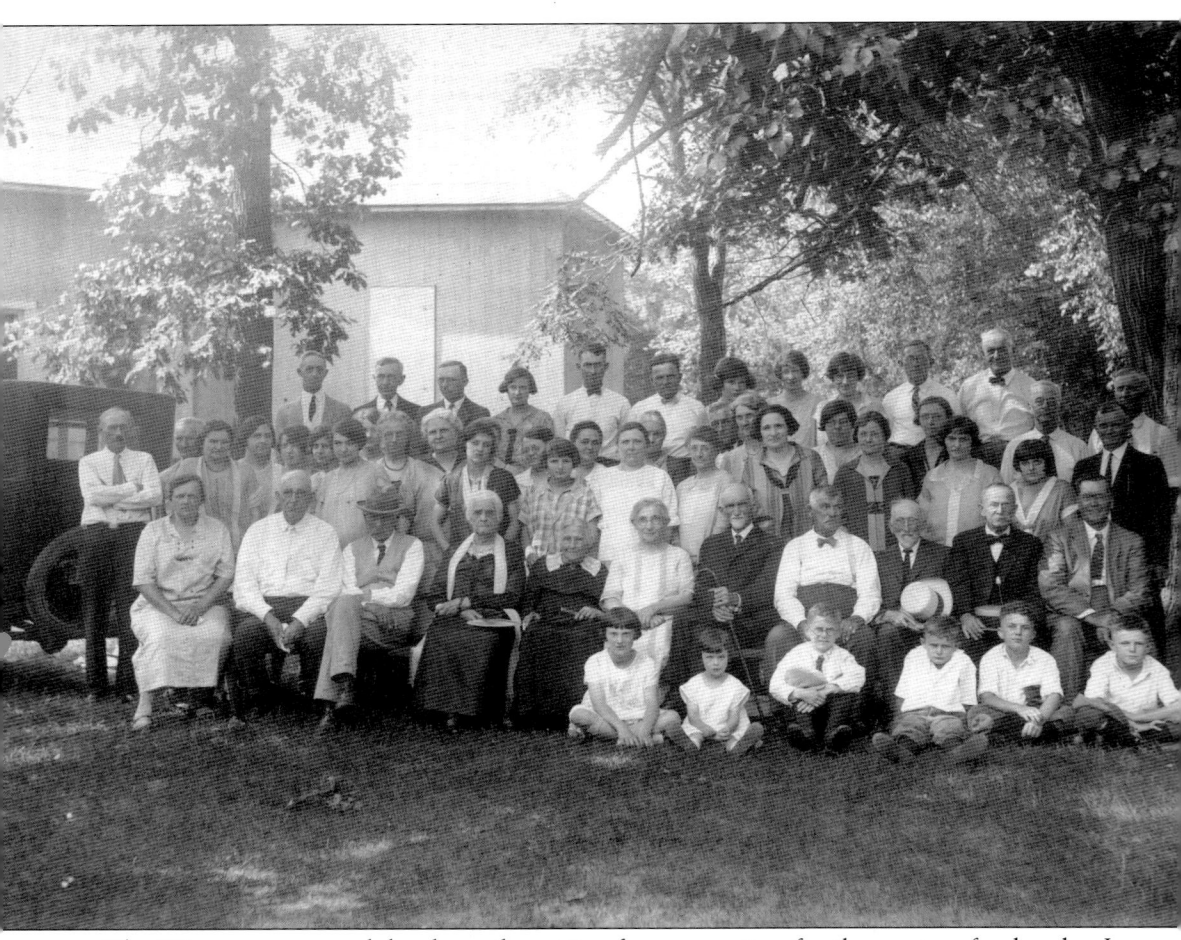

The Winamac town park has been the setting for summertime family reunions for decades. In August 1925, this family gathered for the 80th birthday party of Edmund R. Brown at the park pavilion. Those identified, from left to right, are (first row) unidentified, unidentified, William Starr, Donald Long, Ed Arnold, and Marshall Long; (second row) unidentified, A. B. Diggs, Judge George Burson, Ellen Manders, Elizabeth Keys, Emma Brown, E. R. Brown, Sam Lebo, Adam Breitweiser, John H. Kelly, and Moses A. Dilts. The third row includes E. P. Thompson, Maud Long, Ruby Starr, Lois Keller, Mildred Heston, Elizabeth Holdermann, Delight Holdermann, Katherine Cushing, Myrtle Starr, Anne Holdermann, Dora Keller, Lorene Long, Anna Holdermann, Mrs. William Brown, Clara Dilts, Zona Diggs, Frances Kelly, Mrs. Arnold, Ruth Long, Fred Cushing, and Ed Blue. The fourth row includes John R. Starr, Frank Keller, Ethel Brown, Newt Brown, Louis Holdermann, and Jake Lowry. (PCHS Museum, donated by William Starr.)

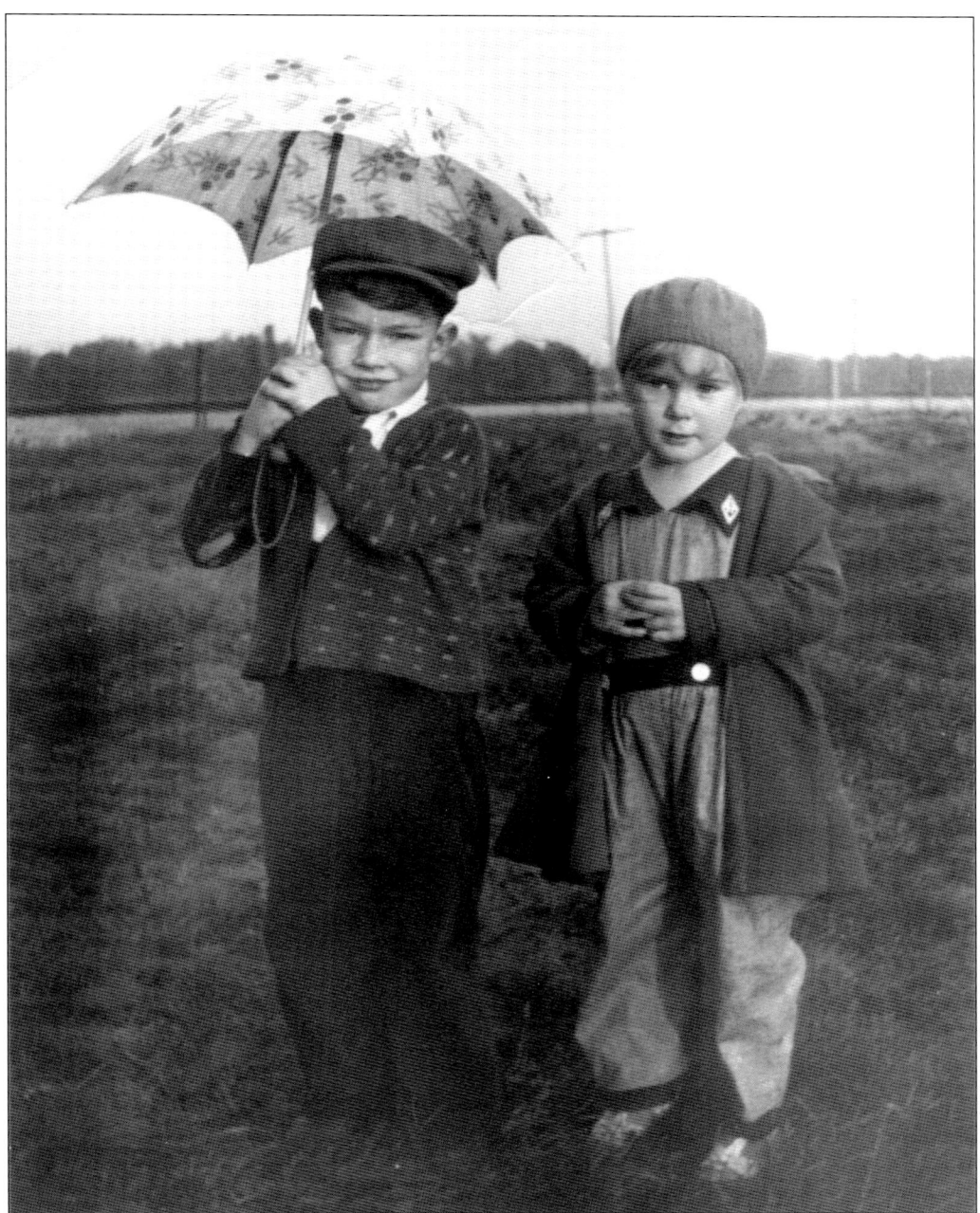

Best friends Harold Long and Shirley Ann Cords were children together, growing up during the Great Depression in the tiny community of Beardstown, north of Winamac. This photograph was taken in 1937 while they played near the Chesapeake and Ohio Railroad tracks. (Shirley Cords Bush.)

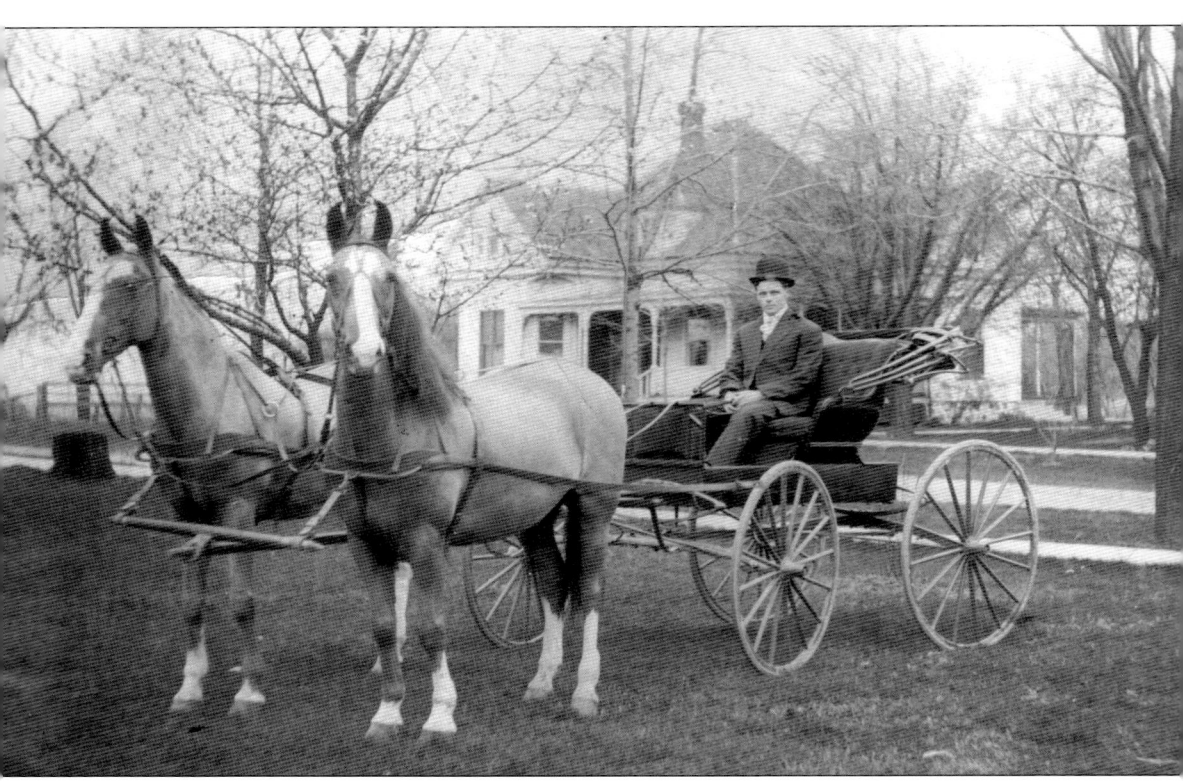

Each spring and autumn, Otis Mull of Star City drove his carriage and ponies to Iowa to visit relatives. Here he is in 1910, ready to depart on the two-day trip. (PCHS Museum, donated by Julia Phillips Fagan.)

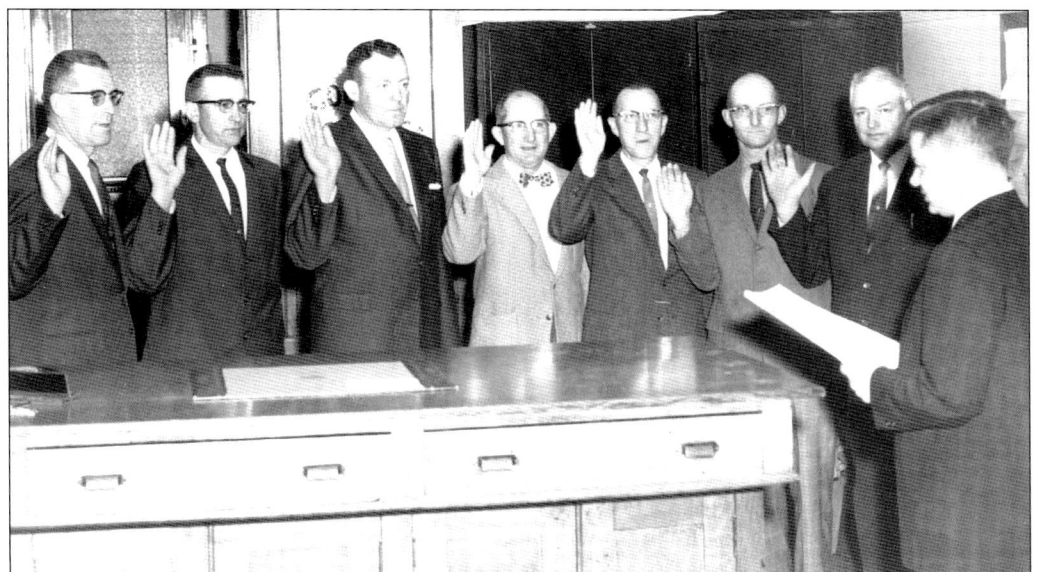

County clerk John Shank (right) administers the oath of office to the first West Central school board members, following the state's school reorganization and consolidation mandate. The board was appointed by Judge Robert Thompson in 1961 and assumed office on January 1, 1962. The board members were Andrew Houston (Gillam Township), Dale Mayhew (Medaryville), Eldon Clark (Cass), Orville H. White (White Post Township), Edward Leman (Salem), Richard Overmyer (Francesville), and Edward Finnegan (Beaver). (Olive White.)

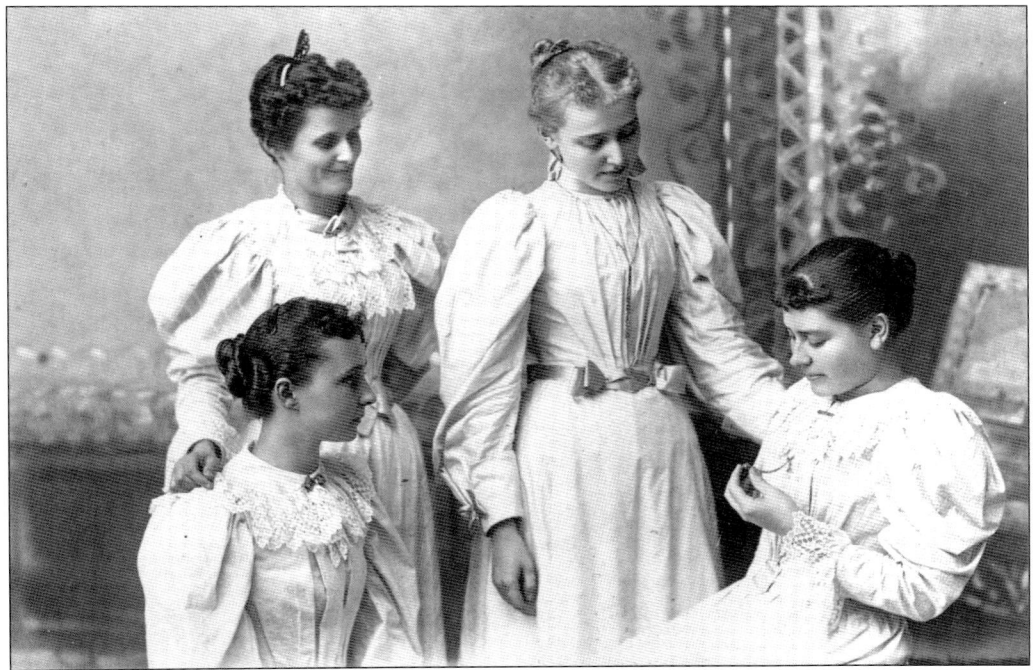

Sharing a girls' moment together in this early-1900s picture, from left to right are (first row) Agnes Shank and Rosa Shank and (second row) Lizzie Weaver and Catherine Horstman. (Brenda Gilsinger.)

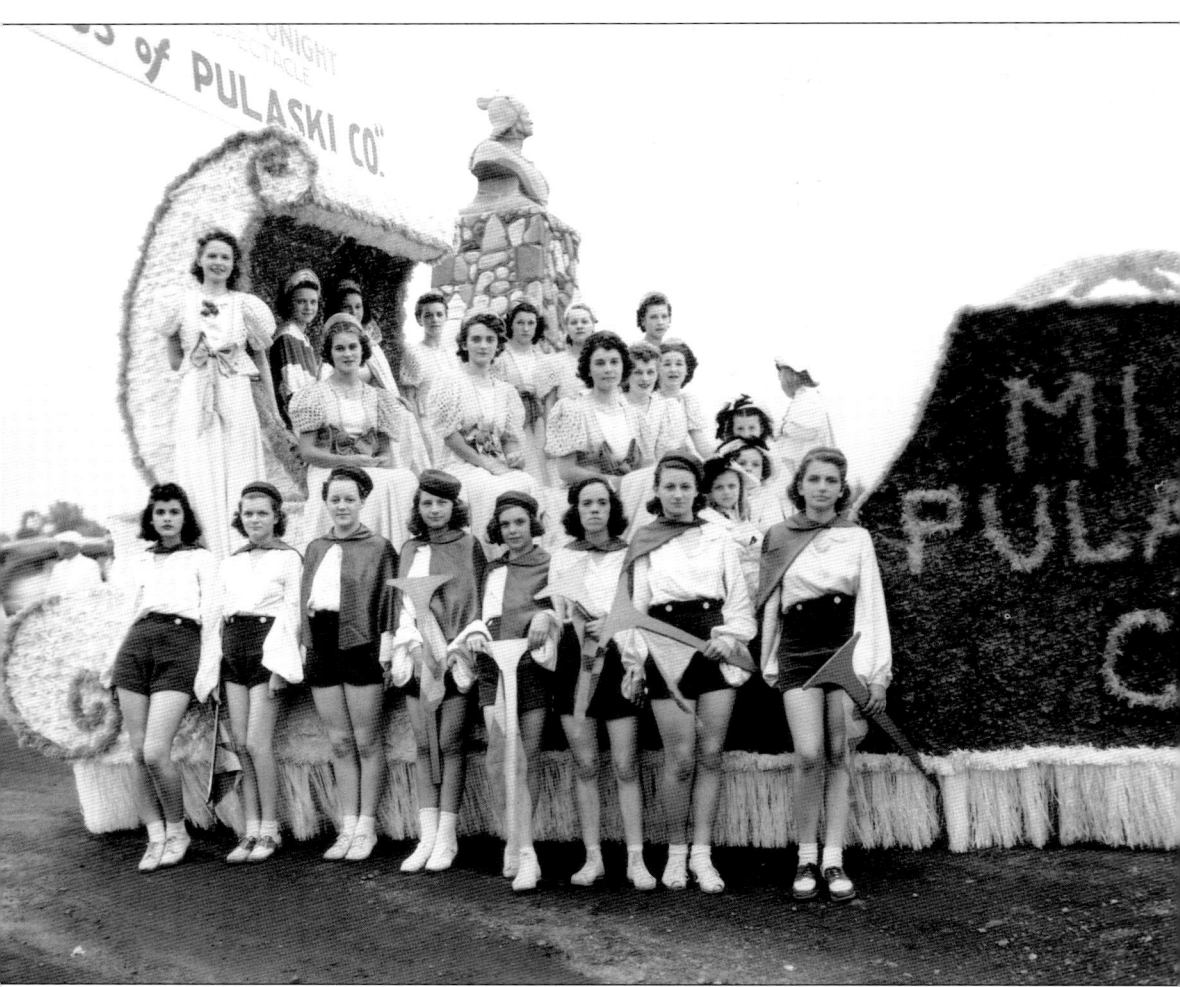

To celebrate Pulaski County's centennial in 1939, a committee was organized to stage a three-day historical pageant, titled Progress of Pulaski County, in August at the Winamac park. Other events included old settlers reunions, band concerts, midway attractions, athletic contests, speeches, 4-H shows, and parades. The centennial queen's float enters the park in this photograph. Imogene Hall reigned as queen. Her title also included a trip to the 1939–1940 New York World's Fair. (PCHS Museum.)

Brothers-in-law J. P. Gilsinger (left), John C. Shank (center), and Frank Miller (right) became among the best-remembered and most-successful mercantile businessmen in Pulaski and later Winamac. The first of their partnerships was formed in 1899 to run dry goods and grocery stores in Pulaski. Shank and Miller moved to Winamac in the 1920s, opening clothing stores. The Gilsinger farm implement business followed in 1958. (Brenda Gilsinger.)

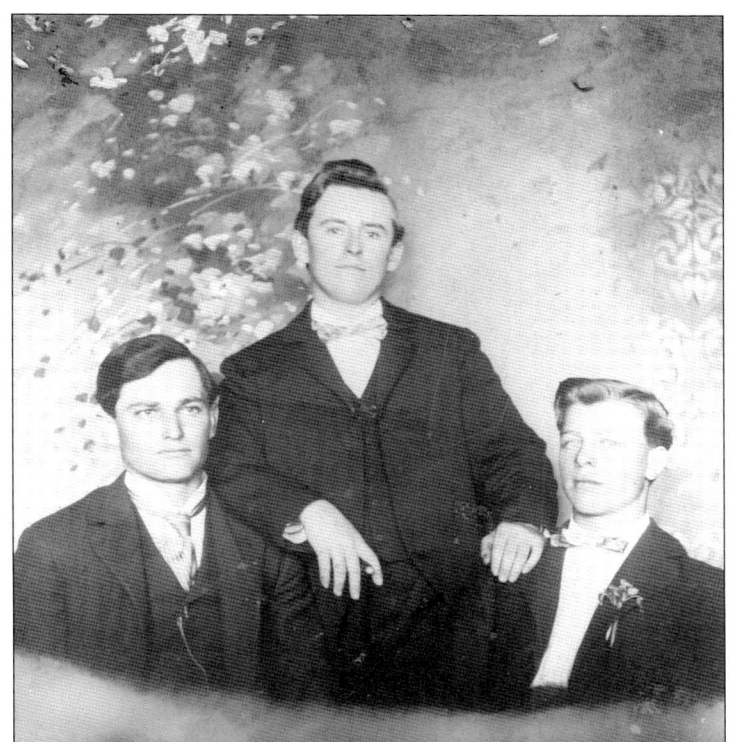

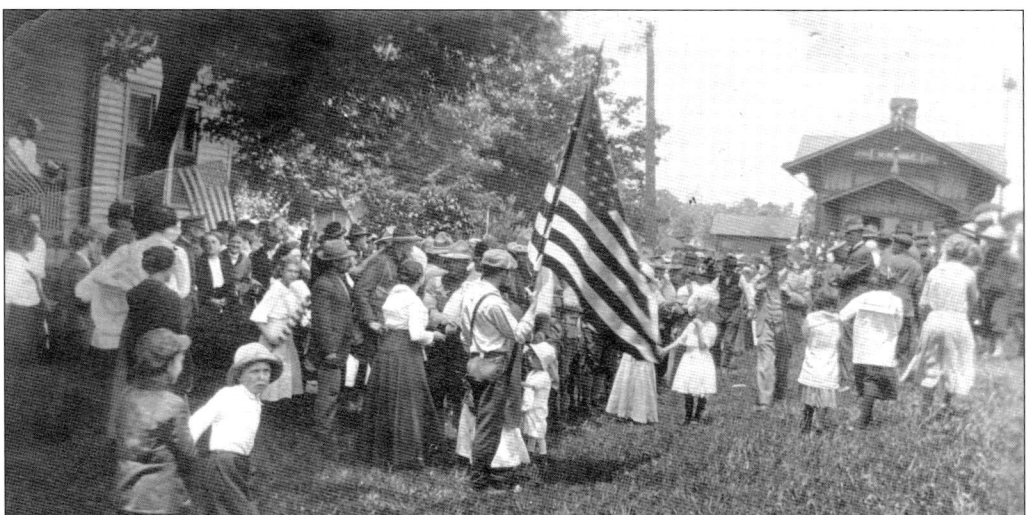

On June 19, 1916, a call went out to the Winamac Militia in anticipation of a possible conflict with Mexico. Revolutionary Pancho Villa had crossed the Rio Grande and raided United States border towns. Pres. Woodrow Wilson resisted calls for war but sent troops under Gen. John J. Pershing to patrol the border. The local militia, after camping across from the courthouse for a few days, boarded a train for Indianapolis on June 23. Winamac residents, young and old, circled the railroad station waving flags in support of the soldiers. Upon arrival at Fort Benjamin Harrison in Indianapolis, the local guardsmen were sworn into the U.S. Army and became Company L, 164th Indiana. (PCHS Museum.)

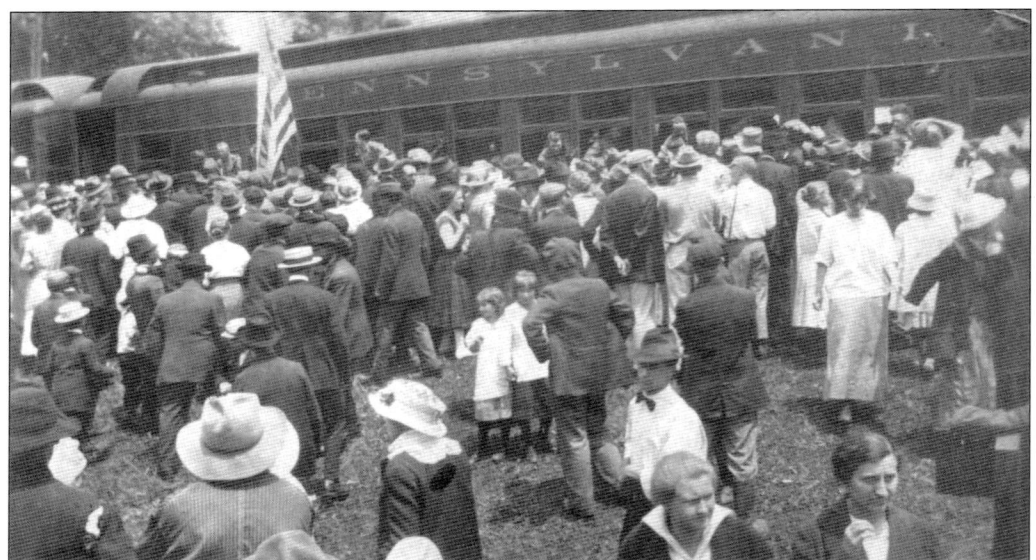

Winamac Militia members, part of the Indiana National Guard, wave to town supporters from the Pennsylvania Railroad passenger cars while they await the train's departure for Indianapolis on June 23, 1916. Most of the militia members had signed up in December 1915, and they drilled regularly and were issued uniforms. However, there were also many new recruits who joined them on this mission. (PCHS Museum.)

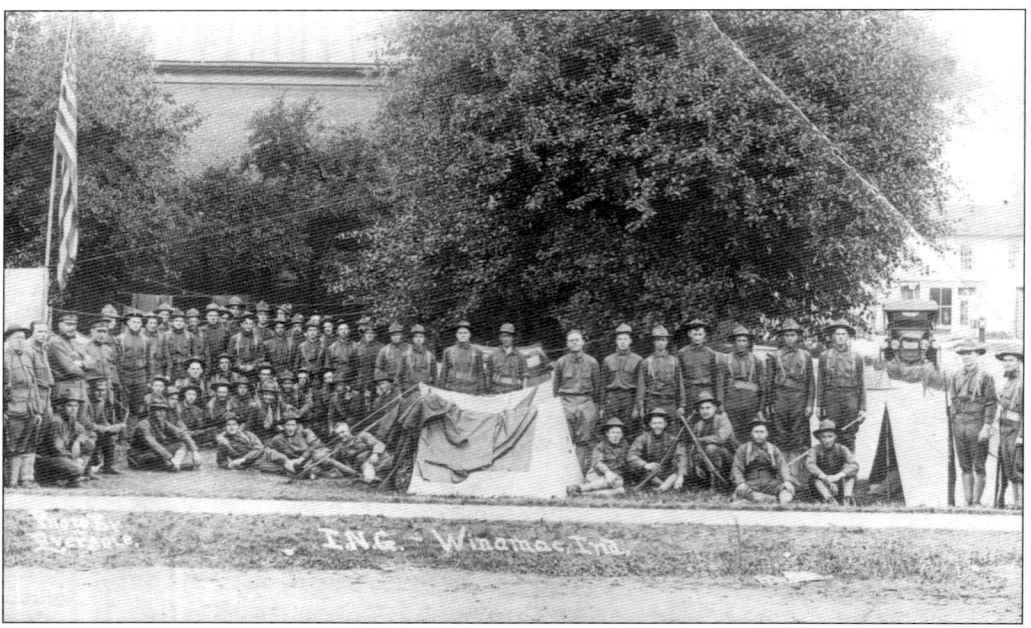

The Winamac Militia members gathered for this photograph in June 1916. Gen. John J. Pershing was successful in chasing Poncho Villa back into Mexico and avoided outright war in spite of much uneasiness with the Mexican government. The Winamac soldiers returned home by Christmas. When the United States joined World War I the following spring, many of these same men reported to duty. (PCHS Museum.)

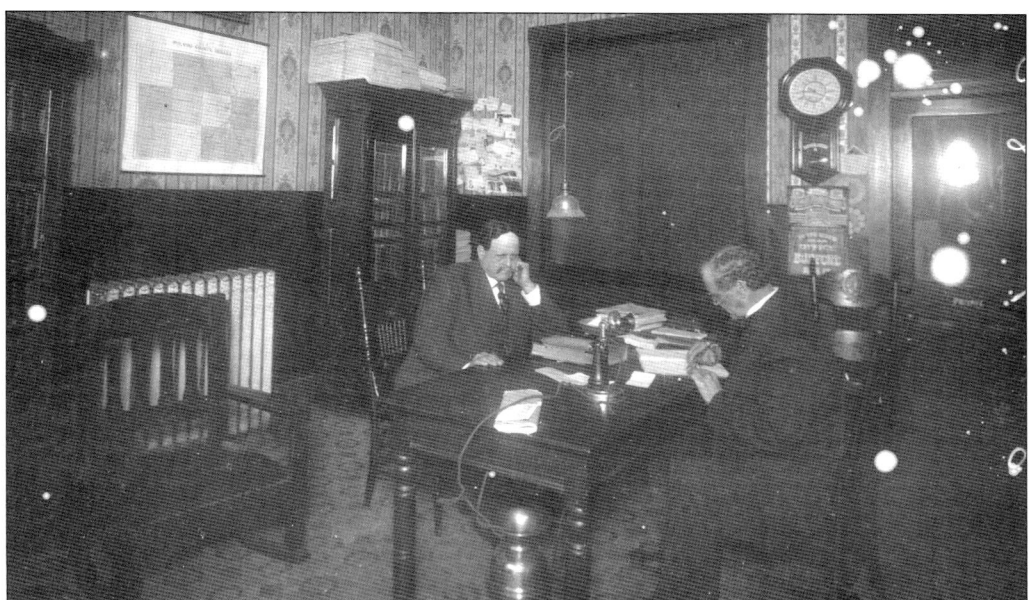

Physicians and brothers Dr. George W. and Dr. William Henry Thompson consult together in their Market Street office in Winamac in this photograph that dates to about 1908. They both practiced for over 50 years. Born on a farm near Royal Center in the 1840s, they completed medical school in Indianapolis and opened their practice in Winamac in the 1870s. They made house calls on patients by horseback and later by horse-drawn carriages. The brothers were also active in church and community organizations. (PCHS Museum.)

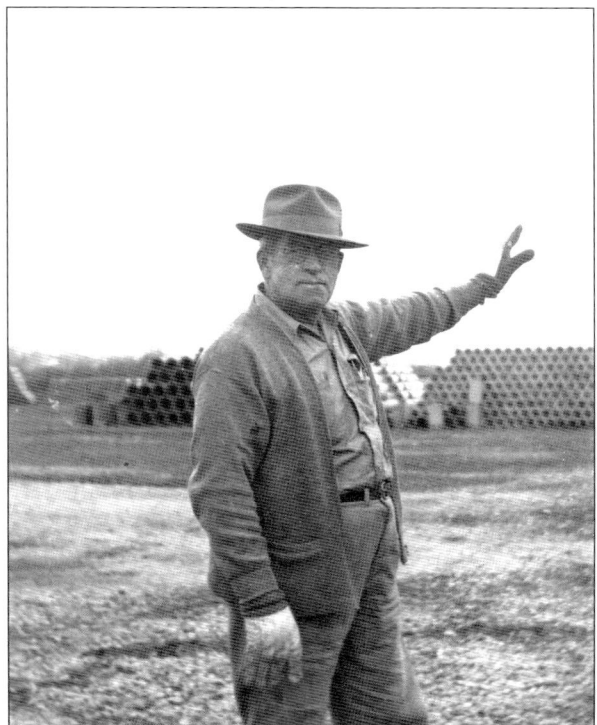

Earl Overmyer, pictured here in 1936, purchased the Francesville Brick and Tile Company in 1923. Later known as the Francesville Drain Tile Corporation, the company manufactures products to drain soil to better produce agricultural crops. The tile was first made of clay, dug locally by hand from the 1920s through 1930s. (Chris Overmyer.)

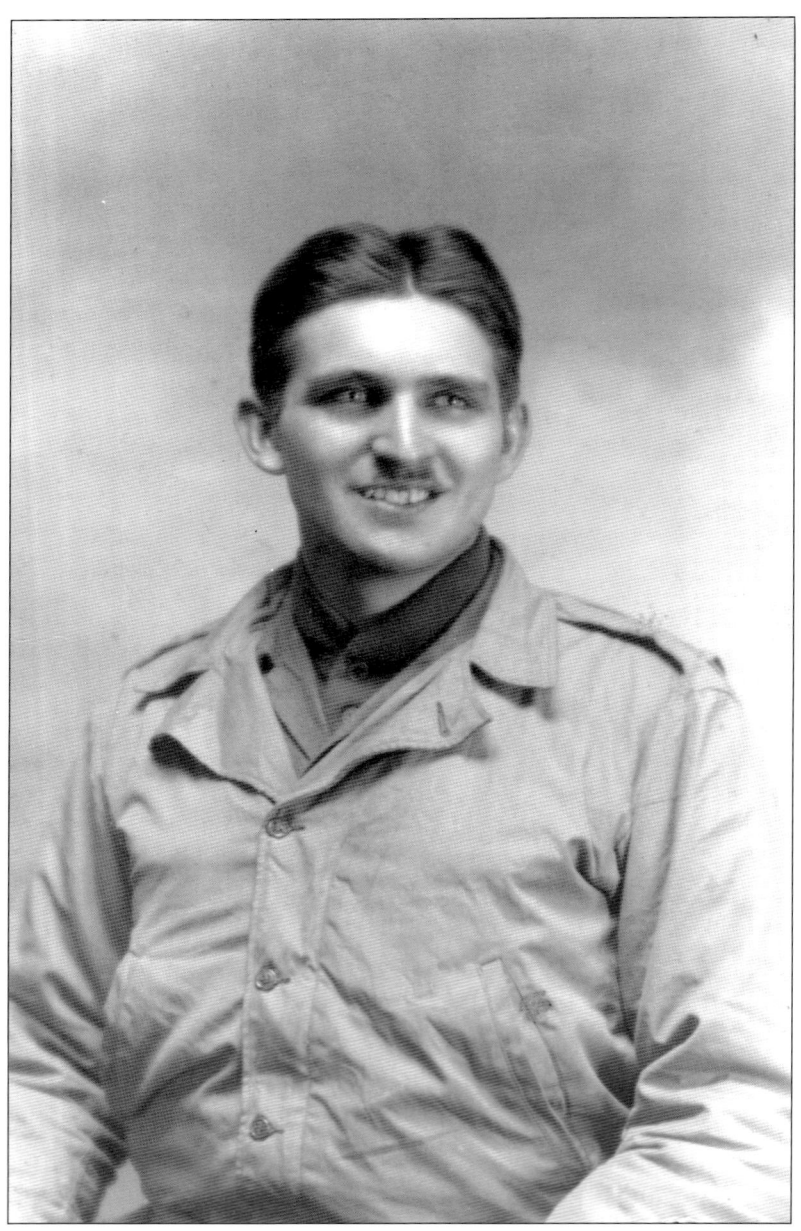

Against his father's wishes, 18-year-old Winamac farm boy Gerald Rife joined the army in May 1943 before completing high school. Thirteen months later, he landed on the shores of Omaha Beach in Normandy, France, during the June 6, 1944, D-Day invasion. Rife landed in the waters in an LST (Landing Ship, Tank) transport as part of the largest buildup and movement of soldiers in history to participate in what was later described as the beginning of the end of Adolph Hitler's brutal five-year grip on Europe. Rife was forever haunted by the memories of the horrors he witnessed that day and never shared with anyone what he saw and experienced during the historic invasion. He participated in the liberation of Paris and in many battles, finally crossing Germany to meet the Russian allies in Czechoslovakia. At the end of World War II, only 15 soldiers from Rife's 200-member unit came home. (Mary Rife.)

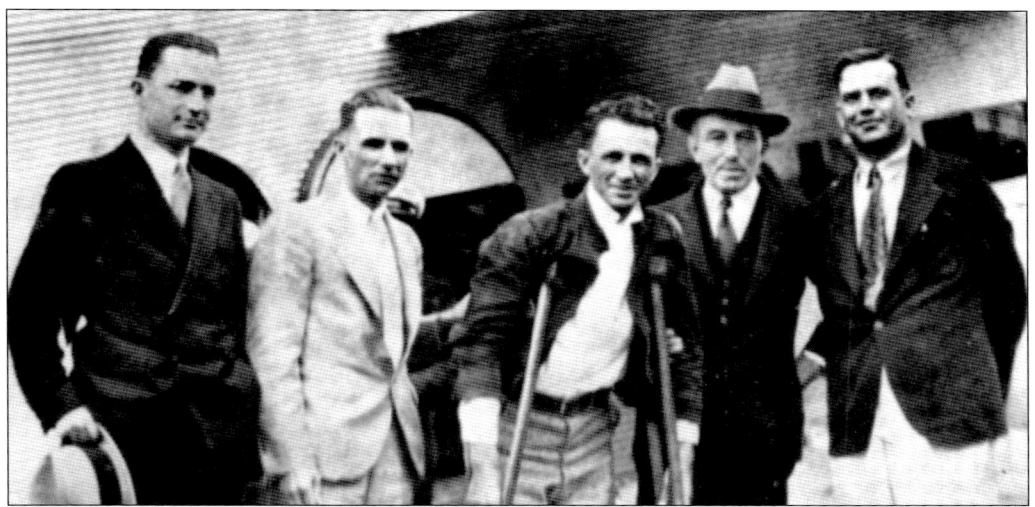

The nation's early aviators were heroes to youngsters. After graduation from Medaryville High School in 1920, Clarence McElroy learned to fly under the training of Capt. Lawrence Aretz. McElroy became a barnstormer and stunt flyer. He was an early airmail pilot and a flight instructor for the air force. In 1932, at age 30, McElroy was employed by Waco Aircraft in Ohio and was assigned to deliver a single-engine airplane to Honduras in Central America. En route, McElroy crashed into a Mexican jungle mountainside during a tropical storm. His companion was killed, and McElroy suffered two broken hips. Crawling down the mountain along a stream, he was discovered 17 days later by a village farm youth. Reports of the pilot's disappearance and recovery made headlines across the nation. The above photograph shows the reception committee who met McElroy (on crutches) in Mexico City weeks after his initial recuperation. From left to right are American vice consul William Cochran, brother Richard J. McElroy, Dr. Goodman, and Medaryville businessman Joe E. Ryden. McElroy later wrote a book chronicling his experience, called *Seventeen Days in a Mexican Jungle*. After his recovery, McElroy quickly returned to flying. He and his wife, Lenore, also a commercial pilot, (below) ferried planes during World War II. (Above, Medaryville History Museum; below, PCHS Museum.)

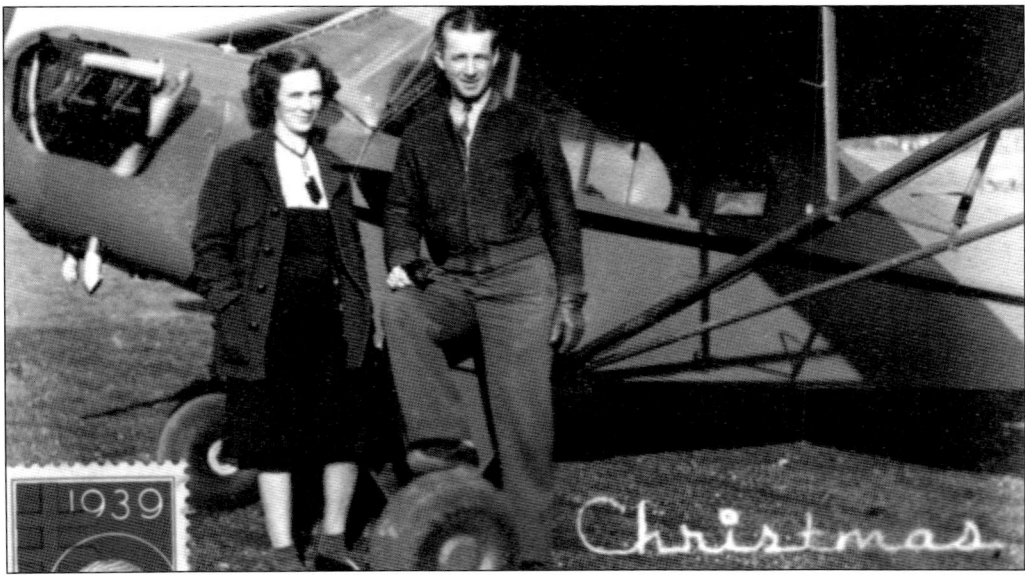

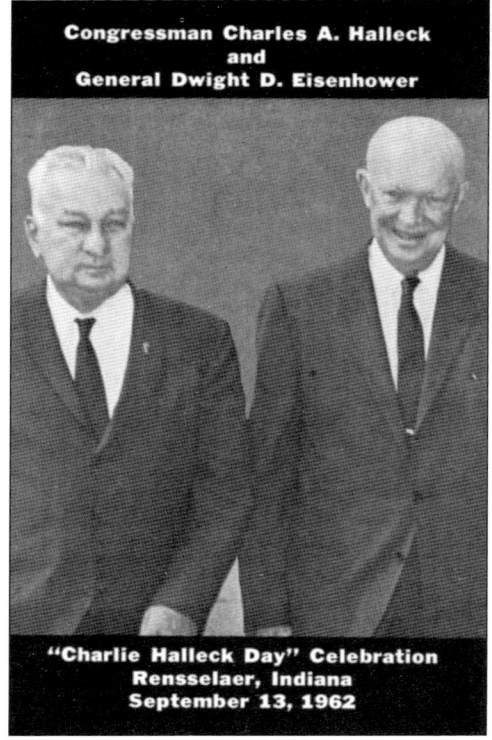

"Charlie Halleck Day" Celebration
Rensselaer, Indiana
September 13, 1962

Charles A. Halleck represented Pulaski County in the U.S. Congress from 1935 to 1969, serving both as Republican Party majority leader and minority leader during his tenure. He was a familiar face at local events, visiting Pulaski County often, particularly as his brother Harold was a beloved Winamac physician. The Hallecks grew up in neighboring Jasper County. Halleck was the subject of a *Time* magazine cover story in June 1959. He is pictured here (left) with former president Dwight D. Eisenhower in 1962. (Thomas Halleck.)

Winamac was, perhaps, the one place where Dr. Harold Halleck was better known than his political older brother. For 50 years, he worked from his office on Main Street. He estimated that he averaged about 25,000 miles per year visiting patients in their homes until the local hospital was built in 1963. He delivered an estimated 3,000 babies. In 1979, the chamber of commerce established an annual community service award in his name. In this photograph from the mid-1970s, Congressman Charles A. Halleck (right) congratulates his brother Harold and sister-in-law Bernice on one of their wedding anniversaries. (Thomas Halleck.)

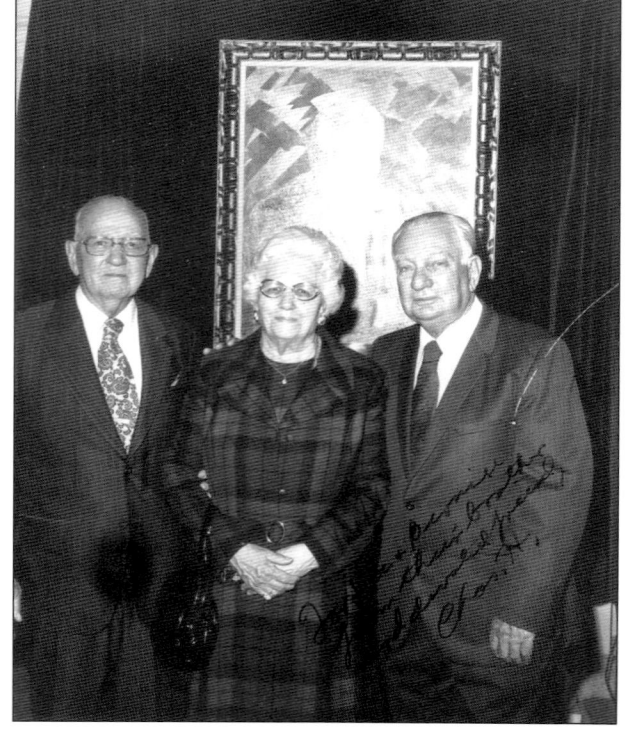

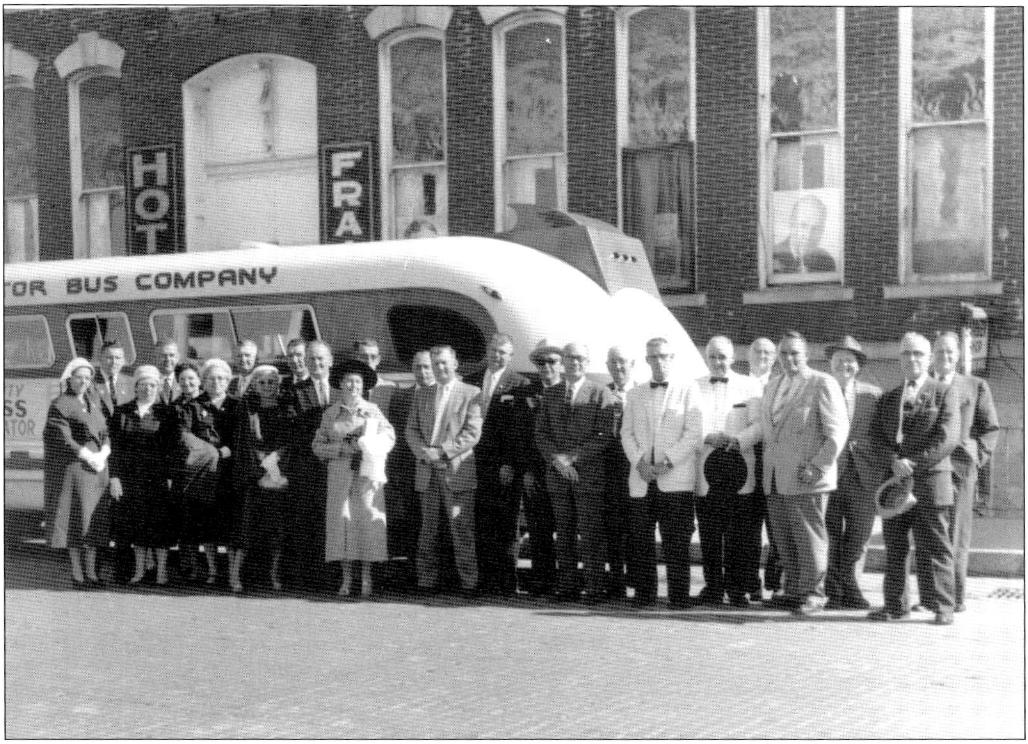

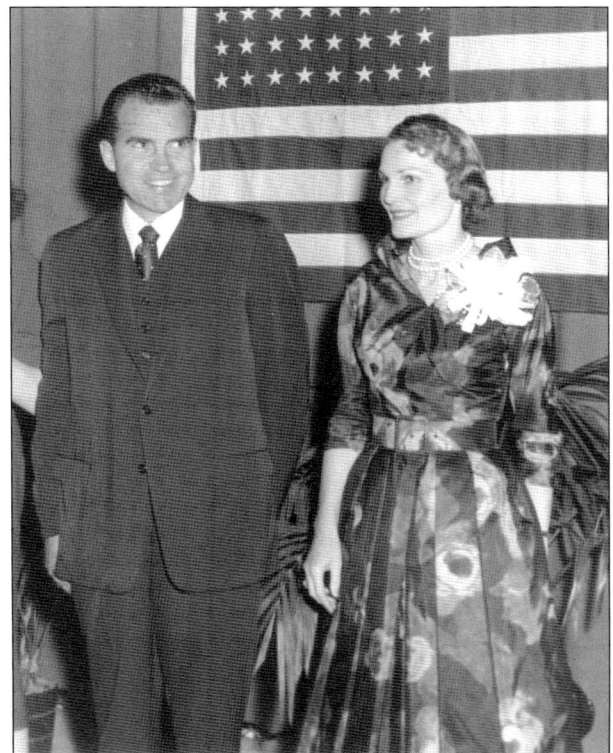

Pulaski County Republican Party officials met in front of the Frain Hotel in Winamac to board this chartered bus on October 6, 1959, to take them to a Charlie Halleck Day rally at neighboring Rochester where Vice Pres. Richard Nixon was the featured speaker. The event was to honor Halleck as party leader in the U.S. House of Representatives and also for his 25th anniversary as congressman. Nixon spoke about his trip to the Soviet Union and also of Premier Nikita Khrushchev's more-recent visit to the United States. Among those identified in the above picture are Max Frain, Harry Smith, Mabel Zellers, Bernice Halleck, Harold Johnson, Bud Cummins, Harry Querry, Harold Halleck, Albert Gudeman, John Dilts, and Lon McKinley. (Sally White, photographs by O. H. White.)

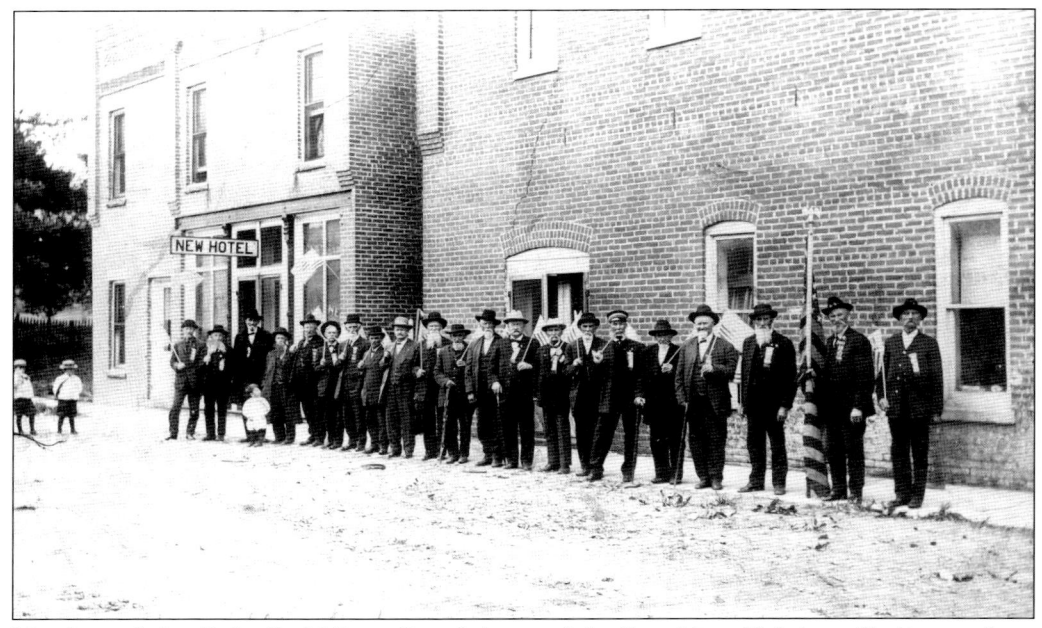

Members of the C. L. Guild Post, Grand Army of the Republic of Medaryville line up for a Memorial Day parade on May 30, 1911. Those identified include Holby Farnsley (far left), John Sebring (seventh from left), Henry Ballard (14th from left), Benjamin F. Faris (third from right), and Frederick Maibauer (far right). (PCHS Museum.)

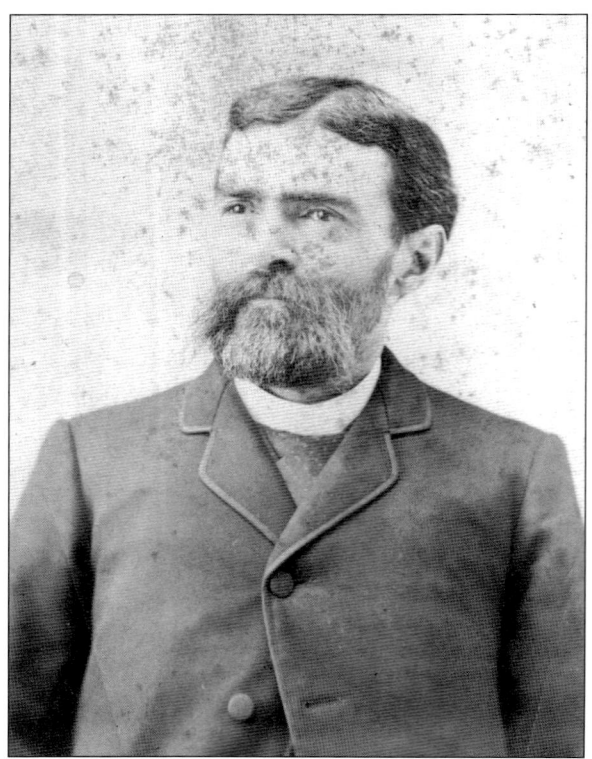

The first attempt to publish a newspaper in Pulaski County was made in the summer of 1858. In the succeeding decades, every town in the county was served by one or more weekly newspapers. Among the most successful editors was Marion H. Ingram, born in 1834 in Ohio and trained as a printer. He came to Winamac in February 1865, a Civil War veteran of the Confederate army. He purchased the *Winamac Herald* from Judge George Burson. Ingram edited this paper for over 30 years, and with consolidation, it became known as the *Winamac Democrat-Journal*. (Author's collection.)

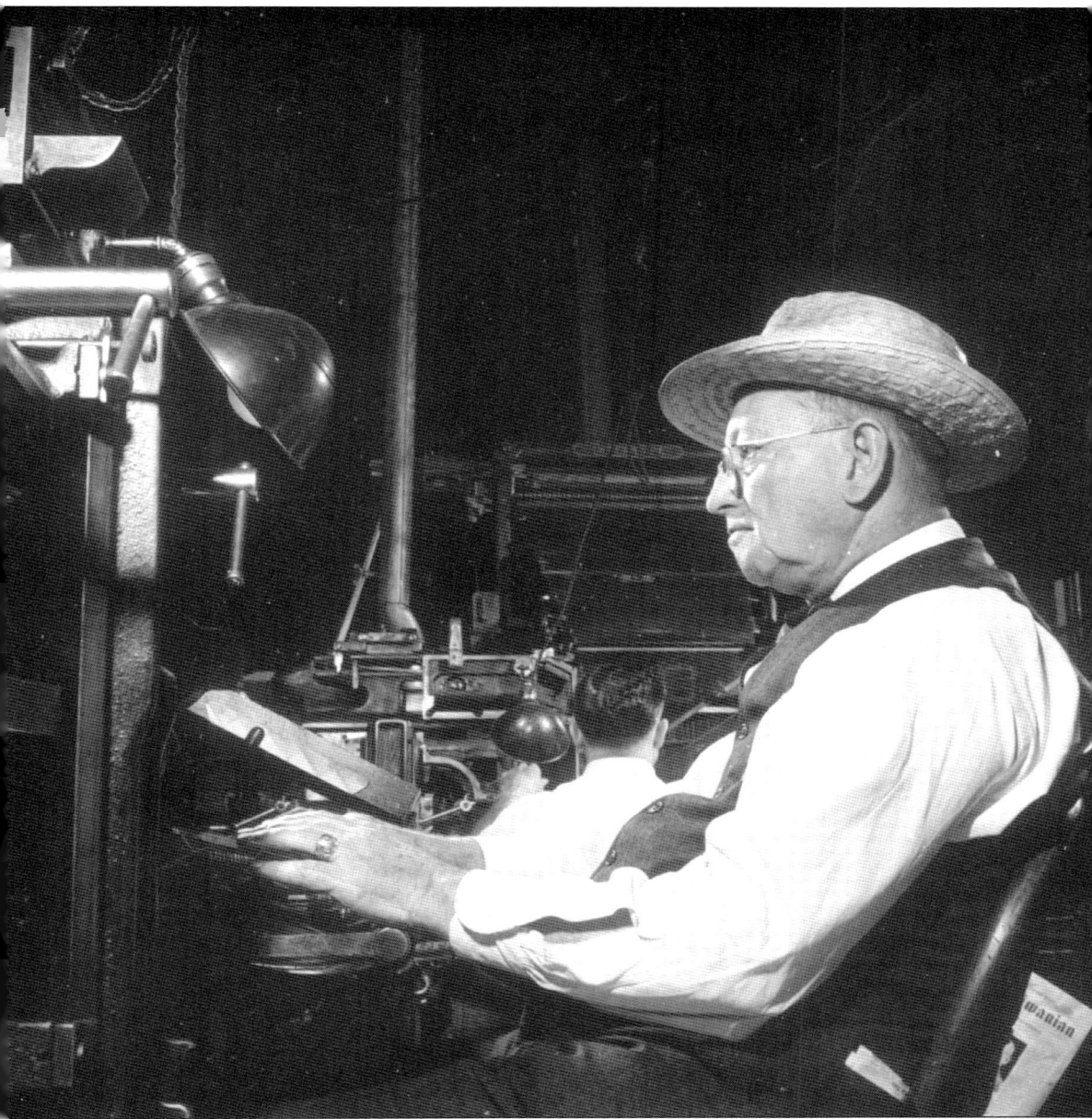

The Old Man at the Desk was the name of editor Edmund (Ned) Gorrell's well-loved column in the *Pulaski County Democrat*. Gorrell was raised in the newspaper business. His father, Joseph, brought the family to Winamac in 1891 after he purchased the *Pulaski County Democrat*. At age 12, Gorrell began his newspaper career as a printer's devil. He advanced to journeyman printer, a linotype operator, and later editor and publisher. He was a progressive voice and activist in the county community and a member of numerous organizations. He was an officer of the Hoosier State Press Association and was also a member of the Indiana Democratic Editorial Association. He was inducted into the Indiana Journalism Hall of Fame by the Sigma Delta Chi Society of Professional Journalists. He remained editor of the *Pulaski County Journal* (the name was changed in 1957) until his death in 1968 at age 89. (Author's collection.)

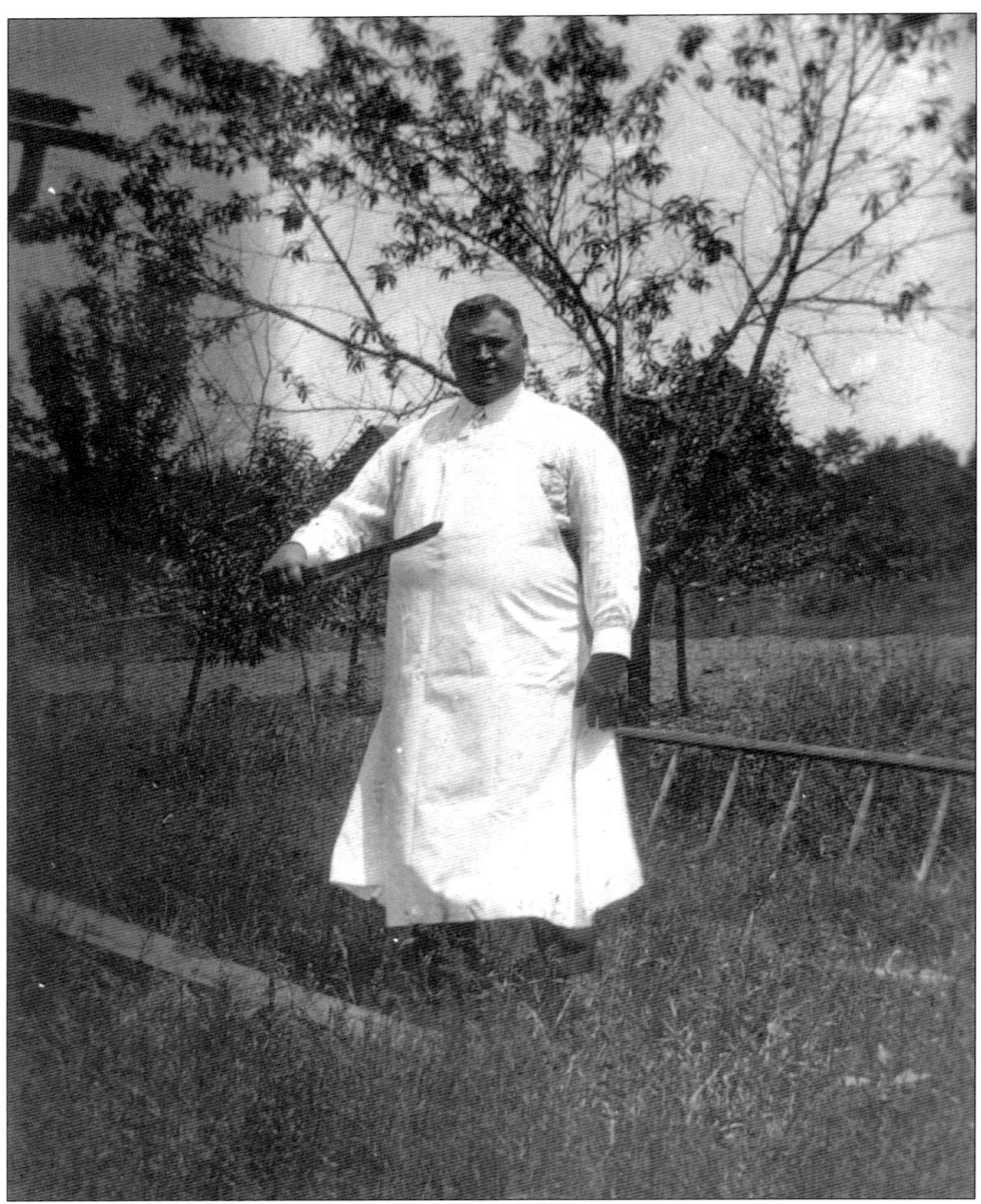

The last grocery store in the village of Pulaski was owned by the Ed Miller family. Miller, the town butcher (shown here in 1912), operated his shop from 1905 until his death in 1934. During that time, he enlarged the business to add grocery items. Three of his children were involved in the business until it was destroyed by fire in 1947. His daughter Annie reopened the store in another building for several more years. The store was closed in the early 1970s. (Brenda Gilsinger.)

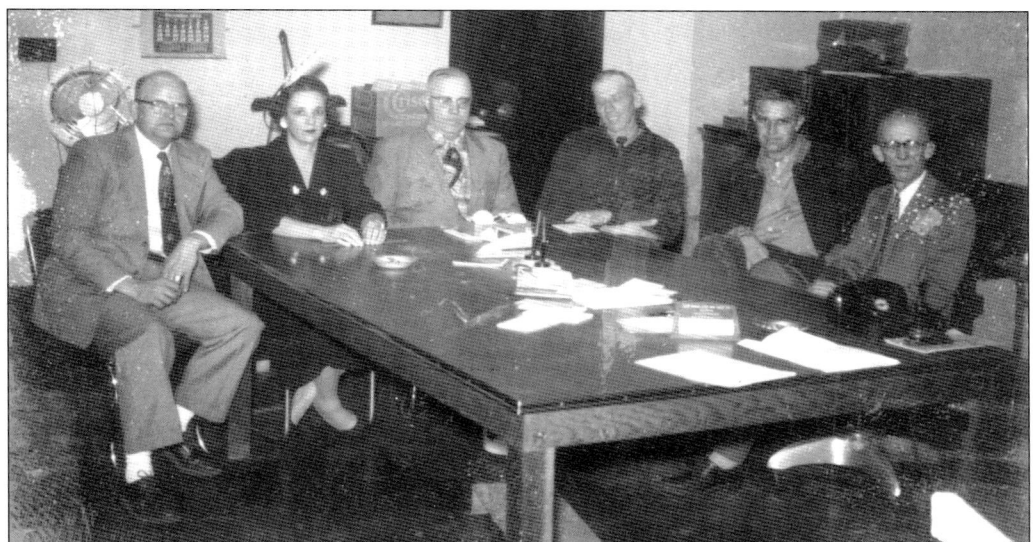

The post–World War II years in Winamac brought continued growth and improvements to the town. The 1950s saw new electric lights and poles put up in the business district. The town waterworks purchased turbine pumps, and a new sewage disposal plant was built. Parking meters were installed in 1953 (and removed about 30 years later), and the county's first traffic lights were installed at four intersections along Monticello Street. Some of these projects were overseen by the 1956 Winamac Town Board, including from left to right, John Kruger, Ruby Taylor, clerk Clay Zellers, James Jenkins, William Larkin, and Richard Dodd. (PCHS Museum.)

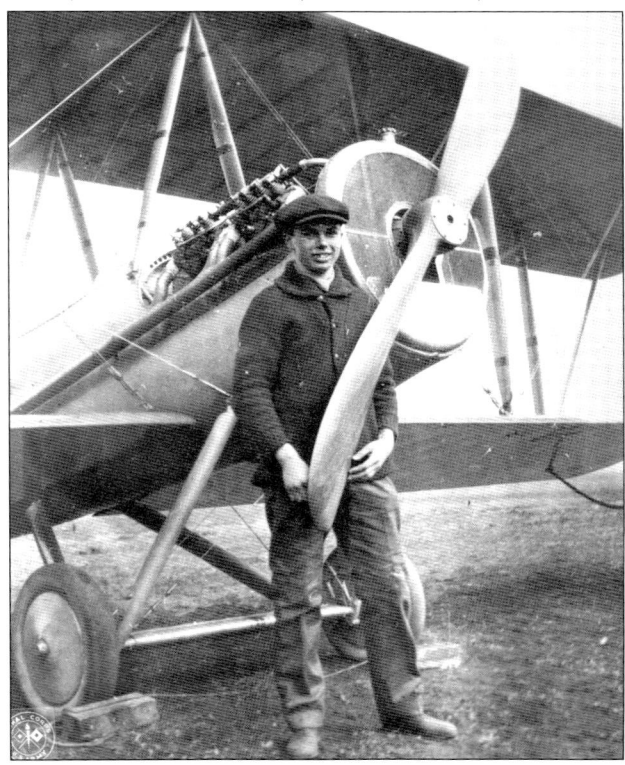

Charles A. Arens (born in 1895), an early aviation enthusiast, constructed a biplane in 1915 and flew at Ashburn Field in Chicago in 1916, qualifying for membership in the Early Birds. Arens became an inventor and manufacturer of controls for the aircraft industry and founded his own company, Arens Controls, in Evanston, Illinois, and a second company in England. In 1944, he retired and moved to Winamac, where his mother, Henrietta Brust Arens, grew up. For the next 22 years, Arens was a civic leader, serving on the chamber of commerce and as first board president of Pulaski Memorial Hospital. He was an advisor on the development of the city/county airport in Winamac, which bears his name, Arens Field. (Author's collection.)

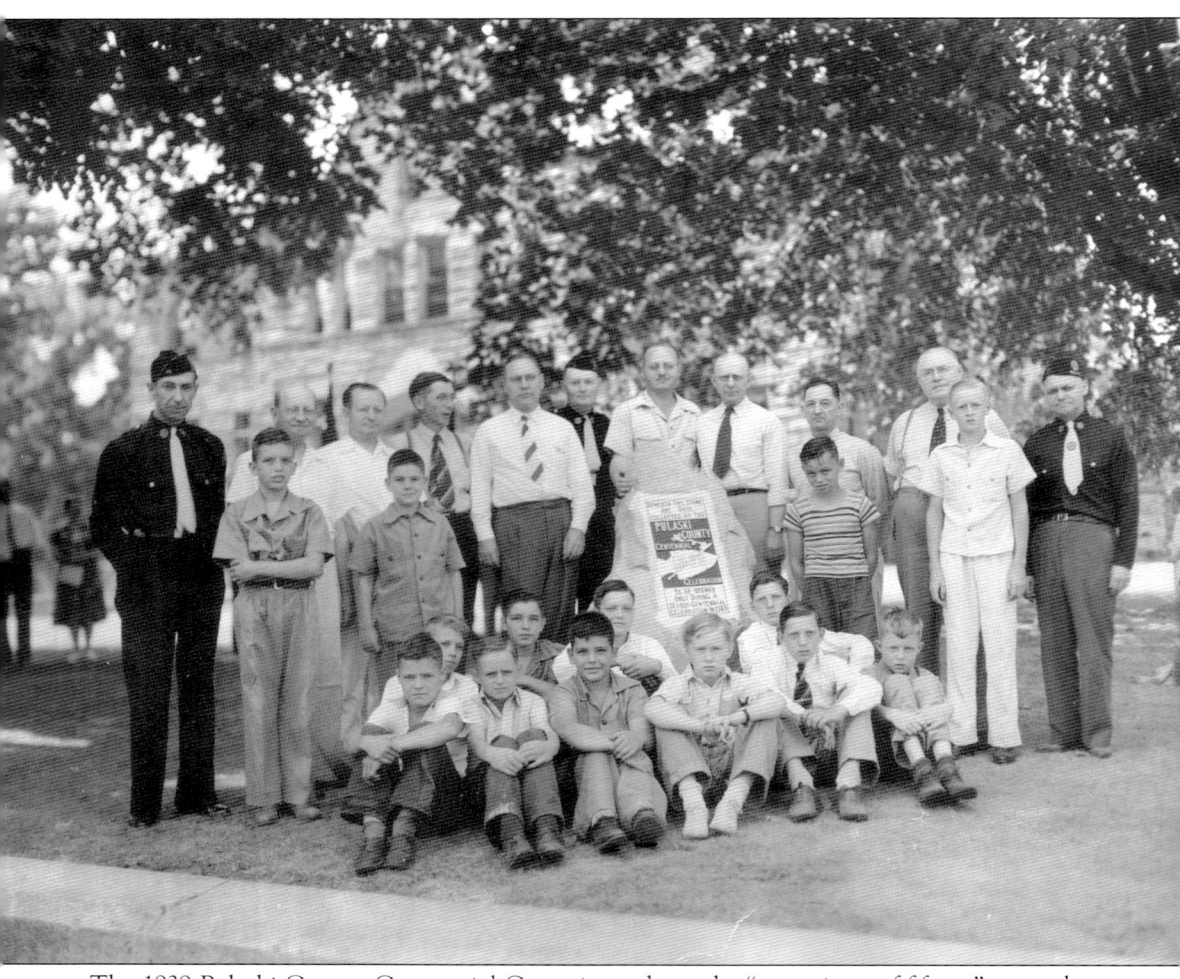

The 1939 Pulaski County Centennial Committee charged a "committee of fifteen" young boys to protect a centennial time capsule buried under a monument on the courthouse square to be opened in 1989 for the sesquicentennial. The boys and community leaders are shown here when the capsule was placed in 1940. From left to right are (first row) Andrew Galbreath, Lawrence McKinley, Robert Dilts, Bill McKinley, Lorwin Henry, and Bill Webb; (second row) Don Boulden, Moses Dilts, Keith Freeman, and Corwin Henry; (third row) Thomas Dilts, David Barr, Jack Fry, John Skillen, and Charles McKinley; (fourth row) Don Boulden Sr., Edmund (Ned) Gorrell, Jim Dilts, Paul Davis, Herman Billerback, Doc Wilbur Yocom, Lon McKinley, Clarence Long, Carl Applegate, John Selle, and Russell Fry. (Charles McKinley.)

Three

GOING ABOUT BUSINESS

By the time he was six years old in 1921, young William L. Starr, whose father operated a grain elevator in Winamac, began spending his boyhood days wandering the brick streets of town visiting the various shops and merchants. The practice of everyday trade left a lasting impression on his young mind. "Growing up in a small town [I] was free of the cares and problems a child faces these days," he recalled decades later. "I knew no restrictions, nor felt any limitations since nearly everyone knew me and my family. My mother did not worry about where I was, knowing full well that when I got hungry I would show up. There were so many places of interest to a small boy, and I was welcomed nearly everywhere."

Dressed in his summer wardrobe of denim overalls, a blue chambray shirt (and one-piece BVD underwear), barefoot, young Starr stopped by Felker's Blacksmith Shop on Monticello Street where he was excited by the sights, smells, and noises of the coal fires, hot metals, glowing forge, roaring bellows, and the pounding hammers on the anvils. He was impressed by the muscular, sweaty workmen dressed in their leather aprons and a little frightened of the powerful horses. Other favorite destinations were John H. Kelly's Hardware Store and the Big Garage next door, operated by Fred Borders and Chester Blinn. Here two fire trucks were kept, one for the county and one for the town. And here also, young Starr was allowed a credit account to pay for the pop and candy he snacked on nearly every afternoon.

Two of Starr's contemporaries, Herb Hoch and Jim Freeman, also remembered that the Winamac streets of their boyhoods in the World War I era were filled with popcorn vendors; numerous groceries; meat markets and dry goods stores; a magnificent hotel; doctors, dentists, and law offices on the second floors of the downtown buildings; an ethnic mix of shopkeepers; summer band concerts; and passenger trains that arrived and departed several times a day.

These same enterprises were booming in the neighboring county towns of Francesville, Medaryville, Monterey, and Star City. Many continued to thrive through the 1960s. Eventually, school consolidation left several of the towns without the bustle of school activities, and the variety of the big shopping malls and the volume discounts of the big box stores began to lure shoppers away from their hometown merchants.

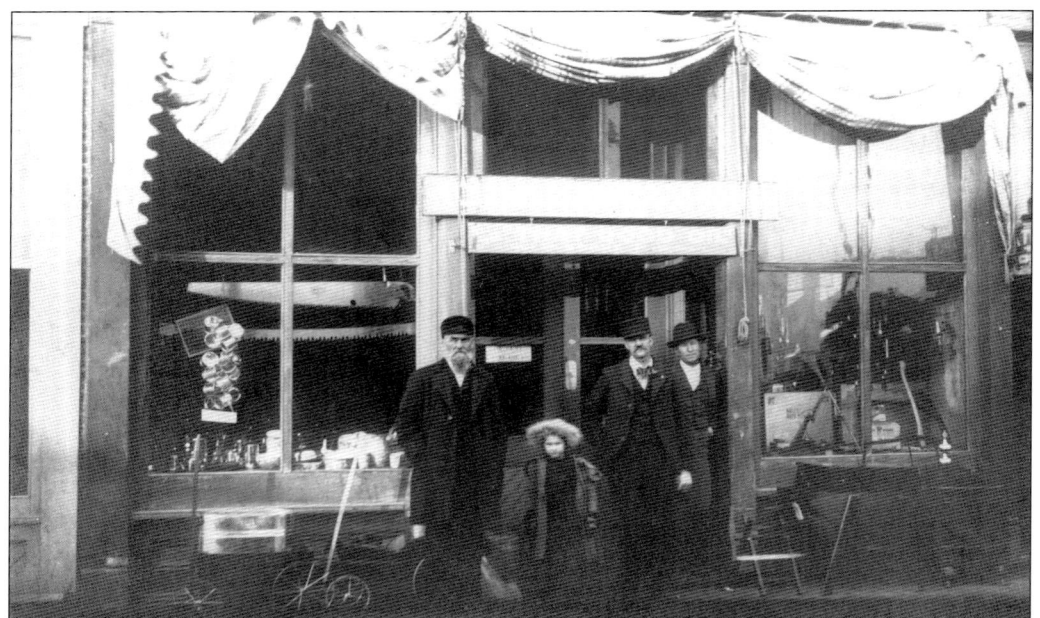

Henry Penry (center), proprietor of Penry Hardware store in Medaryville visits with his father, Eli (left), and older brother Charles. Penry purchased the hardware stock in December 1901 from P. M. Querry of Medaryville. The Penry family moved from Star City to Medaryville in 1902. Their hardware store is believed to have been located on Main Street between a drugstore and a confectionery. The store was sold in December 1907 to a Mr. Darrow and soon resold to the Marbaugh brothers of Monterey. (PCHS Museum.)

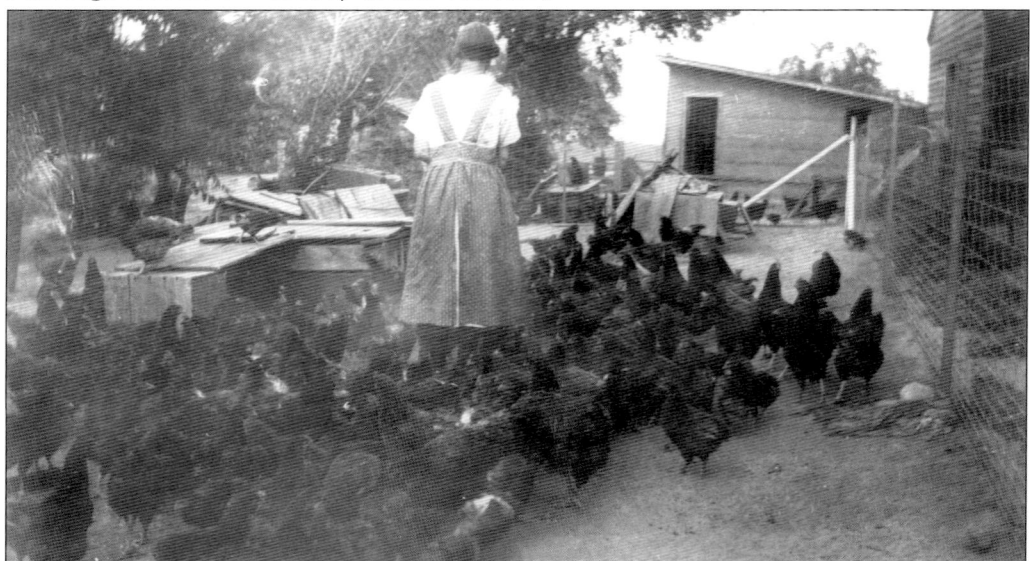

Young Cleo Shank feeds chickens at her home in Pulaski in this undated photograph from the early 1900s. She was the daughter of Agideon and Susannah Weaver Shank and the sister of Rosa Shank Gilsinger. Lucile Degner Roth, who grew up on a nearby farm at about the same time, remembered a "big, black snake" that was allowed to reside in her family's chicken house because it protected the fowl from raccoons and weasels. (Brenda Gilsinger.)

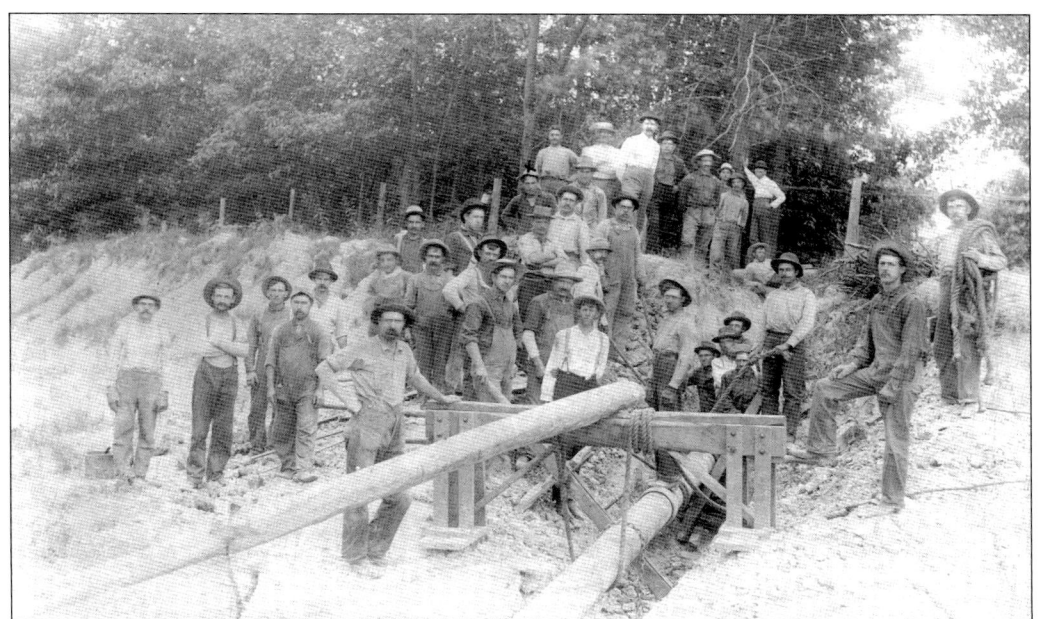

The workmen in this photograph are believed to be laying pipe for the Indiana National Gas and Oil Company. The original line was placed in 1891 but proved to be too small at only eight inches. It was replaced by a 10-inch line in the summer of 1899. This line was supposed to meet up with one running from Greentown. The trench was dug about four feet deep by a crew of 50 or 60 Italians from Chicago. Then the crew pictured here laid the pipe. A handwritten notation on the back of this photograph reads, "the 'X' indicates my brother Chauncey R. Bader, then aged 17 and deceased in 1902." (PCHS Museum, donated by Elmore Jackson.)

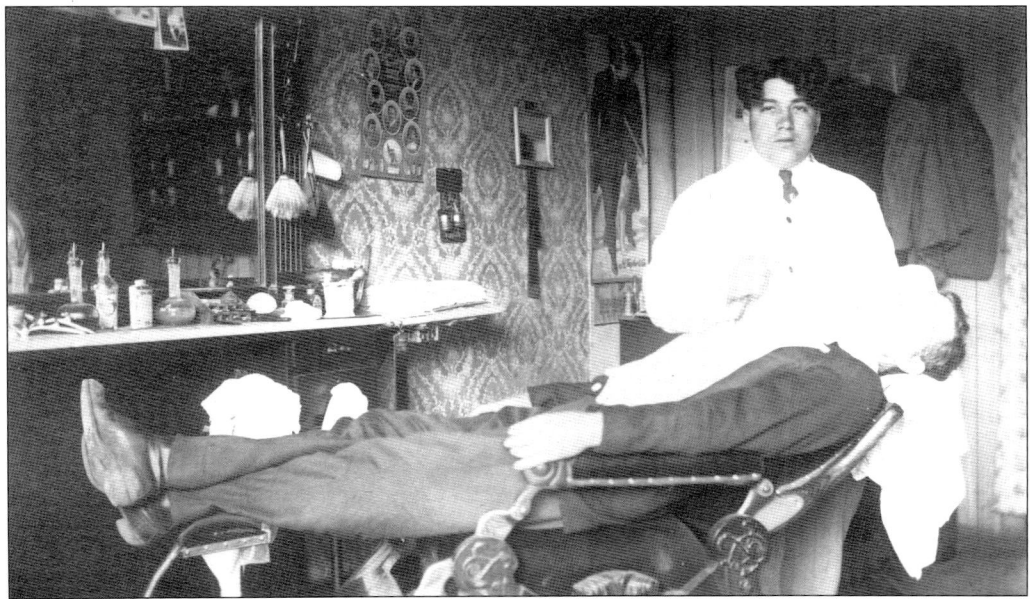

Star City barber Ola (Ollie) Heward shaves customer Skeet Baker in this photograph believed to date to around 1915. Heward was born in 1892 and eventually moved to Michigan. (PCHS Museum.)

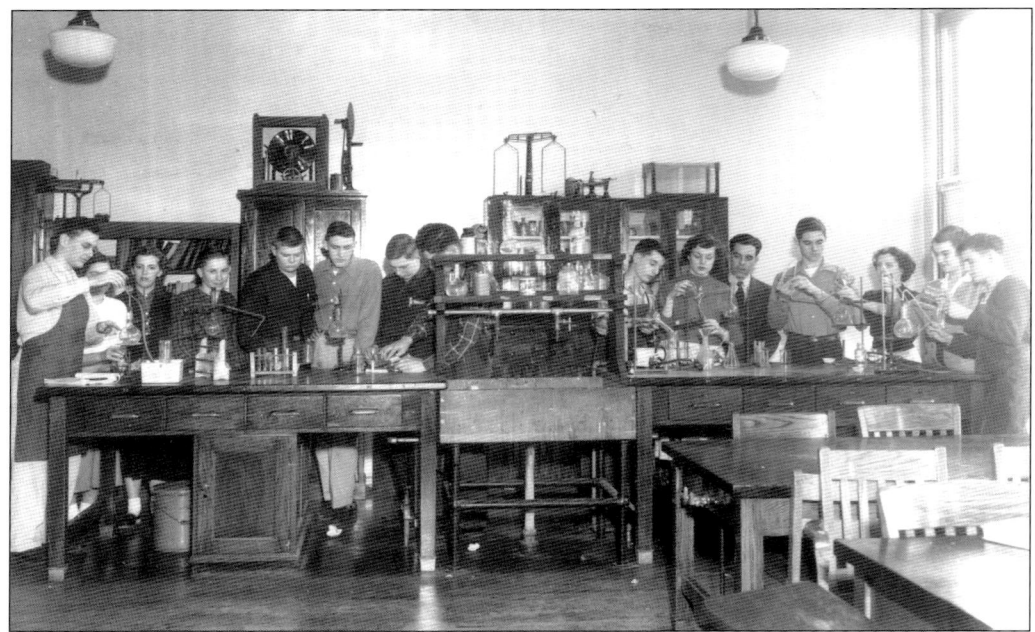

Students at Francesville High School work on a chemistry experiment in this photograph, which dates to about 1955. Enrollment at the high school rose significantly in the 1950s, as country schools were closed. The school building, constructed in 1914, was enlarged or remodeled many times over the decades. In 1953, the students watched the inauguration of Pres. Dwight D. Eisenhower on television. These were also the days of the new polio vaccine. In 1967, the last class graduated from Francesville High School. The school consolidated with Medaryville the next year to form the West Central School Corporation. (Francesville Tribune.)

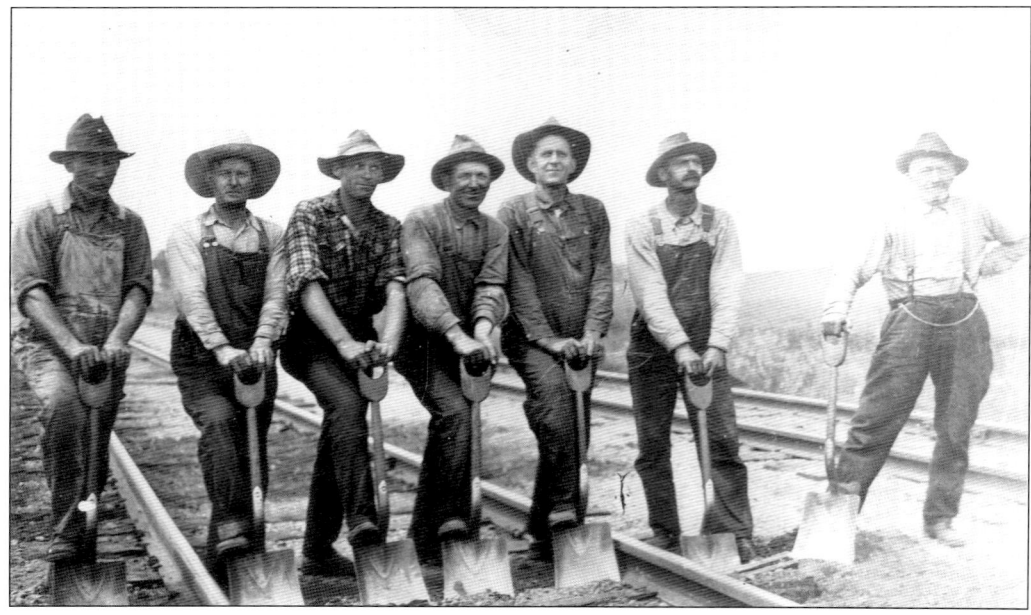

A section gang of a railroad crew working in Winamac poses for this photograph on October 3, 1912. The foreman is John Trapp. (PCHS Museum.)

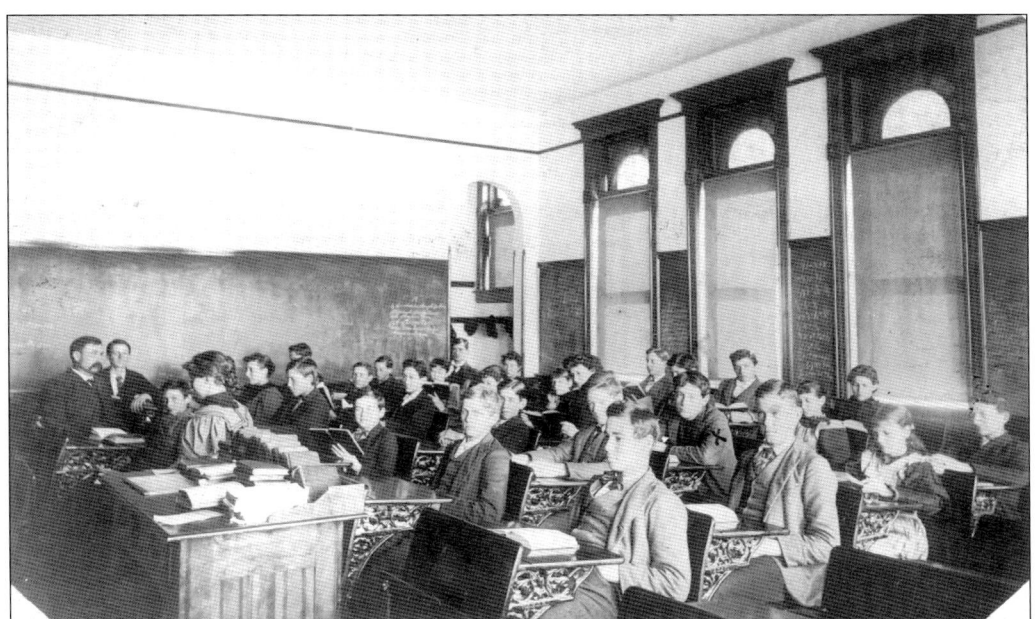

Winamac High School students are shown at their studies in this 1895 photograph. The new school building on Front Street was completed two years earlier. A separate high school building was constructed next door in 1914. By the late 1920s, the two buildings were connected with a new auditorium and gymnasium. Three of the students believed to be in the picture are Chauncey Bader, Charles Kelly, and Nels Zellers. (PCHS Museum.)

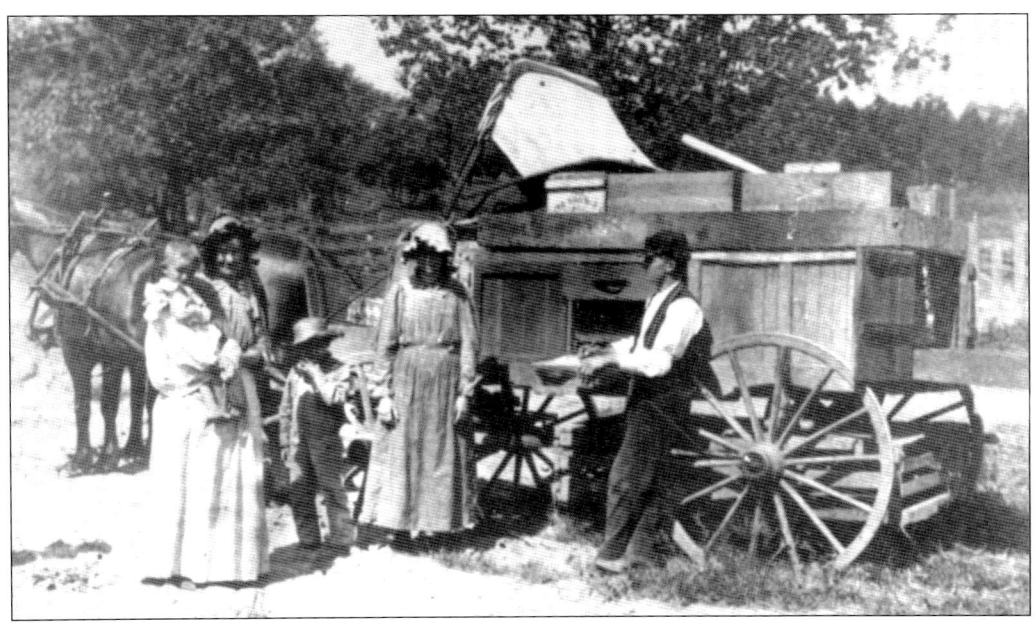

Huckster Henry Wolfe displays his wares to Carrie Metz (holding the child), the Metz boys, and Carrie Freeman in this early-1900s photograph taken in Indian Creek Township. Wolfe drove six weekly routes out of Pulaski. The traveling hucksters were a welcome sight with their wagonloads of treats. (PCHS Museum.)

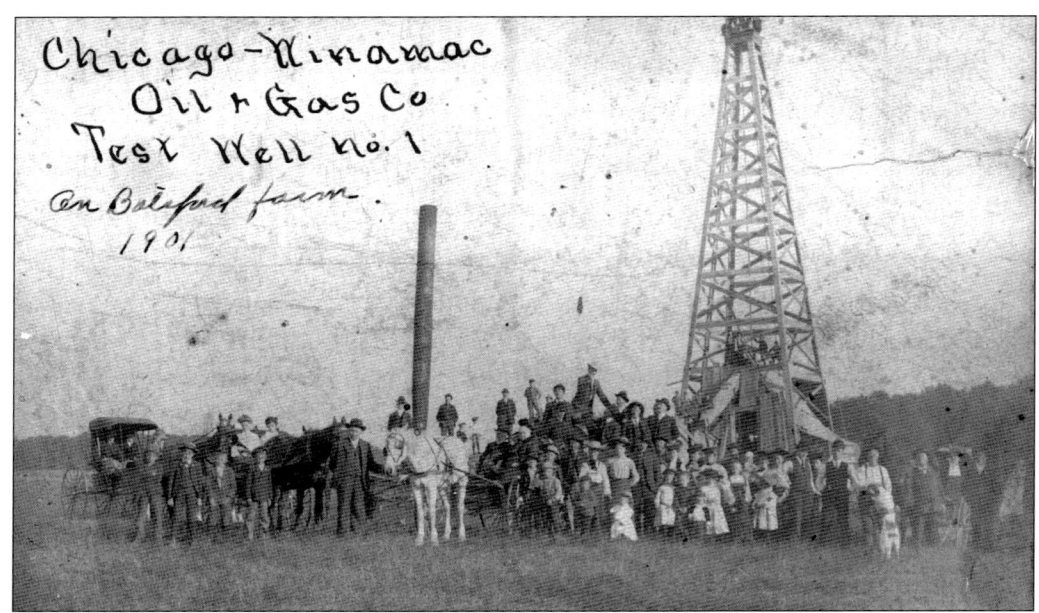

Gas and oil fever swept through Indiana in the mid-1880s. Wells were drilled everywhere without regard to geology. Gas was discovered as early as 1867 near Francesville. More wells were drilled there between 1887 and 1889, but the gas piped into town lasted only four years. A test well was drilled on this farm near Winamac in 1901 by the Chicago-Winamac Oil and Gas Company. The effort left only a hole in the ground and dashed hopes. (PCHS Museum.)

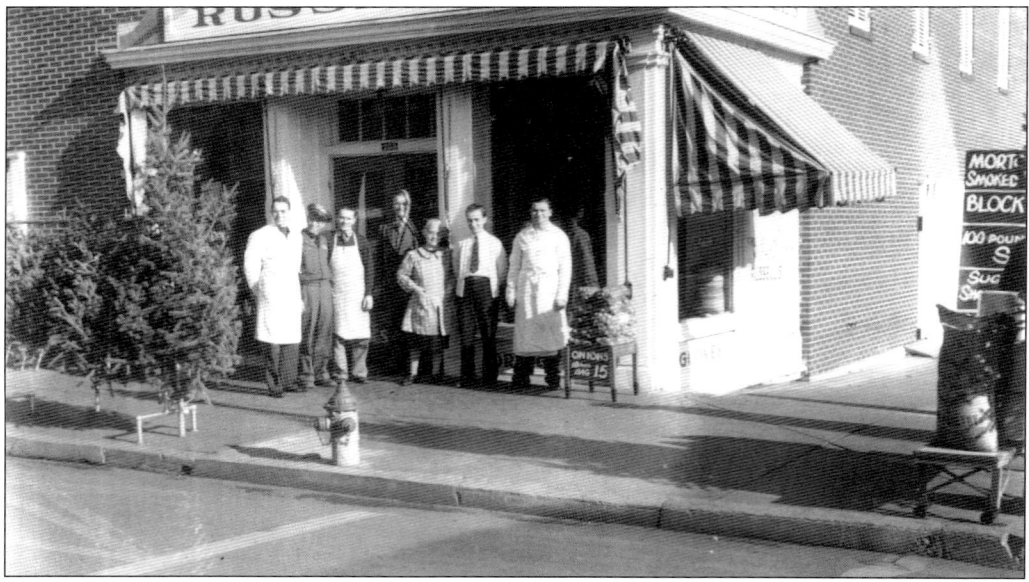

Russell's Old Trading Post in Winamac was extensively remodeled in 1939, and a brick veneer was added to the exterior of the store. Family members and employees gathered for this picture soon after completion. Then in January 1940, an early Sunday morning fire destroyed the building. Local papers called it Winamac's most disastrous fire in a quarter century. The Russells immediately announced plans to rebuild, and by the end of May, a new structure (minus the second story) was opened. (Emily Russell.)

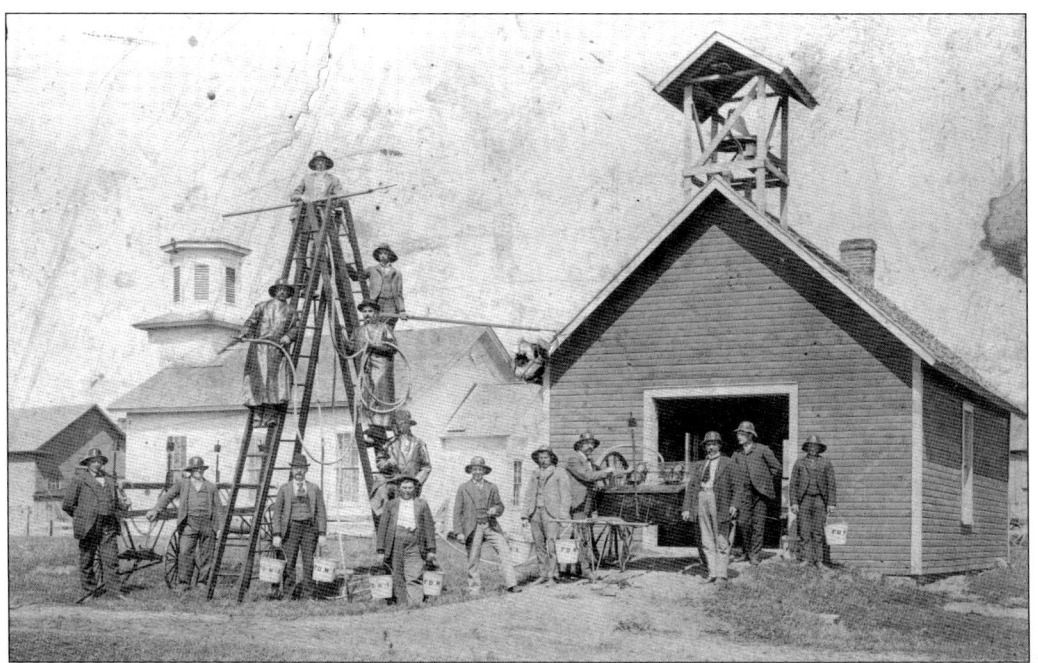

Monterey's first firehouse and firefighting equipment are displayed by the firemen in this photograph, which was taken about 1917. The cart-type engine and hook-and-ladder wagon were both "man-drawn." (Monterey-Tippecanoe Township Library.)

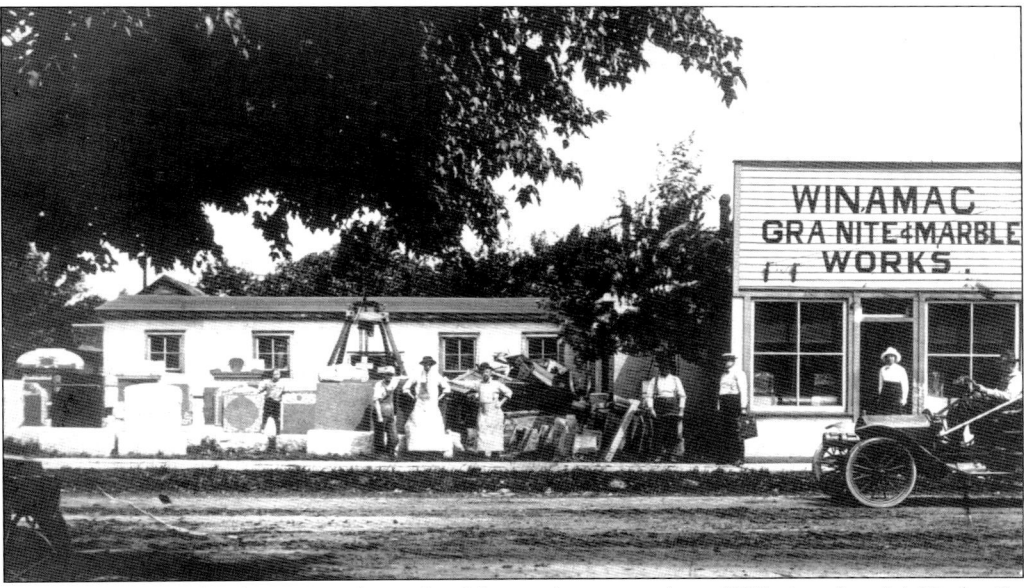

A rock and a chisel—these were the tools of the tombstone trade in 1895 when Lon McKinley Sr. purchased the Winamac Granite and Marble Works. More than 100 years later, family members continued to run McKinley Monuments on Pearl Street. Pictured in this 1912 photograph from left to right are Obie McKinley (boy), stonecutters McWilliams, Rearick, and Lindsy, Lon McKinley Jr., owner Lon McKinley Sr., Frank Long, Mrs. Flander, and Cal McKinley. (Charles McKinley.)

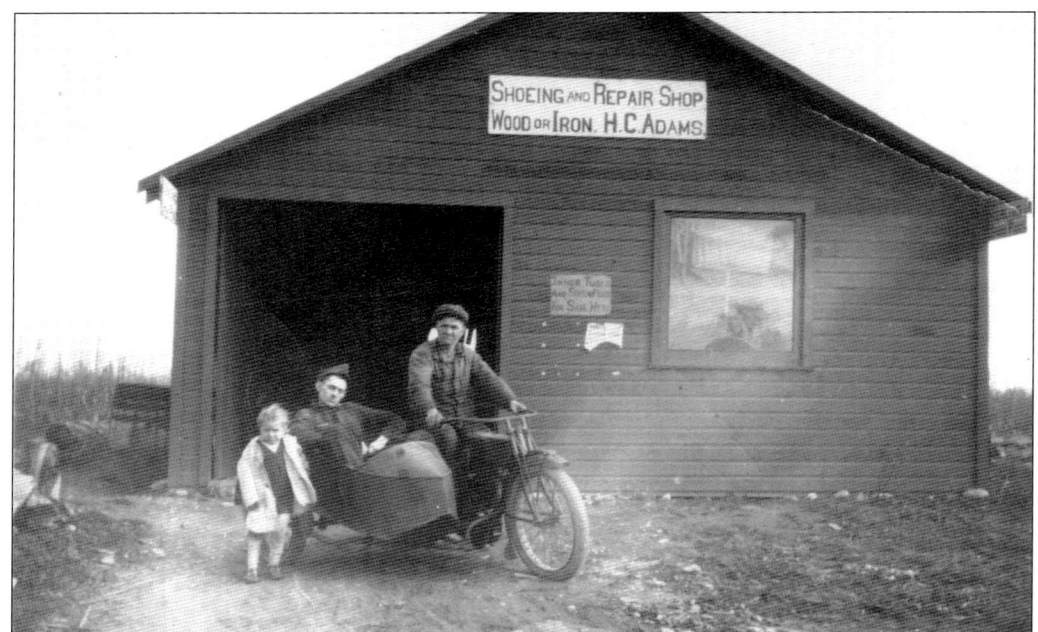

Harry C. Adams (on the motorcycle) operated this blacksmith shop in Star City. He is shown with his son Cassius Elmer Adams who is wearing his World War I uniform. The little girl is believed to be Harry's daughter Corine. The photograph was probably taken between April 1918 and April 1919. (Janet Onken.)

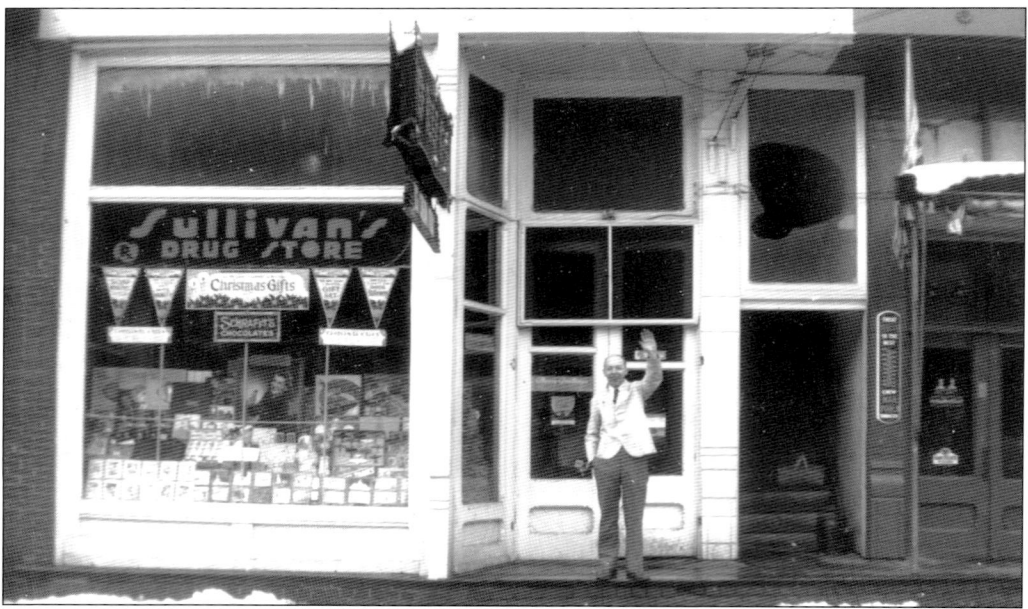

Hank and Maxine Sullivan operated their drugstore in Francesville for over 47 years. Sullivan's Drug Store opened in 1937 in the business block, which was destroyed by the Christmas 1944 fire. Sullivan purchased Gunny Gunnerson's repair shop garage across the street, remodeled it, and reopened the store a few months later. The drugstore was sold to Fagen Pharmacy in March 1985. (Betty Kruger.)

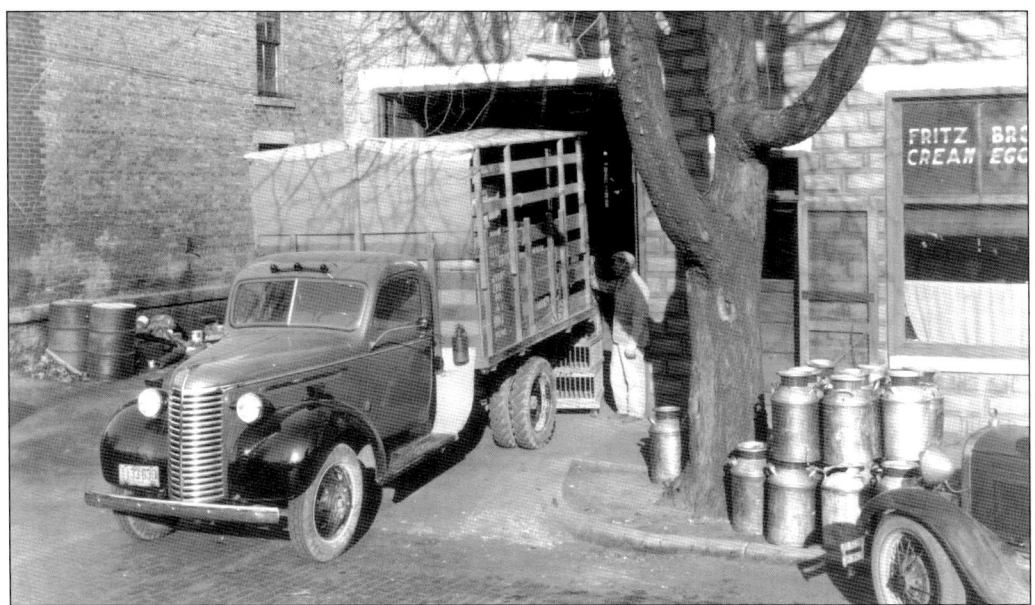

Brothers Alfred and Burley Fritz purchased the Baker Feed Barn on Logan Street in Winamac in 1925. They removed the old building and constructed a new concrete block one where they operated a cream station and purchased eggs and poultry. Sam Key manufactured the block and laid the walls. This was a 60-foot clear span building, which was very unusual in 1925. Burley is shown with the 1937 Chevrolet truck in this 1938 photograph. (Charlene Fritz.)

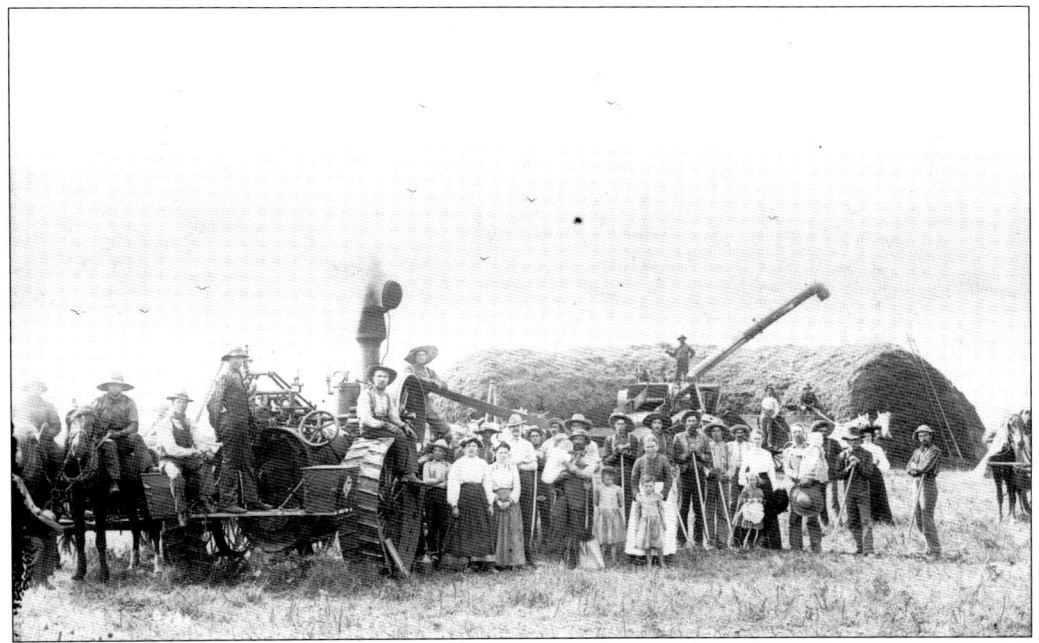

The Thrasher and Rainer families of rural Francesville are shown with the threshing crew in this early-1900s photograph. Farmer Stephen Thrasher was a Civil War veteran. Threshing time was memorable for its neighborly cooperation, for making up the crews to thresh the wheat, and for the huge threshing dinners made and served by the women. (Alyce Onken.)

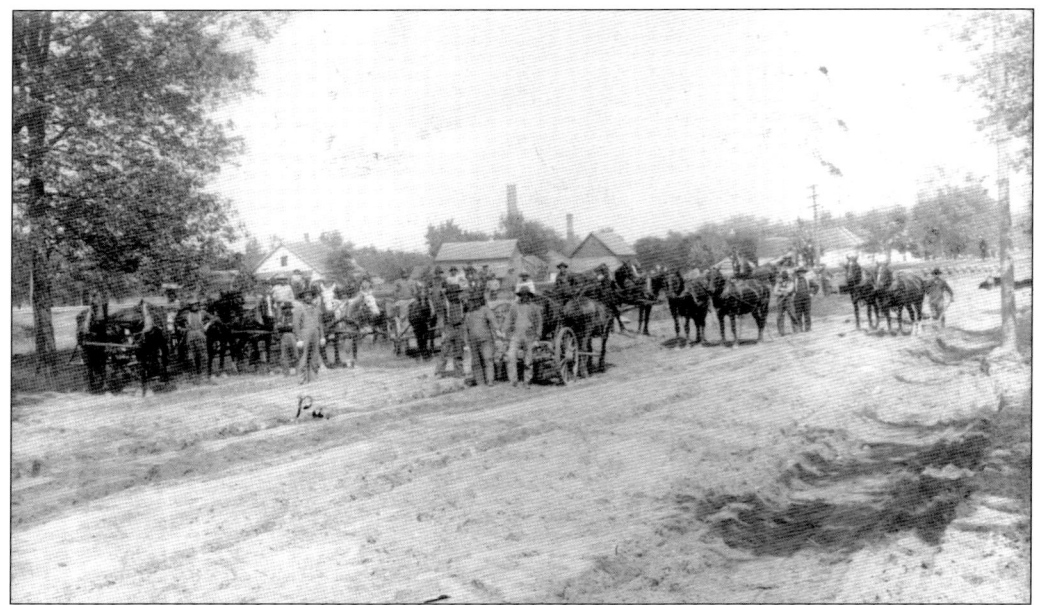

Construction began on the railroad viaduct on Eleventh Street in Winamac in 1909. This view looks east toward town. The job was contracted to Frank M. Williams for removal of 12,800 cubic yards of soil, which was used to fill a couple of gravel pits. The entire project was powered by horses and slip scoops. Railroad traffic was not affected. A total of 17 horse teams and 25 men were employed to complete the job. At least three of the teams belonged to Williams, and one team was purchased especially for this job. At the far right behind the tree trunk, a man can be seen standing in the hole being dug under the tracks, while another man stands on the railroad tracks behind him. The tracks run behind this group of workers and horses and in front of the buildings. Railroad service ended in downtown Winamac in the early 1980s, and the 77-year-old viaduct was removed in 1986. (Sara Slaven.)

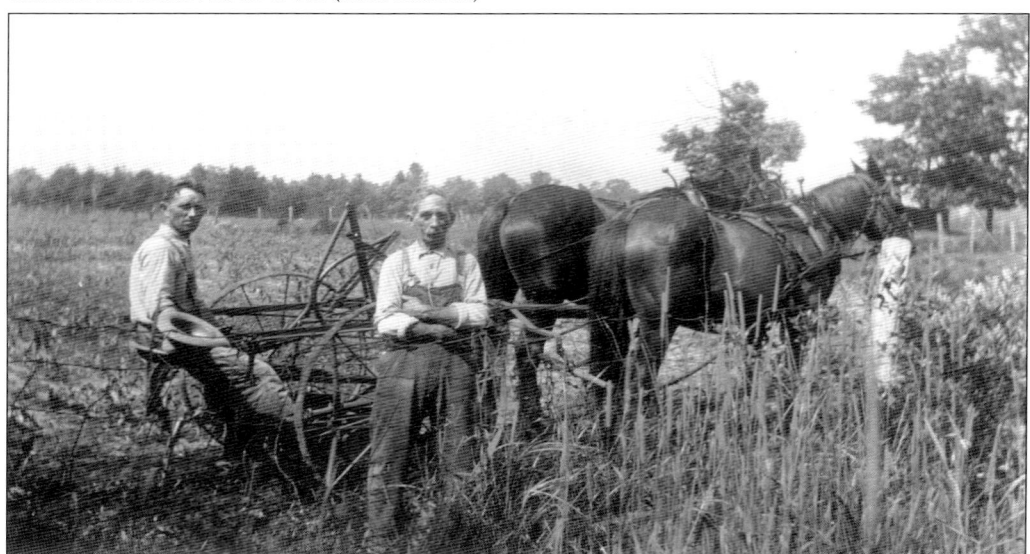

Franklin Township farmers Ira Bridegroom (left) and Charles Bridegroom pause for this undated photograph while plowing a field. The horses' names are John and Prince. (Janet Onken.)

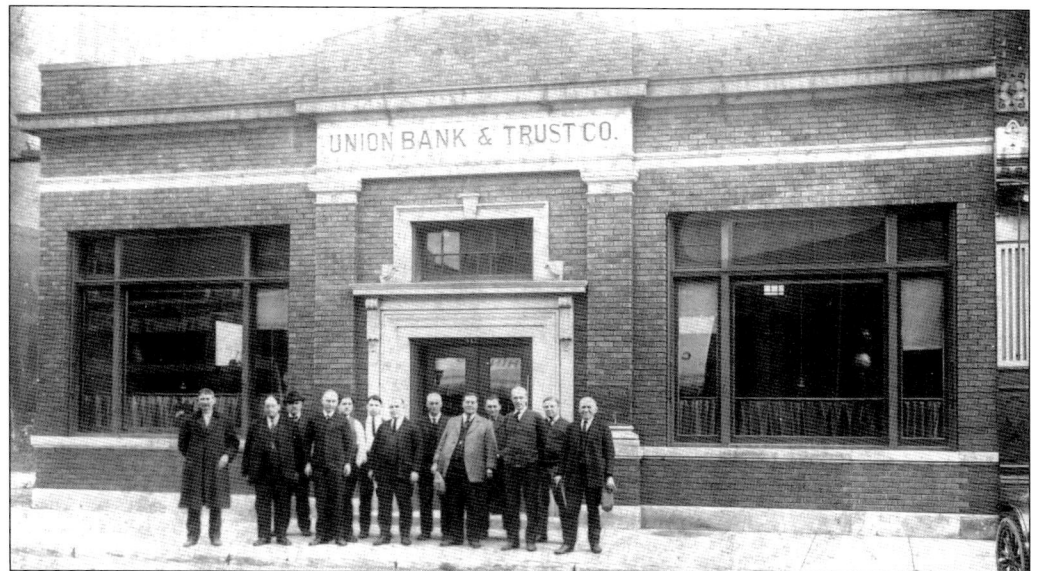

The Union Bank and Trust Company of Winamac was formed in 1921 with the consolidation of the Citizens National and the First Trust and Savings banks. This bank was located on mid-Market Street downtown. To survive during the Great Depression, Union Bank and Trust again consolidated with the First National Bank in 1931 to form the First Union Bank and Trust Company. The men shown in this photograph are believed to be bank stockholders. (PCHS Museum.)

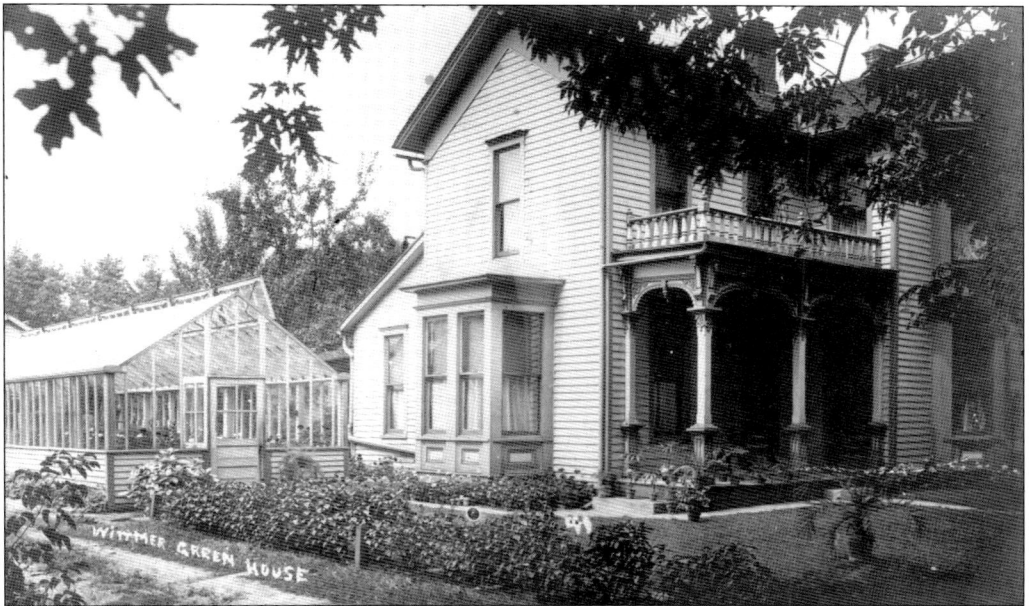

The Wittmer home and greenhouse on Market Street in Winamac is seen as it appeared in this undated postcard picture that was probably taken about 1908. The Winamac Greenhouse and Floral Shop was later operated by John and June Saidla. In 1943, Edward and Myrtle Haag purchased the business when he was 63 years old. They continued to run it for nearly 30 years. (Sara Slaven.)

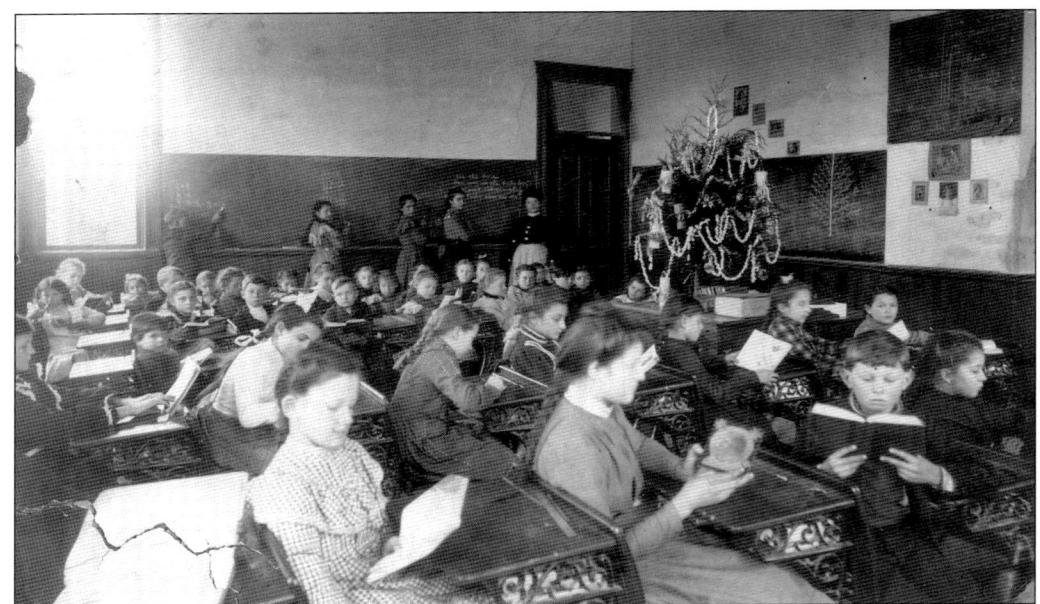

Students work on a variety of tasks at the schoolhouse in Pulaski, as seen in this photograph believed to date to December 1904 or 1905. The girl in the front desk in the second row from the camera is Sylvia Lowry. Behind her in the plaid dress is Nellie Leasure. They are the only identified pupils. Grades one through eight met in this classroom. This was Pulaski's first schoolhouse, built in 1896. (PCHS Museum.)

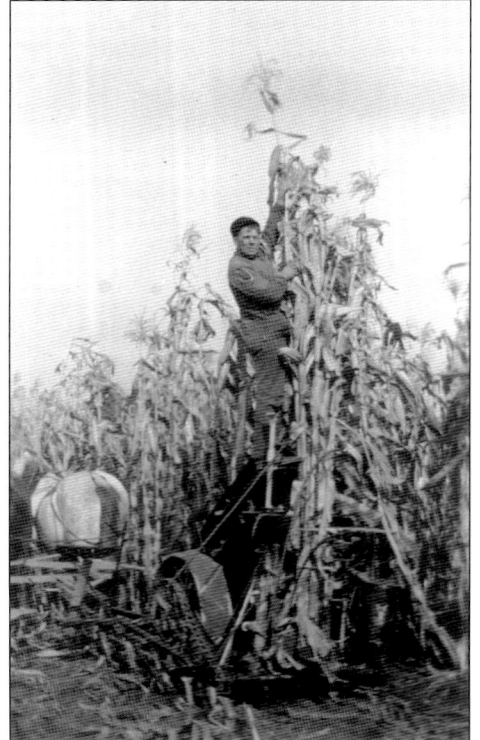

Herman Busch of Francesville shows off his tallest stock of corn in this 1920s photograph. He is standing on a horse-drawn corn binder. Born in 1870, Busch was among the first commercial fertilizer dealers in northern Indiana when he formed the Herman H. Busch and Son Company in 1913. The fertilizer, shipped in boxcars in 150- and 200-pound burlap bags, consisted of animal by-products and bone marrow with tobacco filler. The fertilizer was distributed by wagons to customers' farms. (Shirley Cords Busch.)

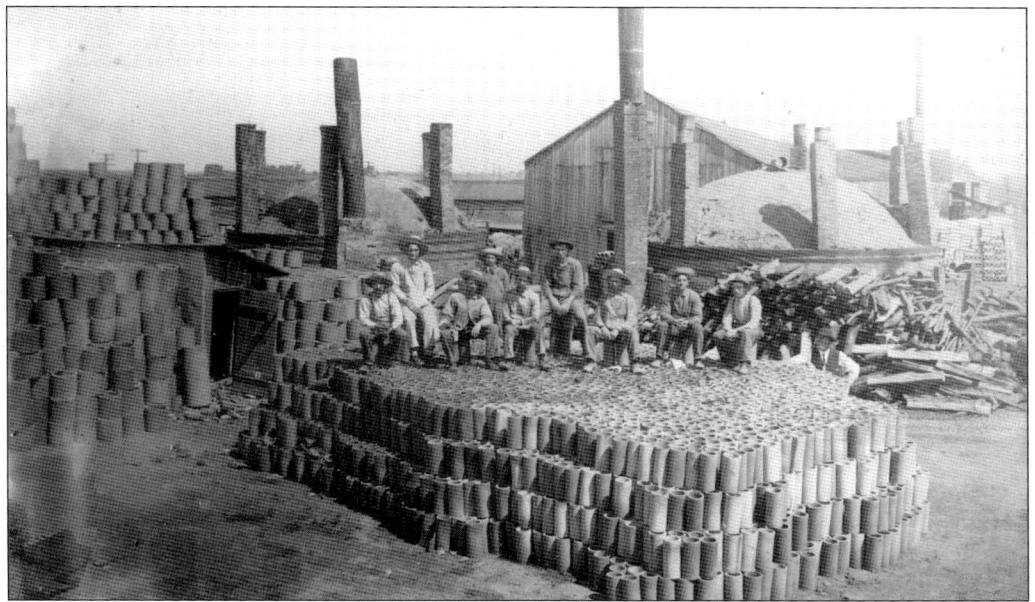

The Francesville Brick and Tile Company was founded in 1880. The plant is seen here in 1905. The company was reorganized in 1907, and the name changed to Francesville Clay Products Company. In the 1920s and 1930s, the clay was dug by hand. The tiles were used for farmland drainage. At one point in time, the company had four beehive kilns to fire the clay products. (Chris Overmyer.)

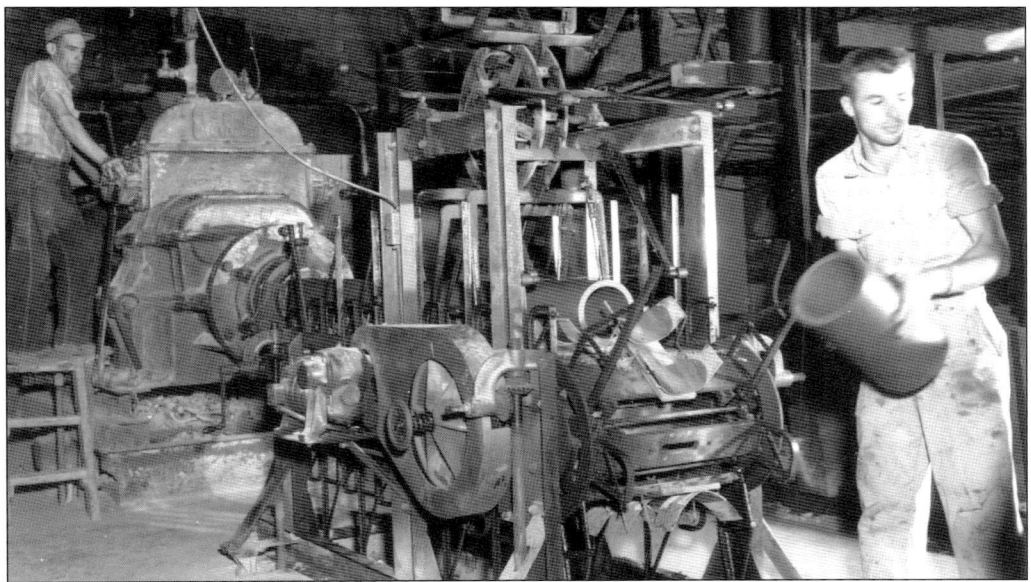

In 1923, Earl Overmyer became the sole owner of the tile company on the north side of Francesville. Three sons, H. Lee, Richard, and John joined the firm. The company incorporated in 1956. This 1958 photograph shows Jon Kopka (left) operating the F-R-H Hummer Extruder and an unidentified coworker. By the mid-1970s, the company made the conversion from clay tiles to corrugated plastic drain tubing. In 1997, the fourth generation of the Overmyer family assumed company operations. (Chris Overmyer.)

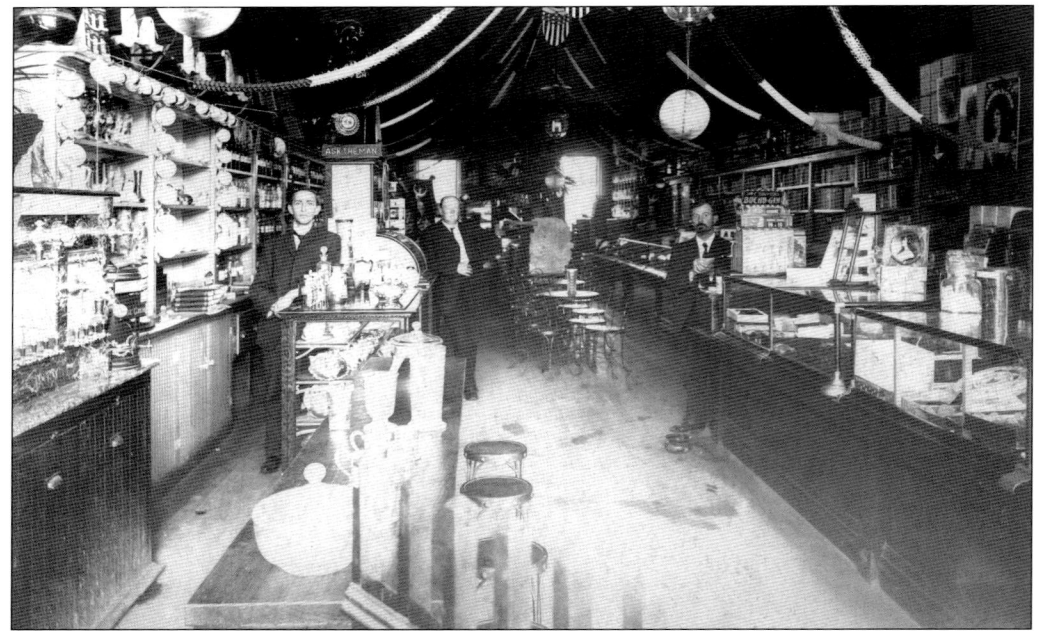

The "Blue Front" drugstore in Francesville was owned by Ed Detamore (left). This interior photograph of the store was taken around 1910. Charles Kruger (center) was an employee. Detamore emphasized that prescriptions were "compounded by a registered pharmacist." The store also advertised itself as the "home of the best malted milk." (Alyce Onken.)

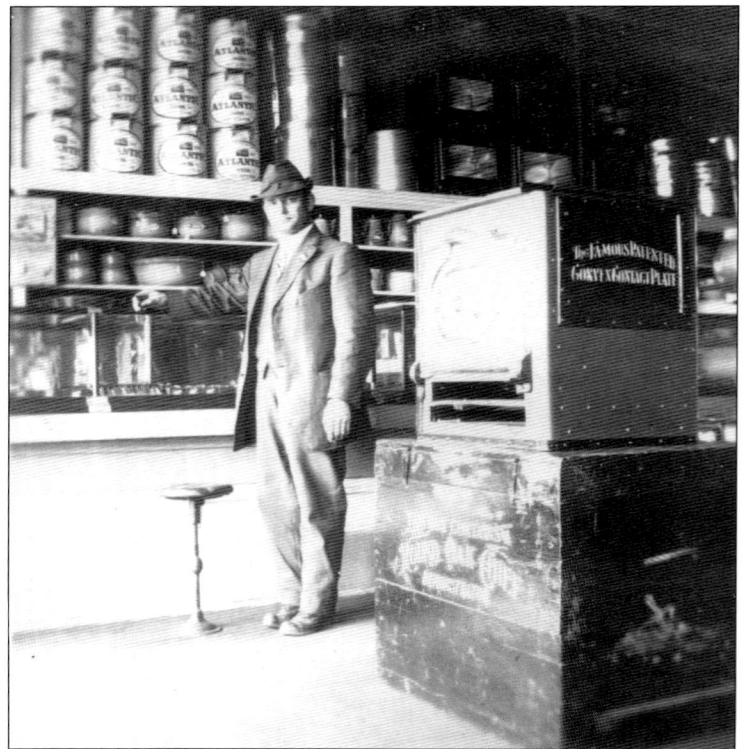

Born in 1874, Joseph P. Gilsinger was a successful mercantile businessman in the village of Pulaski. He was also active in community projects, such as building a sidewalk to connect the Presbyterian and Catholic churches. He brought the first telephone service to the town, provided water service from his store to several homes, and offered electricity to the town from a power plant in his building. For a time, a post office also occupied space in the store. (Brenda Gilsinger.)

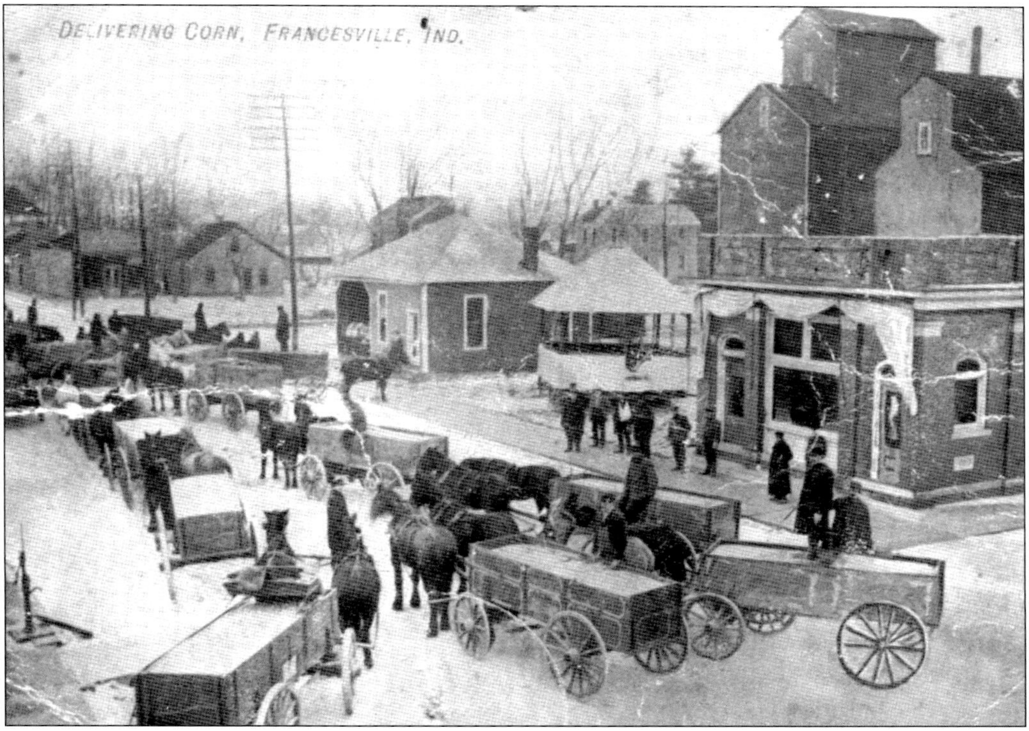

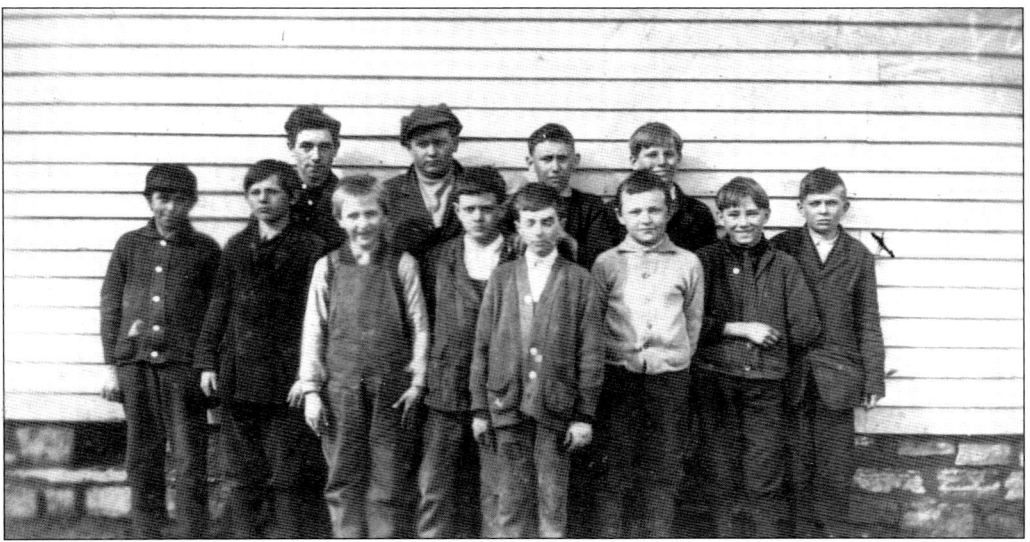

Farmers line up in their horse-drawn wagons to deliver their newly harvested corn from the field to the grain elevator in Francesville in this early-1900s photograph. The Francesville State Bank stands on the corner, with the elevator rising behind it. (Francesville Tribune.)

A group of schoolboys gathered for this photograph outside the Denham school in about 1914. The only one identified is Gustave Schuttrow at far right. The first schoolhouse in Denham was a crude, log structure build in 1855 at a cost of $75. The Denham School served the community until the 1950s when the students and their peers from the rest of Rich Grove Township were transferred to North Judson. (Patrick Schuttrow.)

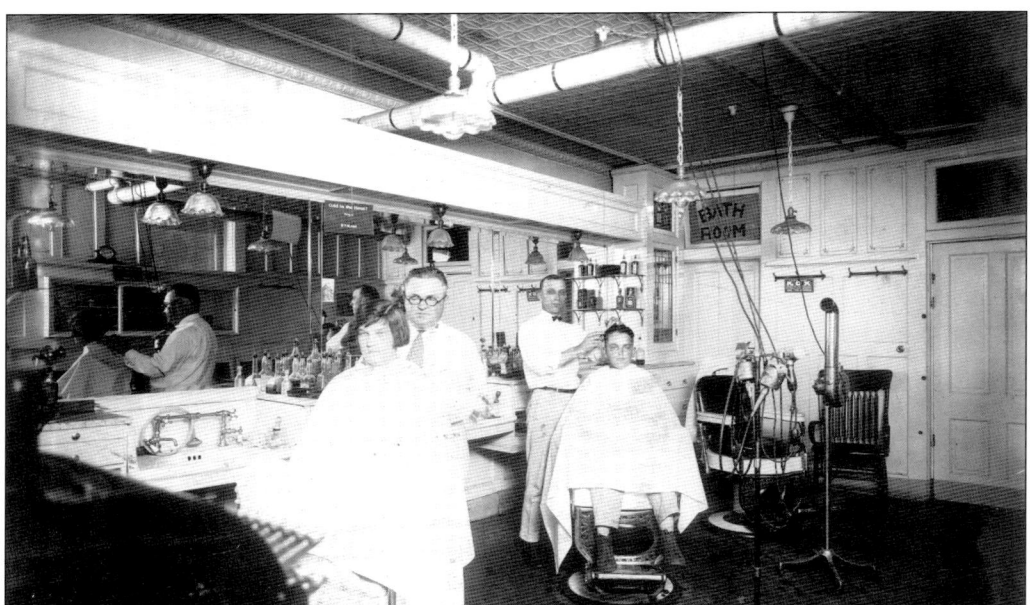

This barbershop was located in the basement at the west end of the old Frain Hotel, located at Main and Market Streets in Winamac. The barbers are Oscar "Pat" Boyles (left) and Frank Hair. The boy getting a haircut at right is John Dilts. The date of the photograph is believed to be about 1929. The Frain Hotel building was constructed in 1880 and demolished in 1965. (PCHS Museum.)

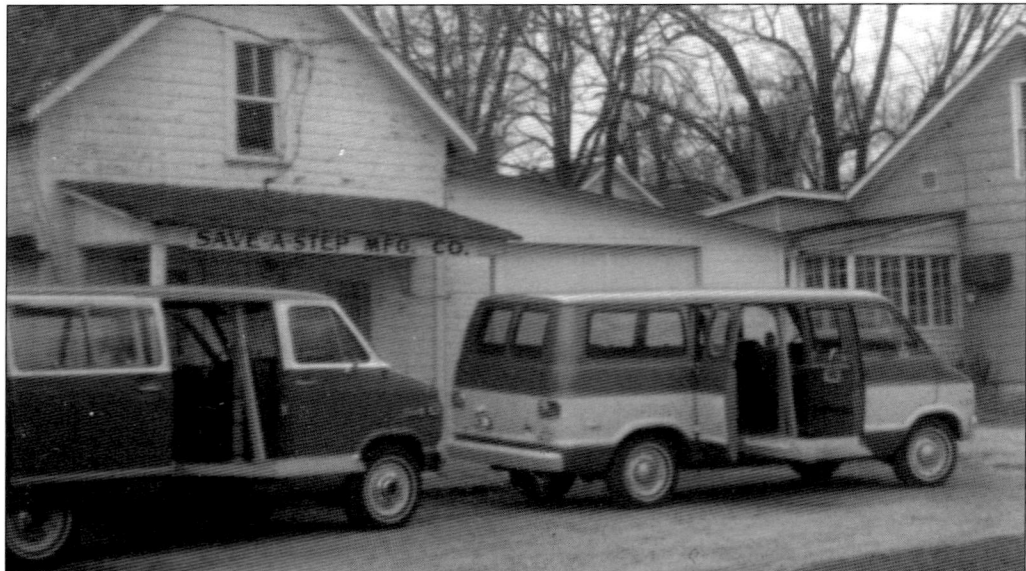

The Braun Corporation, an international leader in the manufacture of products to mobilize the handicapped, was founded in the 1960s in a humble Winamac garage, beginning with a motorized chair developed by a young man who wanted more than anything to deal with his muscular dystrophy by getting around on his own. By the 21st century, the company became the county's biggest employer, and Ralph Braun was getting around by motorized carts—and private jets and even hot air balloons. (Braun Corporation.)

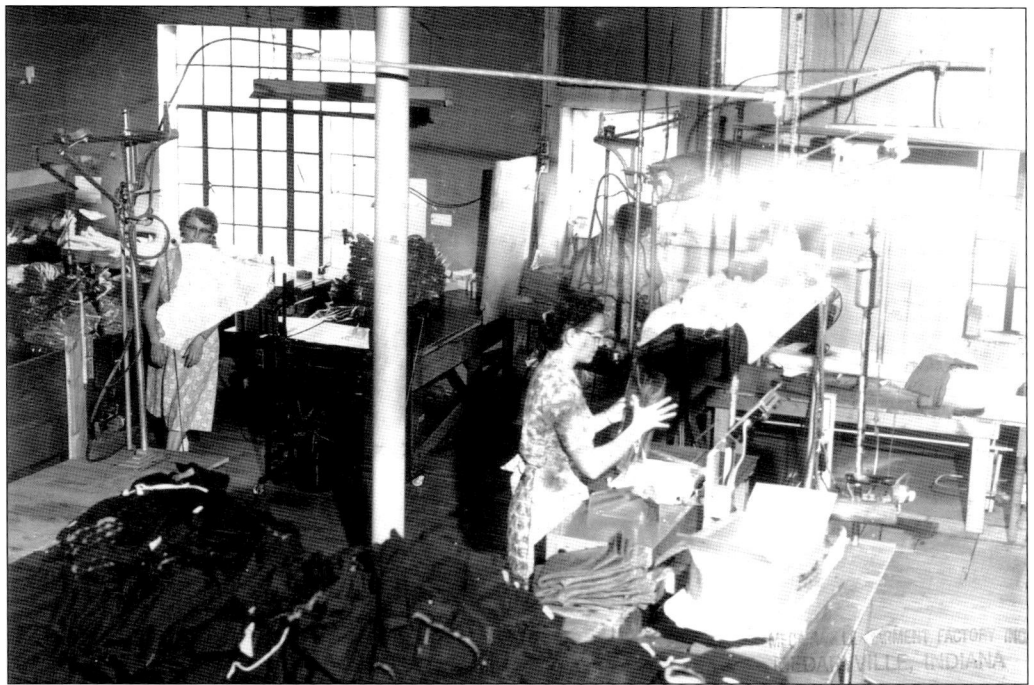

Above, Goldie Stout and Dorothy Burium work in the folding room at the Medaryville Garment Factory, while coworkers sit at the sewing tables (below). The pictures are believed to date to 1948. At one time, there were 150 employees. In 1989, there were 50 employees who produced 500 dozen work garments each week. The Medaryville factory was in operation from 1922 to 1996. (Medaryville Historical Museum.)

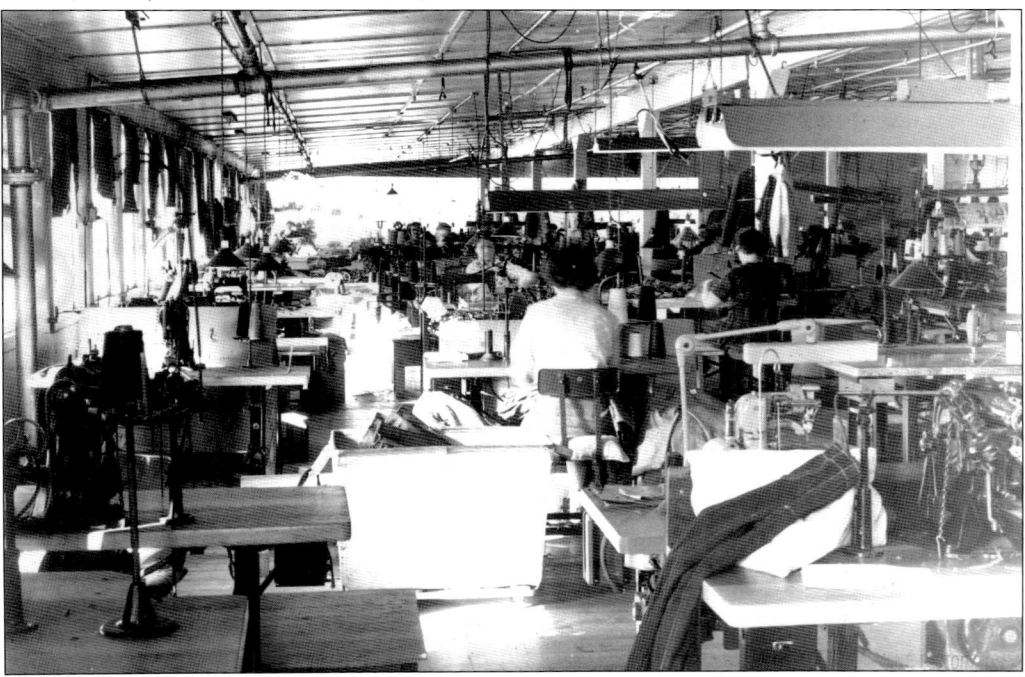

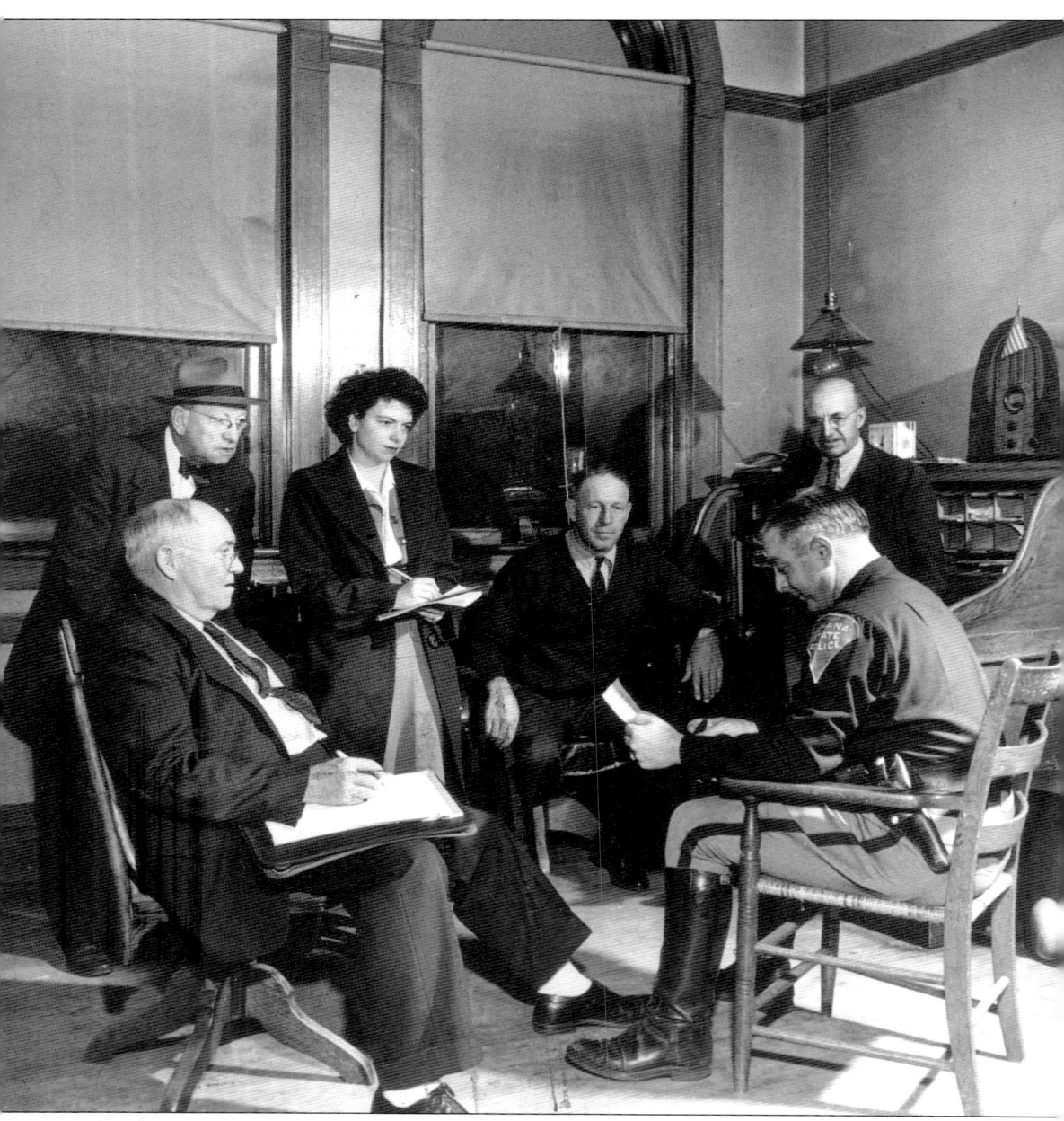

Parade magazine published a feature story on Edmund (Ned) Gorrell and his *Pulaski County Democrat* in 1946. This photograph was staged for the article. Pictured from left to right are (first row) prosecuting attorney George Collins and state trooper Delvie Masterson; (second row) Ned Gorrell, Janet Gorrell, Sheriff Jim Bruce, and Deputy Sheriff H. W. Wolfe. (Author's collection.)

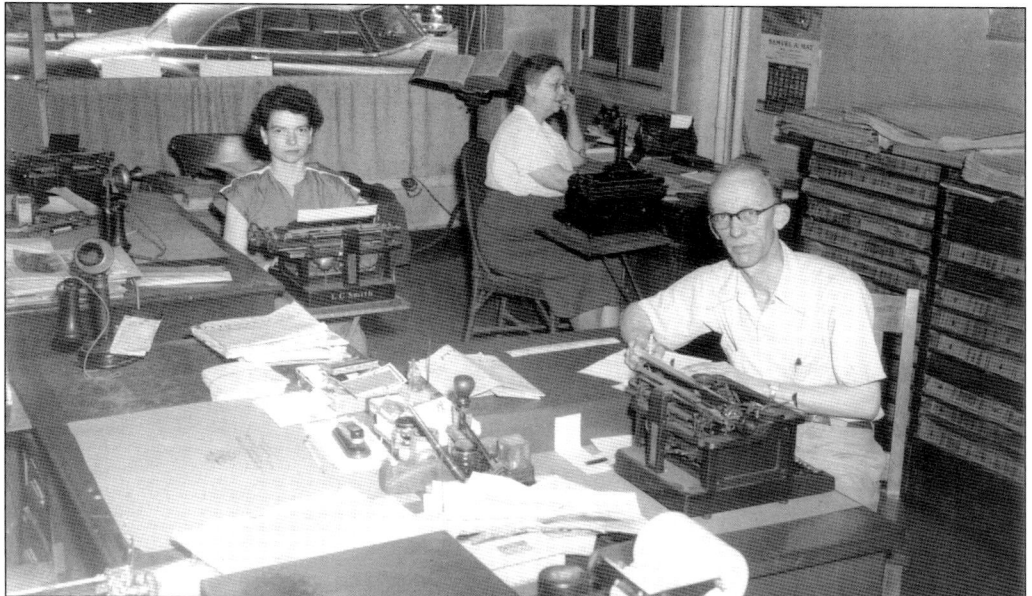

Working against a deadline in the front office of the *Pulaski County Democrat* in 1951, from left to right, are Janet Gorrell Meyer, Nell Davis, and Richard Dodd. The Gorrell family owned the weekly newspaper from 1891 until 1970, with three generations working in its offices. Under the leadership of editor Ned Gorrell, the paper was honored by the Hoosier State Press Association as the state's best weekly paper in the late 1930s. (Author's collection.)

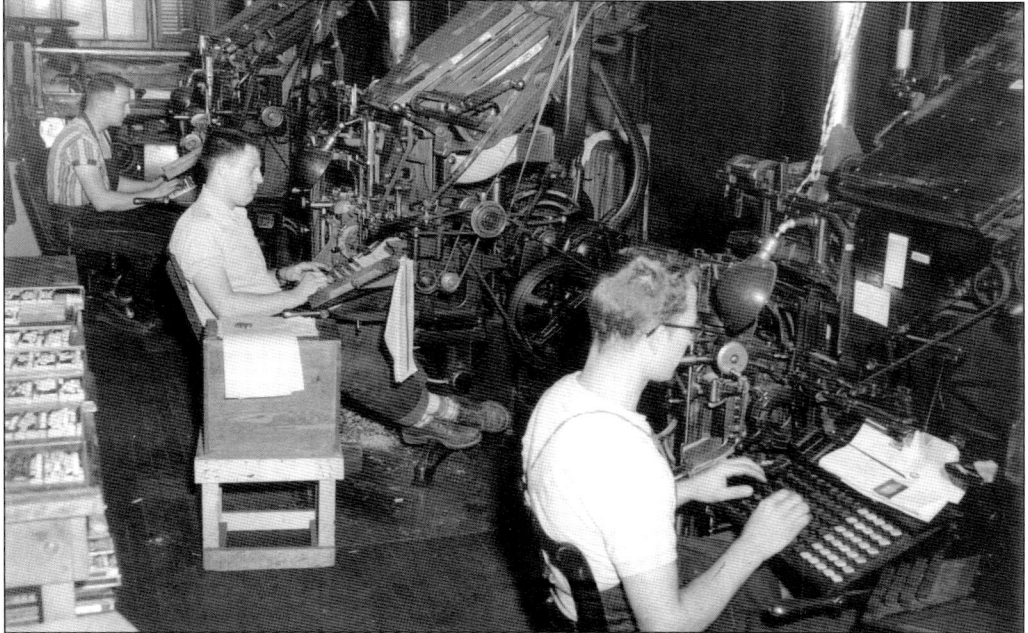

The *Pulaski County Democrat* building on Main Street in Winamac was constructed in 1911, 20 years after the newspaper enterprise was purchased by J. J. Gorrell. Typesetting equipment, newspaper presses, and a print shop were located at the back of the building. Setting type in 1951, from left to right, are Bill Webb, Corwin Henry, and Tom Knouff. (Author's collection.)

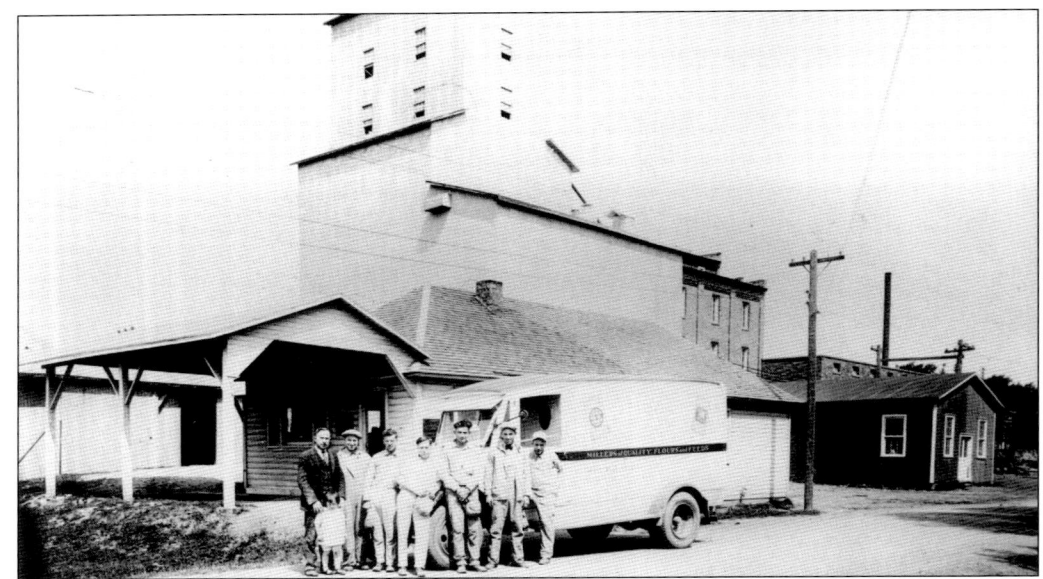

The Gutwein Milling Company was founded in Francesville in 1920. The Gutwein family came to the United States in 1906 from Hungary, where Philip Gutwein Sr. had operated a grain milling company with his brother-in-law. This photograph dates to the early 1930s and was taken in front of the Gutwein Elevator and Milling Company. Those in the picture include Adam Gutwein, John Gutwein, Arthur Getz, Emel Ryans, Alvin Boehning, Herman Wuethrich, and Phillip Schubert. The little girl is Margaret Gutwein. (Betty Kruger.)

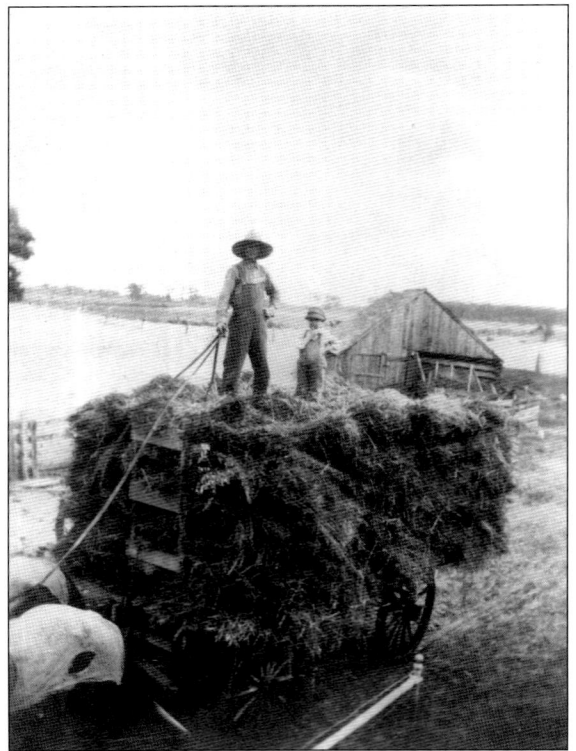

Shocked grain is carried from the field to the threshing machine on a bundle wagon driven by an unidentified farmer and child. This wheat threshing took place at the Busch farm in Beaver Township in September 1917. It took 16 men or more to do the work on threshing day, including a couple of workers to pitch these shocks onto the threshing machine, which separated the grain from the straw and chaff. (Shirley Cords Busch.)

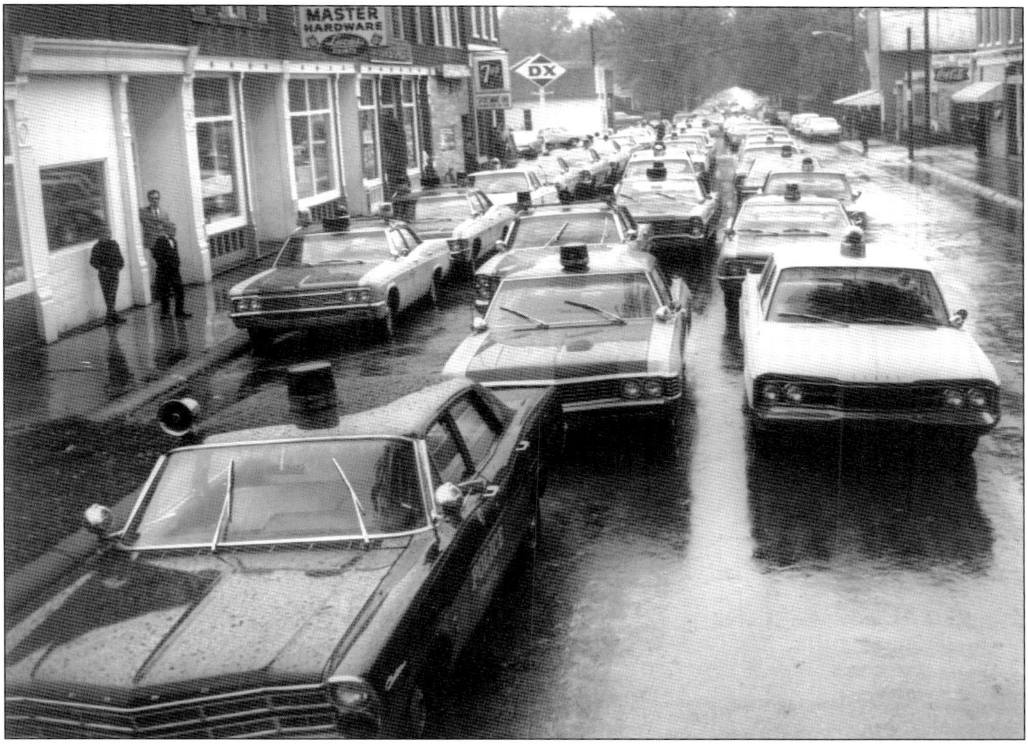

The funeral procession for slain Pulaski County sheriff Milo Lewis proceeds through his hometown of Monterey in October 1967. At age 50, Lewis (right) served as sheriff for 10 months when he was shot on October 11 by a prisoner who was being held at the county jail. The prisoner was attempting an escape, using a gun smuggled to him by a girlfriend. Lewis died hours later at Pulaski Memorial Hospital. He was survived by his wife and four children. One other county sheriff was killed in office. Sheriff Charles Oglesby was shot while attempting to arrest three hobos stealing a ride on a Pennsylvania Railroad freight train in October 1907. (Above, Monterey-Tippecanoe Township Library; right, Jeanne Lewis Stinemetz.)

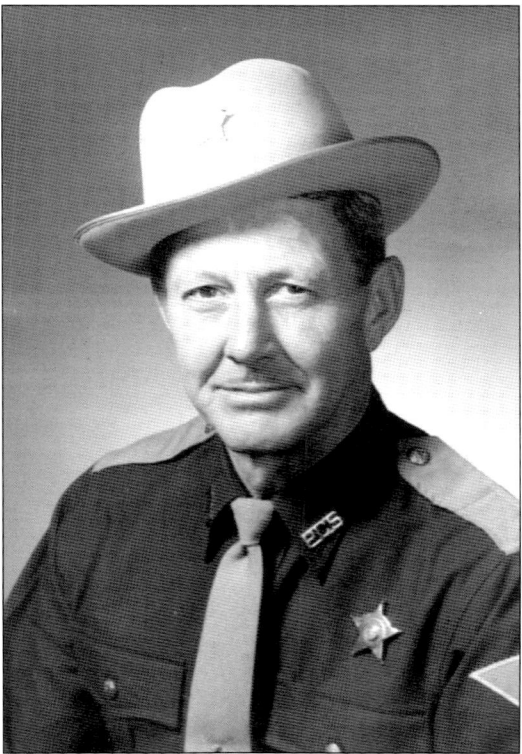

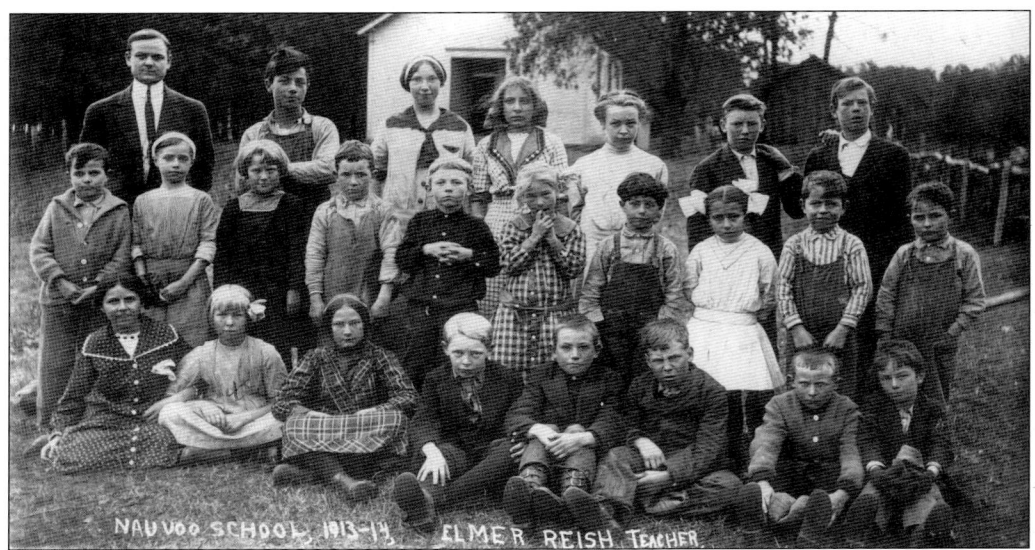

The Nauvoo School in rural Salem Township was typical of the small country schoolhouses that dotted the county. Students during the 1913–1914 school year are pictured here with their teacher, Elmer Reish. From left to right are (first row) Mabel Webb, Mildred Harbrecht, Myrtle Elston, Russell Wiley, John Wentz, ? Whitlow, Verl Webb, and Robert Elston; (second row) Robert Webb, Thelma Strong, Loretta Wentz, ? Whitlow, Bill Exen, Edna Exen, Kenneth Strong, Flora Morris, ? Webb, and ? Webb; (third row) Reish, Roy Strong, Lola Harbrect, Helen Webb, Freida Wiley, Ruel Whitlow, and Verl Elston. (PCHS Museum, donated by Lola Tetzloff.)

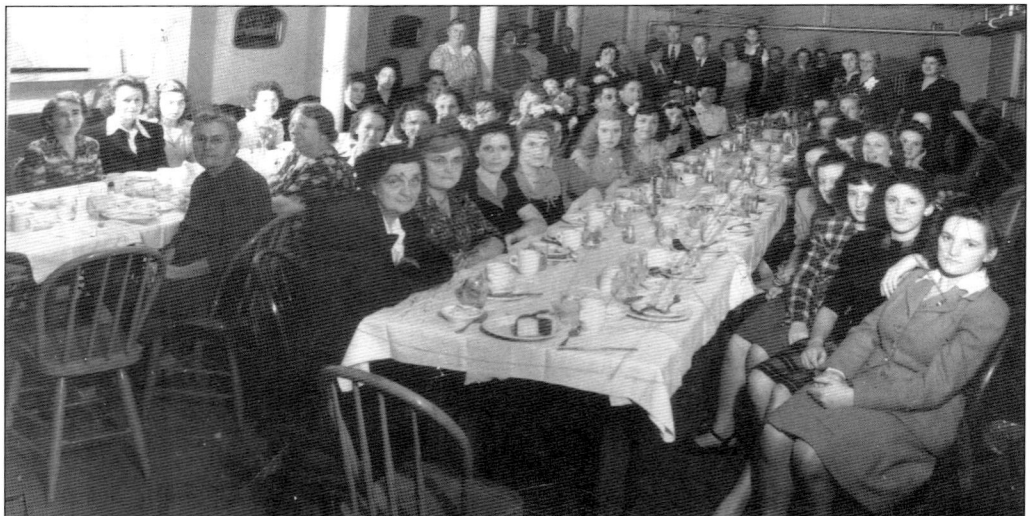

The employees of the Rice Corporation in Winamac attend a banquet at a local church hall in this picture dating to about 1950. The company was a sewing factory that made blue jeans and overalls for J. C. Penney, Spiegel, Hudsons, L. S. Ayres, and other department stores. It was located on Pearl Street, and from 1948 to 1964, it also had a branch in Monterey. James Freeman of Winamac joined the firm as its business manager in 1947 and acquired ownership of the company in 1953. At its peak, the Rice Corporation employed 180 workers at its two branches. It closed in 1974, when competition from imports made the business unprofitable. (Jean Nicholson.)

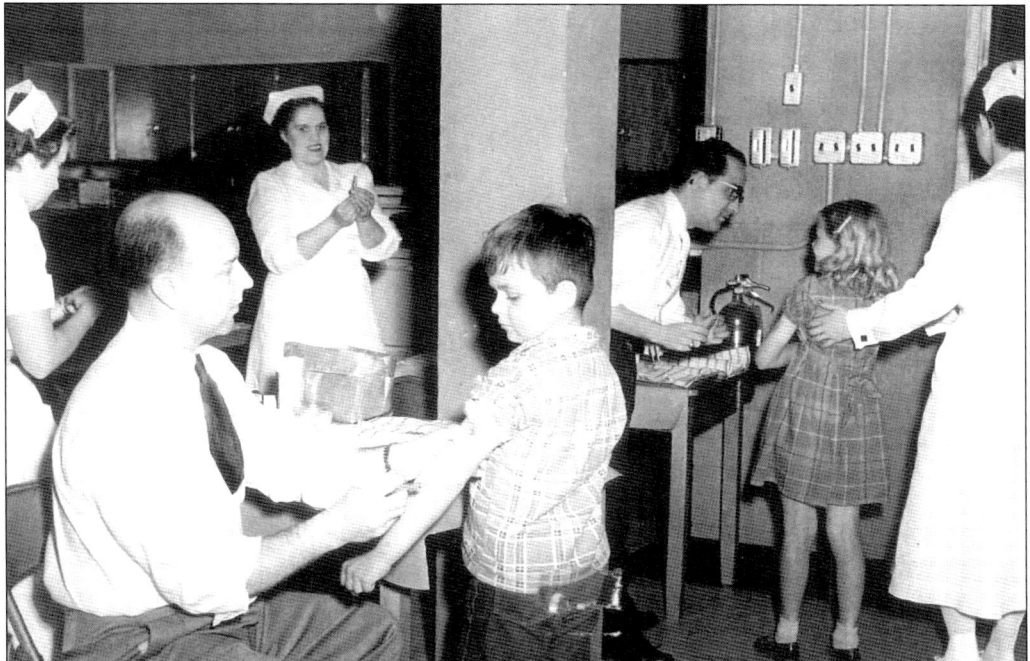

The first polio vaccinations at the Medaryville schools were given on April 19, 1955. Preparing to administer the shots are Dr. William Thompson (seated); registered nurses, from left to right, Lenora Gilsinger, Olive White, and Rosemary Coburn; and Dr. John Karnes. The children are Steve Nielsen and Thelma Tanner. (Olive White.)

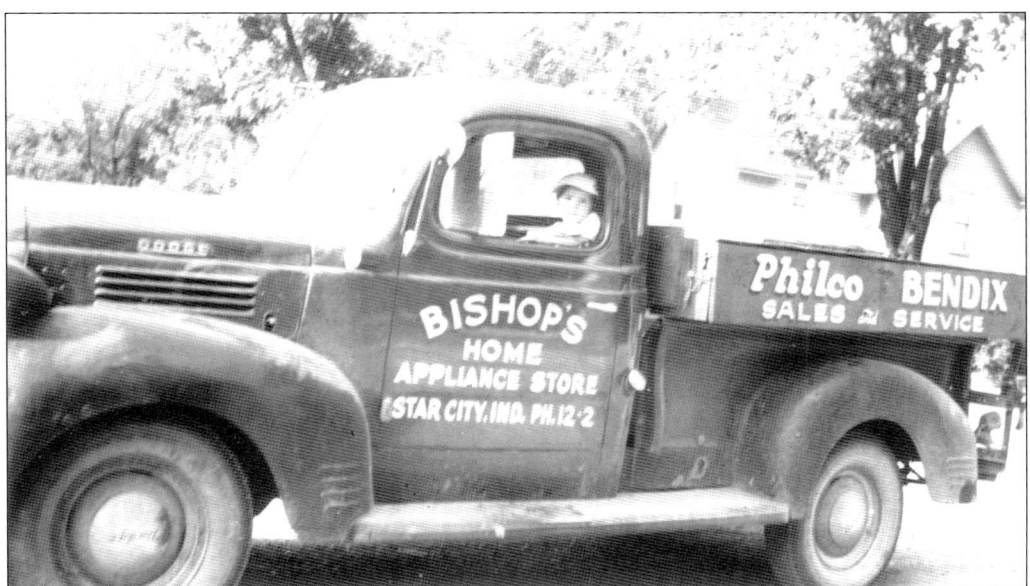

Ralph and Leah Bishop opened a garage business in 1924 and then expanded into home appliance sales and service in Star City. They sold their first electric refrigerator in 1927. Grandson Larry Heater sits in the driver's seat of the Bishop Store's Dodge pickup truck in this 1953 photograph. The Bishops continued in business into the 1990s. (Lois Bishop Heater.)

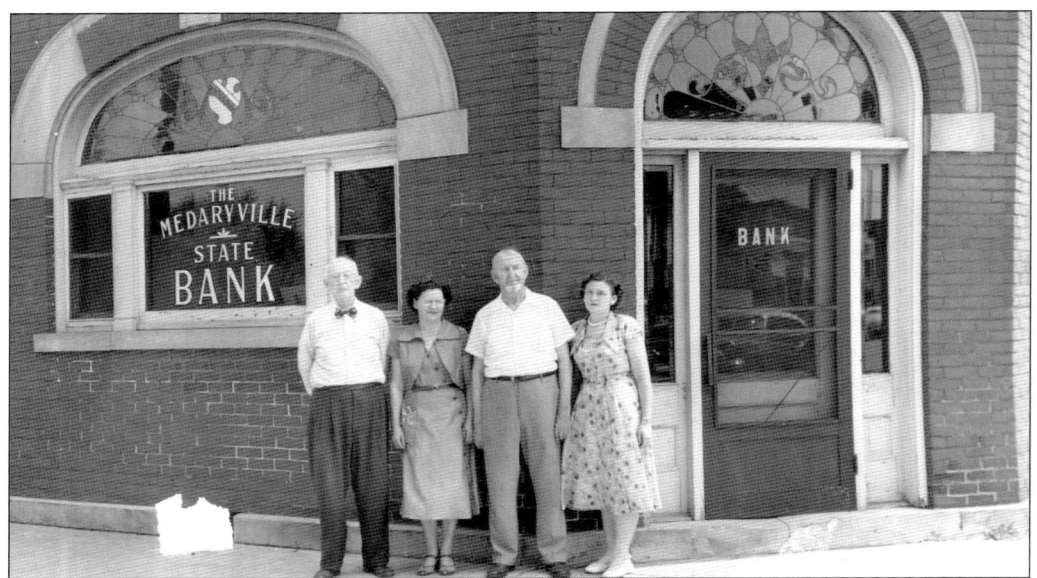

The Medaryville State Bank was chartered in 1907 and was located in the Horner Block on Main Street. Working at the bank in 1953 from left to right are Claude Horner, Dora Williams, Owen Horner, and Jeanetta Freshour. The Horner brothers were sons of the bank's founder, E. W. Horner, who first opened a private bank in his store. In 1957, the bank merged with the First Union Bank and Trust Company of Winamac, whose president was another brother, Ralph Horner. (Medaryville History Museum.)

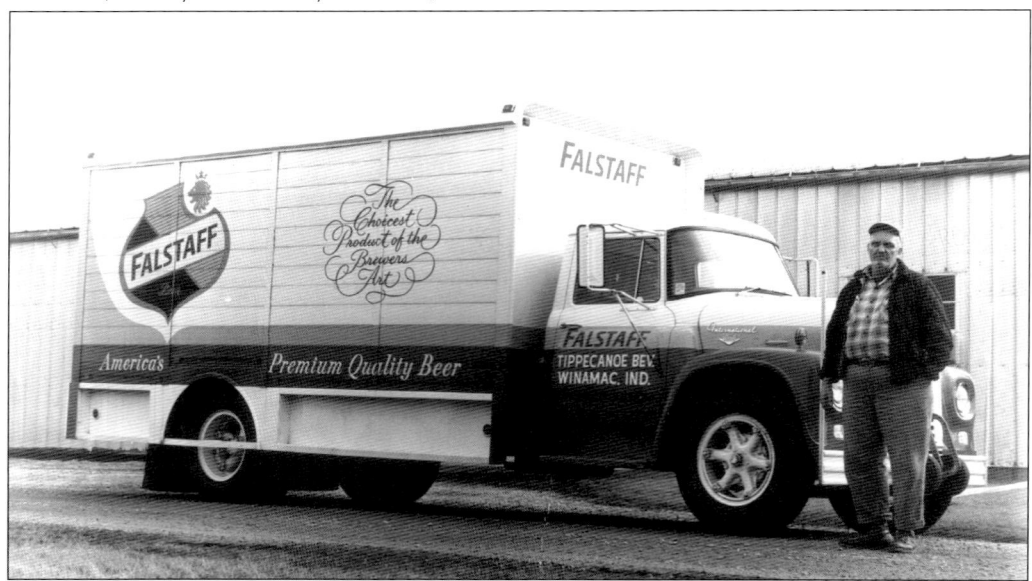

Tippecanoe Beverages of Winamac was founded in 1955 by George Zahrt and Clarence Battenfield. The business began as a distributor of Sterling beer, which was brewed in Evansville. Within 10 months, the new firm became an Anheuser-Busch distributor. Zahrt bought out his partner a few years later. The business celebrated its 50th anniversary in 2005, operated by Zahrt's sons Fred and David. Employee Dewey Wickizer is shown in this early company photograph. (Fred Zahrt.)

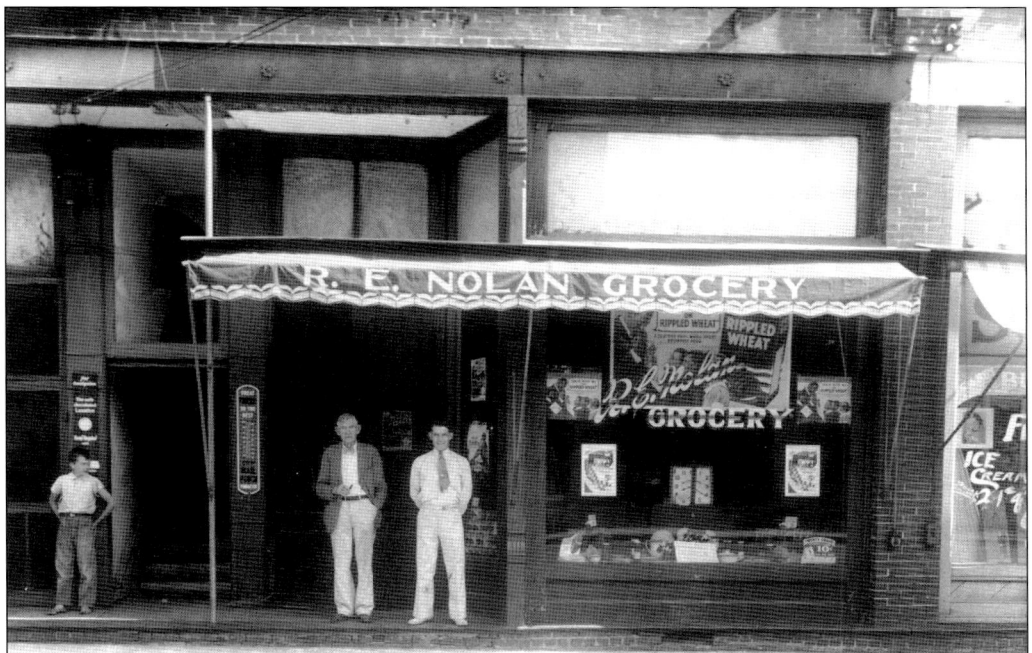

The "Red Front" grocery store in Francesville was operated by Ross E. Nolan (left), shown here with Harry White, who served as a clerk in the store in the early 1930s. Nolan and his brother Frank were engaged in business at this location in 1890. This grocery store was one of several businesses destroyed by fire on Christmas in 1944. (Alyce Onken.)

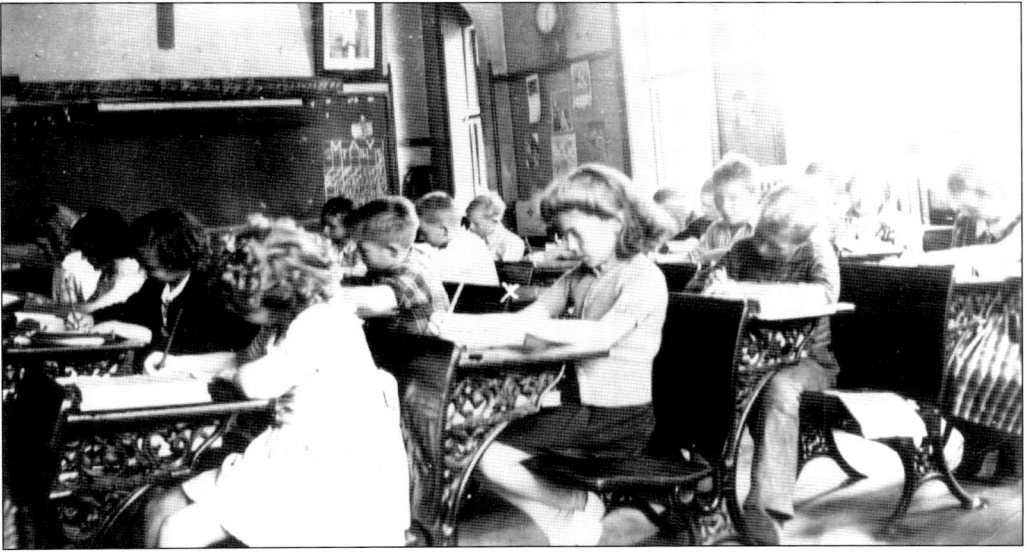

With summer vacation days away and World War II raging across both oceans, these fourth-grade students at Winamac Elementary School are hard at work on an assignment in this May 1943 photograph. From left to right are (first row, front to back of classroom) Mary J. Fry, Carolyn Smith, Dick Lebo, and Abagail Crosby; (second row) Jean Kasten, Tommy Galbreath, Gerald Hewitt, and Norma Poor; (third row) Jean Garling, Charles McKinley, Dick Lebo, and Raymond Smith; (fourth row) Eleanore Fry, unidentified, Dick Baske, and unidentified. (Shirley Cords Busch.)

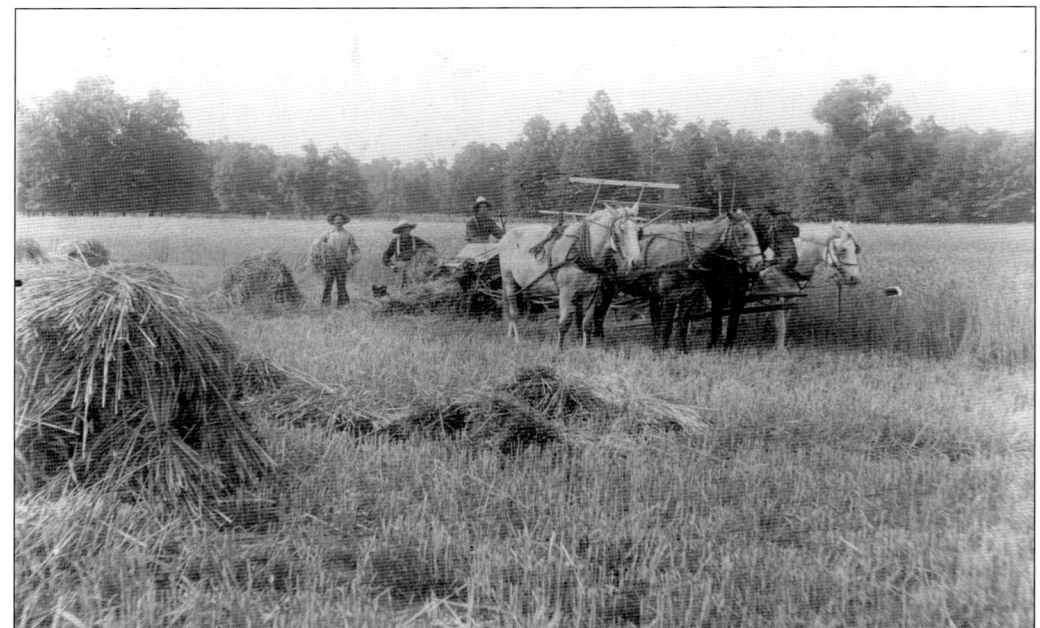

A bumper crop of wheat is harvested at the Fred Reidelbach farm in Beaver Township. The work crew is using the horse-drawn equipment to bind and shock the wheat for the threshing machine, which arrived a few days later. The date is unknown. (PCHS Museum, donated by Harold Budd.)

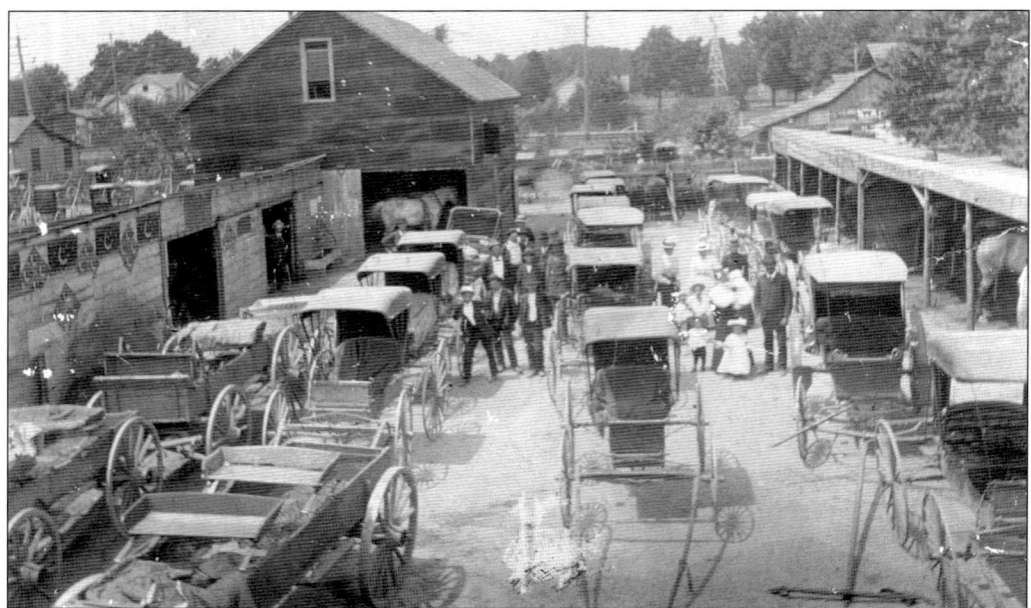

The Wyant Feed Barn and Livery Stables were located on Logan Street in Winamac behind the Christian church. Robert Wyant built his new livery and feed barn in September 1896 on the lots just north of George Frain's machine shop. He sold out to Joe Hepp in June 1904. This undated photograph was taken by James M. Engle, a photographer who took many pictures of Winamac at the dawn of the 20th century. (PCHS Museum.)

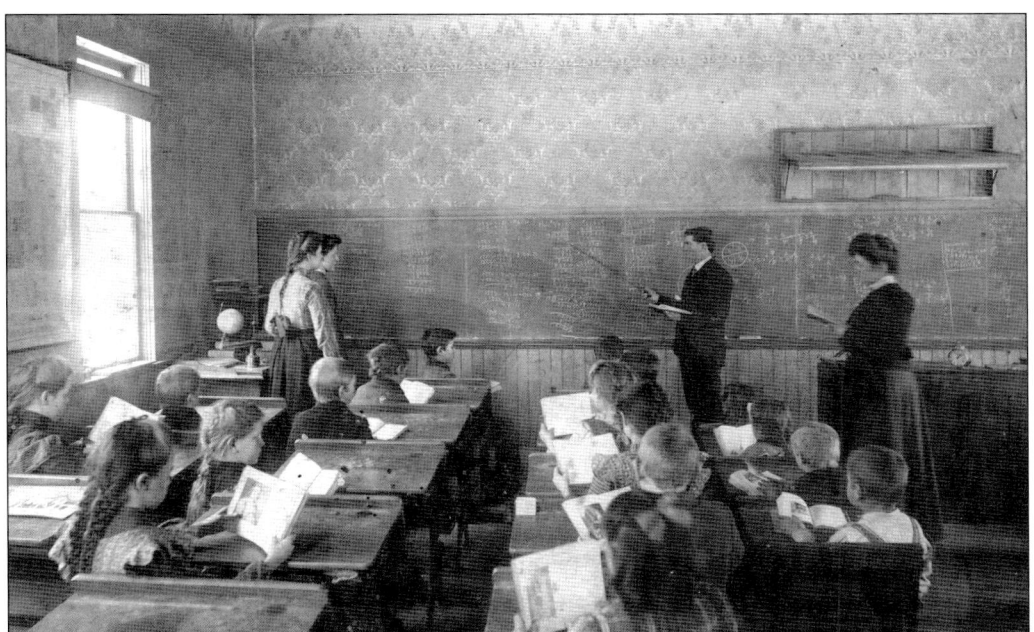

Two of the older pupils at the Wade School in Tippecanoe Township work with the schoolhouse teachers on arithmetic problems, while the younger students observe or work on their own individual assignments in this vintage photograph, which dates to the early 1900s. There were about 90 such schools in the county during this time period. (Monterey-Tippecanoe Township Library.)

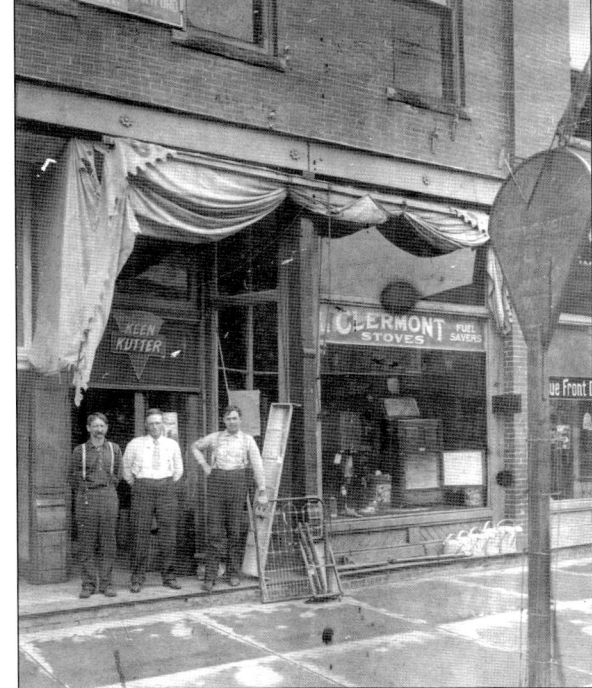

Wolfe's Hardware Store was in business for only about a year in Francesville, but was captured for posterity in this 1915 photograph. The business was located on the north side of Montgomery Street. Charles Wolfe (right) visits with Bill Boehning (left) and an unidentified customer. (Chris Ann Gutwein, provided by Alyce Onken.)

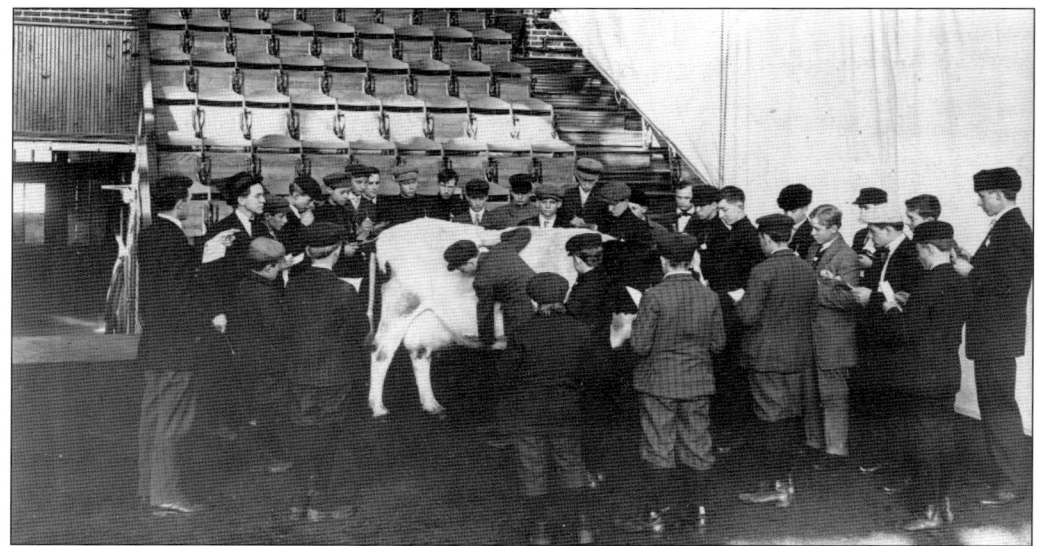

When Purdue University first offered a degree program in agriculture, it had a difficult time convincing Indiana farm families of the need for advanced education to make a living in farming. In 1887, Purdue offered its first winter short course for young, rural people who were interested in less than a full degree. The agriculture short courses proved quite popular, and by 1909, over 1,000 were enrolled in the classes of various lengths and subjects. This undated photograph shows a group of Pulaski County boys participating in one of the short courses. (PCHS Museum.)

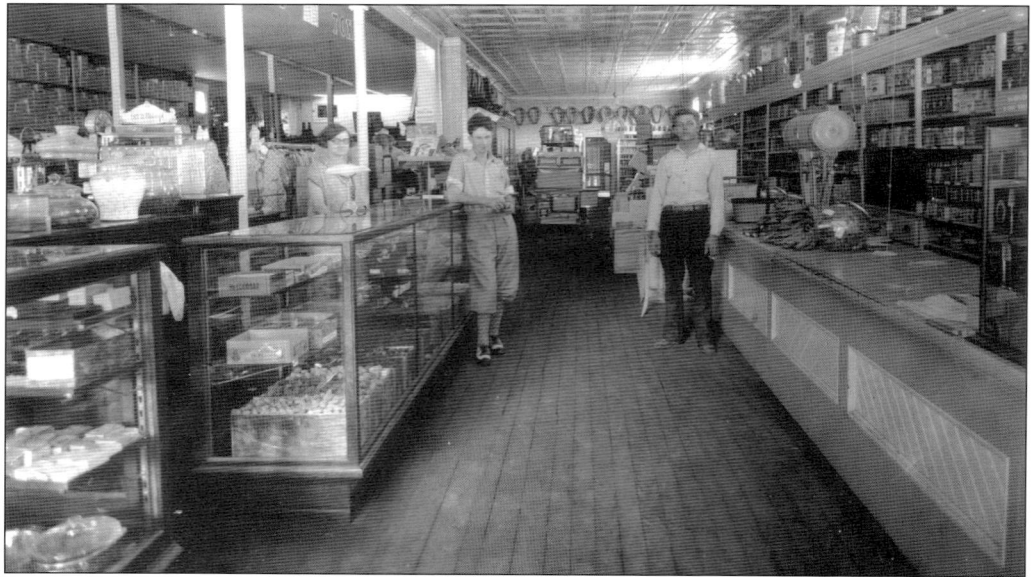

Customers could purchase almost anything they needed at the Gilsinger Store in Pulaski, from clothing to farm implements or Jell-O and Mr. Goodbars. Max Gilsinger, right, son of owner J. P. Gilsinger, visits with friend Ed Dwyer while clerk Virgie Bowers is busy behind the counter. This photograph dates to the 1930s when Max worked for his father until he joined the U.S. Army Air Corps in 1941. He later returned to the business where he remained until his death in 1971. (Brenda Gilsinger.)

The development of nearby William Gehring farms in 1939 had a significant impact on Medaryville's economy. With underground drainage, about 6,000 acres of marshy muck land was converted into rich farmland for raising onions, potatoes, mint, and similar crops. Here workers load Limberlost brand onions in 1941. One year during World War II, the federal government bought the entire onion crop. They were shipped in refrigerated railroad cars out of Medaryville. The farm operation closed in the 1970s. (Nick and Rose Capouch.)

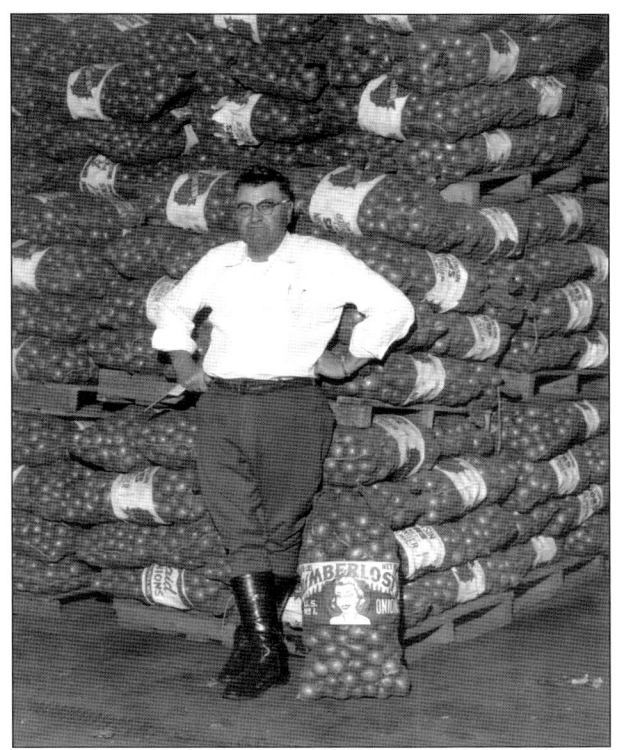

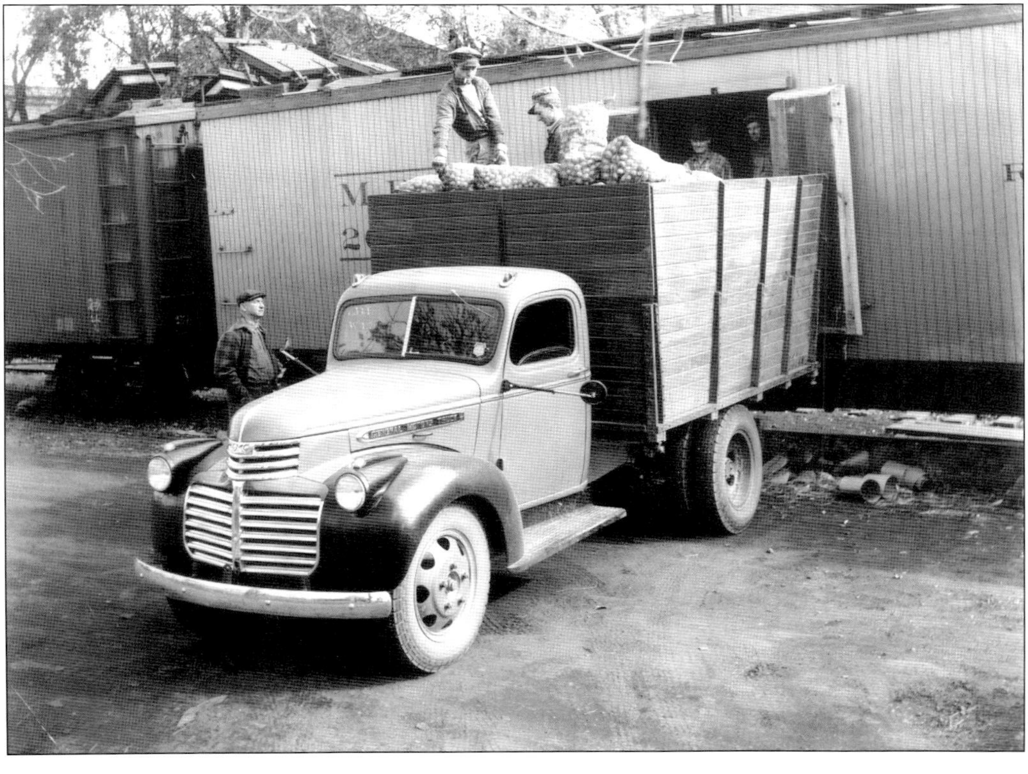

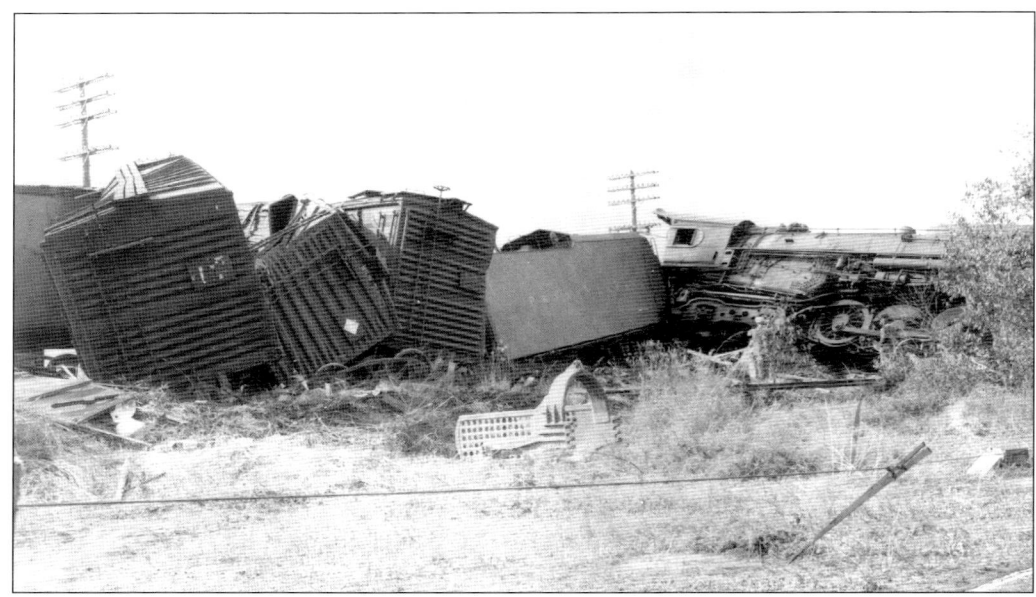

The 350-ton locomotive and freight cars of this train are piled along the Pennsylvania Railroad tracks following a wreck in Winamac on October 24, 1949. The accident occurred when this train plowed into the rear of a standing freight train on the tracks parallel to Burson Street on the south side of town. The caboose and cars of the standing train are on the opposite side of this scene. Cartons of groceries spilled from a broken car. (R. Marshall Fritz family.)

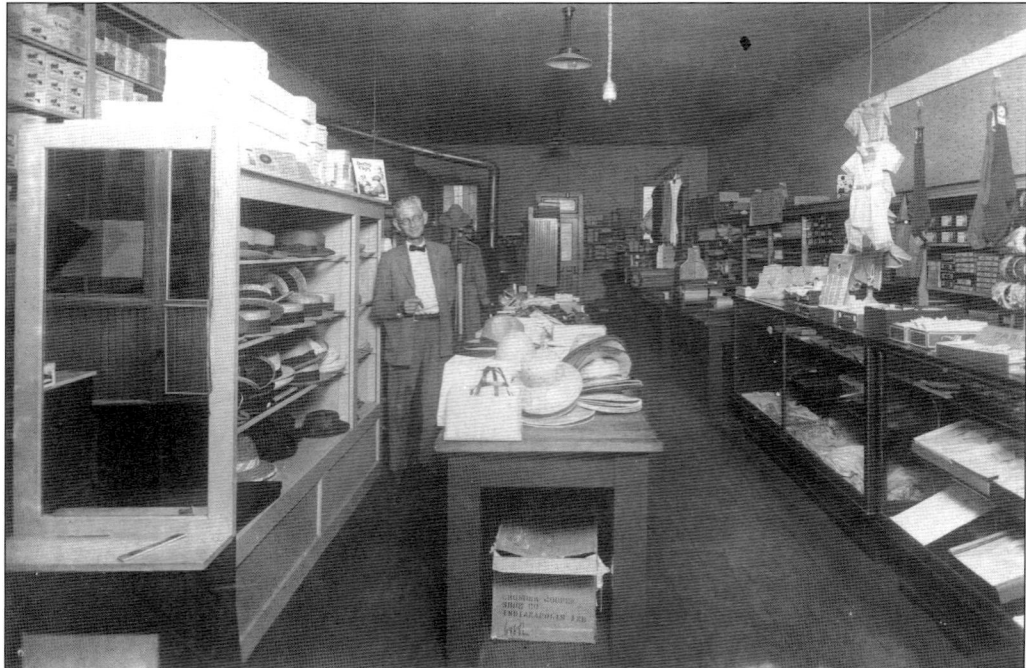

Frank Nolan was a pioneer businessman in Francesville, beginning operations there in 1890. He displays merchandise in his clothing store in this photograph probably taken in the 1920s. This store was among those destroyed in the Christmas 1944 downtown fire. (Alyce Onken.)

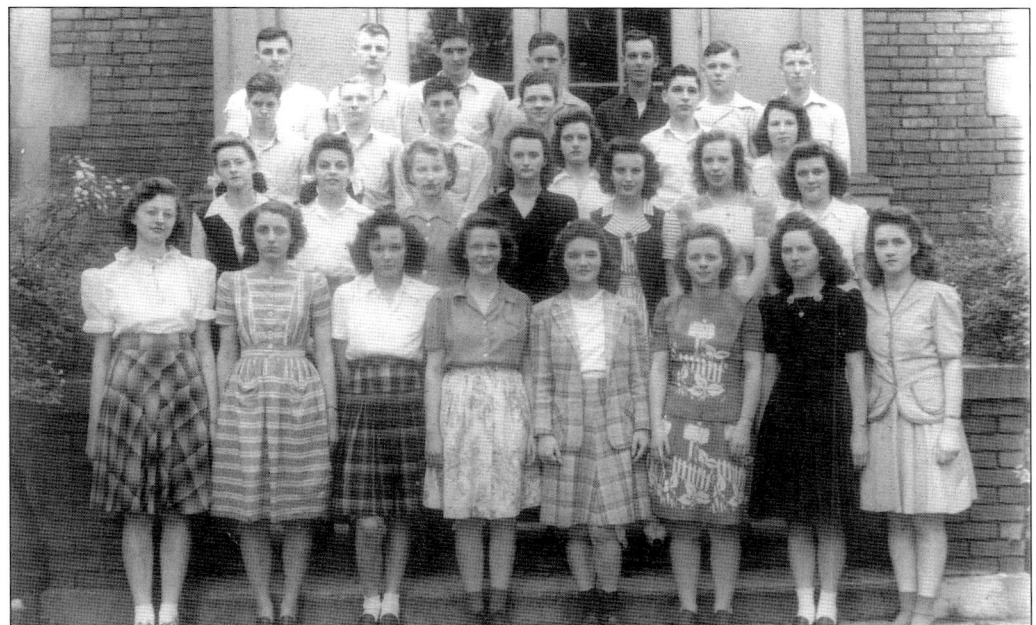

The future looked brighter for the Winamac High School graduating class of 1945 as World War II was brought to a close that summer. The graduates are, from left to right, (first row) Juanita Fletcher, JoAnn Lange, Emma Lou Nims, Wilda Mohr, Helen Brown, Rosalie Kruzick, Irene Redlin, and Jessie Morgan; (second row) Joan Skillen, Ida Miller, Joan Fry, Peg Brown, Lois Hair, Joan Boulden, and Mary Ann Hatfield; (third row) Bill Fites, Bill McKinley, George Kruzick, Tom DePoy, Margaret Kruzick, Mose Dilts, and Genievive Zimba; (fourth row) Erven Zink, Brooks Roudebush, Bob Shaw, Bill Hooks, Jim Gordon, Harold Baker, and Dick Conn. (Mary Rife.)

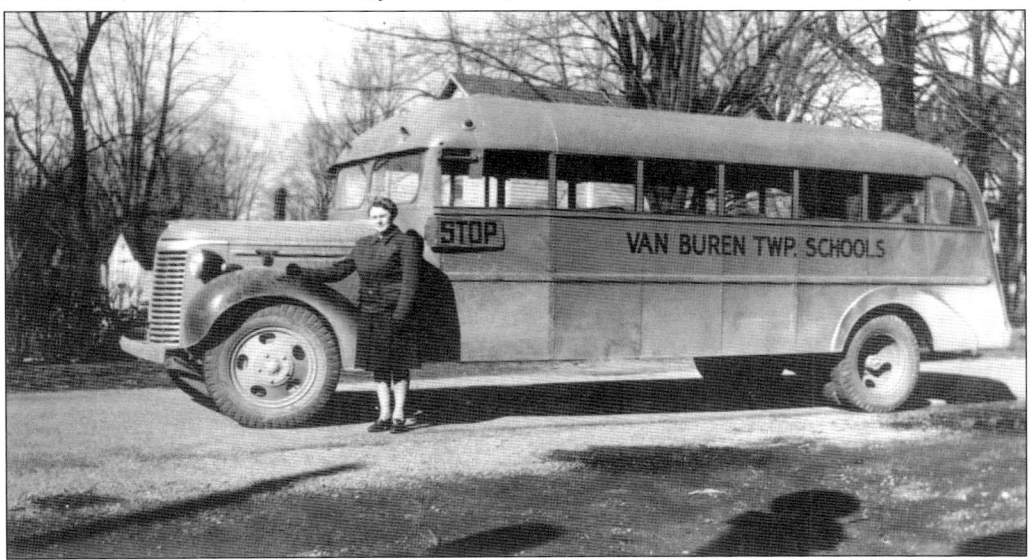

Leah Bishop was the first woman school bus driver in Van Buren Township. She took over her husband Ralph's route during World War II while he worked away from home at the Kingsbury Ordinance Plant. Ralph had also worked as a U.S. Army Air Corps mechanic in World War I. (Lois Bishop Heater.)

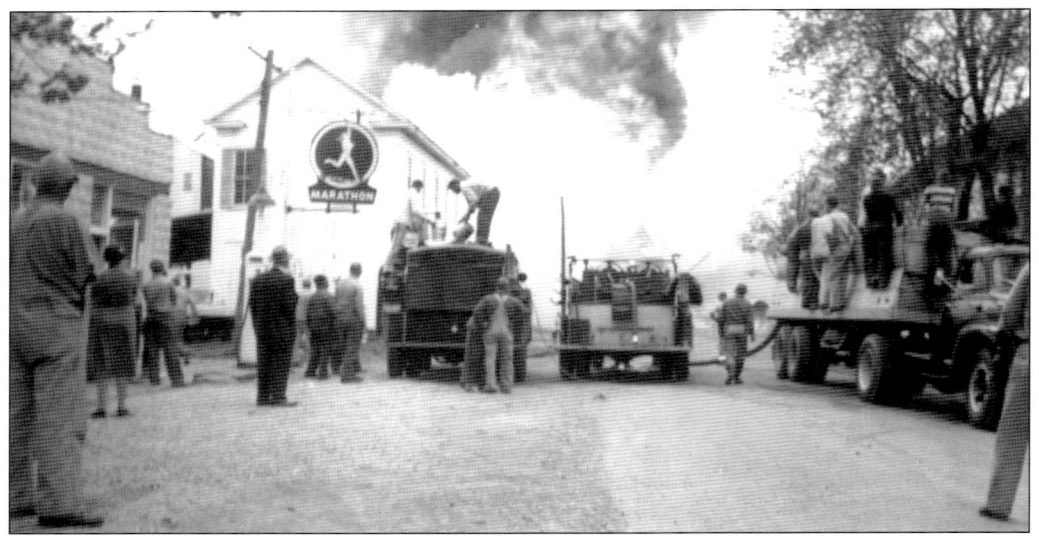

An April 1954 fire destroyed the Star City grain elevator. Flames leaping up through the 110-foot elevator could be seen for miles around. Fire departments from five surrounding towns joined the Star City volunteer firemen to extinguish the blaze. Efforts were hampered by a lack of water, as Star City had no city water supply, but residents offered their hoses, and nearby farmers brought in water to fill the fire trucks. (Lois Bishop Heater.)

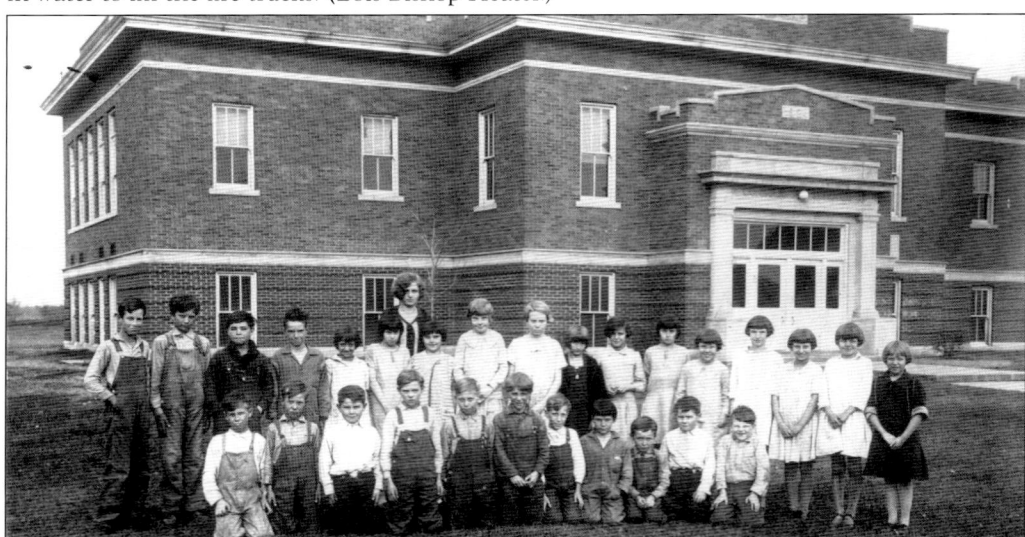

The Thornhope School, which served students in grades one through eight when this photograph was taken in 1928, closed in 1939 and was sold in 1943. The school included three large classrooms plus a gymnasium, a stage, a library, indoor restrooms, and a health room. This picture shows the students in grades three through five. From left to right are (first row) unidentified, unidentified, Johnnie Haselby, unidentified, Tom Skillen, Jim Kochel, Ralph Allen, Galen Russell, Charles Fisher, Harlan Haselby, and James Zeider; (second row) unidentified, Walter Strong, Woodrow Shidler, Max Russell, Mildred Strong, Geneva Day, Verla Haselby, Lovie Batty, unidentified, unidentified, Maude Ellen Batty, Janetta Day, unidentified, Thelma Swartzell, Mary Thompson, Ruth Ellen Swartzell, and Anna Kochel. The teacher is believed to be Marie Skillen. (Mary Powers.)

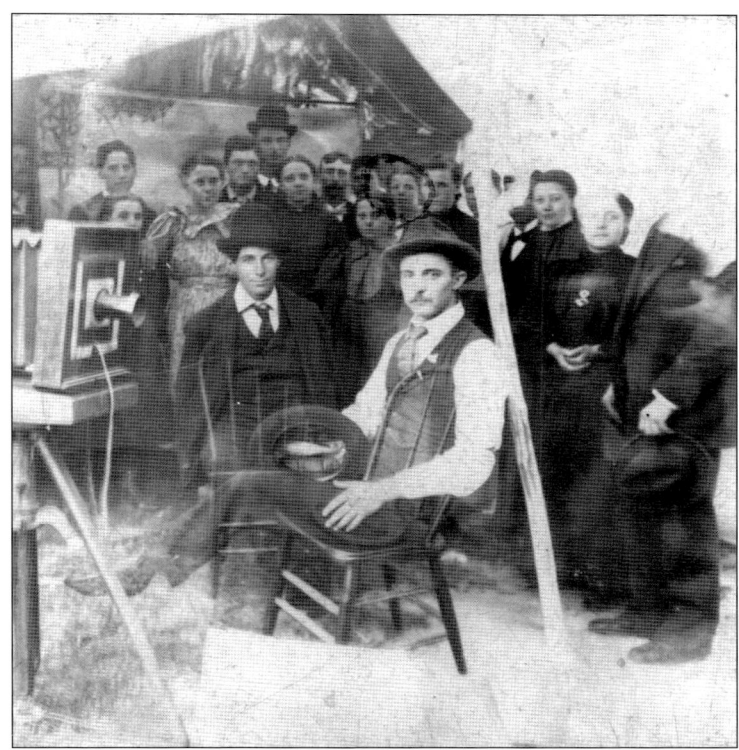

The Needmore Store was owned by Benjamin Franklin Kochel and located about three miles west of Thornhope from about 1890 to 1905. Seated in the front are Bill Geier (left) and Ed Kochel. The others in the picture include Fermanda Sheetz, Lillie Kochel, Mollie Conn, Mart Moyer, Lillie Moyer, Mertie Kochel, Cassie Moyer, Ike Kochel, Lew Geier, Pearl Moyer, Edith Kochel, Bill Conn, Bell Geier, Andy Pasley, Ethel Kochel, and Frank Kochel. (Lois Bishop Heater.)

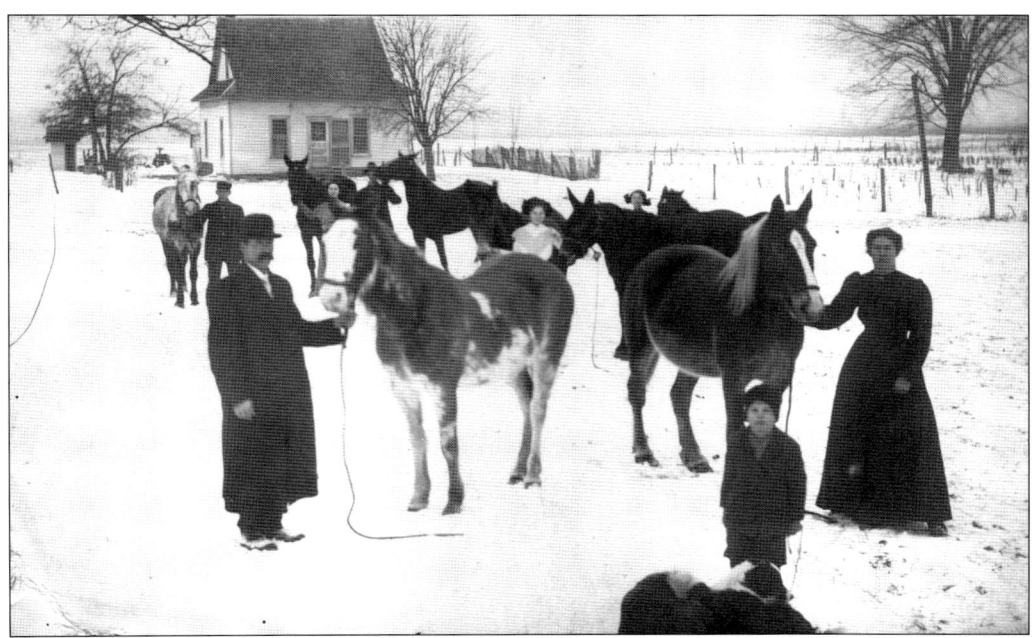

William F. Scott and his family display their horses in this photograph taken at their Jefferson Township home in about 1910. They were a farm family, and Scott was a well-known trapper in the area. Hunting and trapping of wild animals was a source of food and extra income from the fur pelts. (R. Marshall Fritz family.)

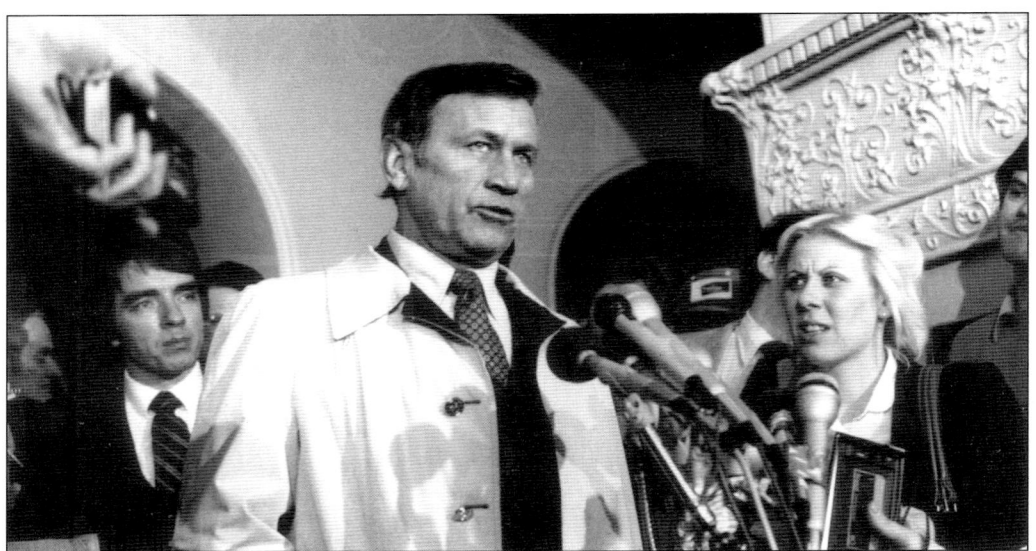

Pulaski County made national news in 1980 with the groundbreaking Ford Pinto trial. The *State of Indiana v. Ford Motor Co.* case marked the first time a manufacturer was brought to court on criminal charges for marketing an allegedly dangerous product. Charges stemmed from a fiery August 1978 Pinto car crash, which claimed the lives of three teenage girls in Elkhart County. Media, including national television networks, crowded the daily press conference. Local residents participated in the trial as jury members, legal team advisors, courthouse employees, and media reporters. Ford hired former Watergate prosecutor James Neal of Nashville (above), Tennessee, to head up its million-dollar defense team. One of his first moves was to have the trial venue moved out of Elkhart County. After a nine-week trial with Pulaski Circuit Court judge Harold Staffeldt presiding, Neal won acquittal for Ford. Elkhart County prosecutor Michael Cosentino (below) operated on a shoestring budget with many volunteers as he navigated the landmark case. He was frustrated by motions filed by Ford that he believed prevented the prosecution team from presenting its full case. (Author's collection.)

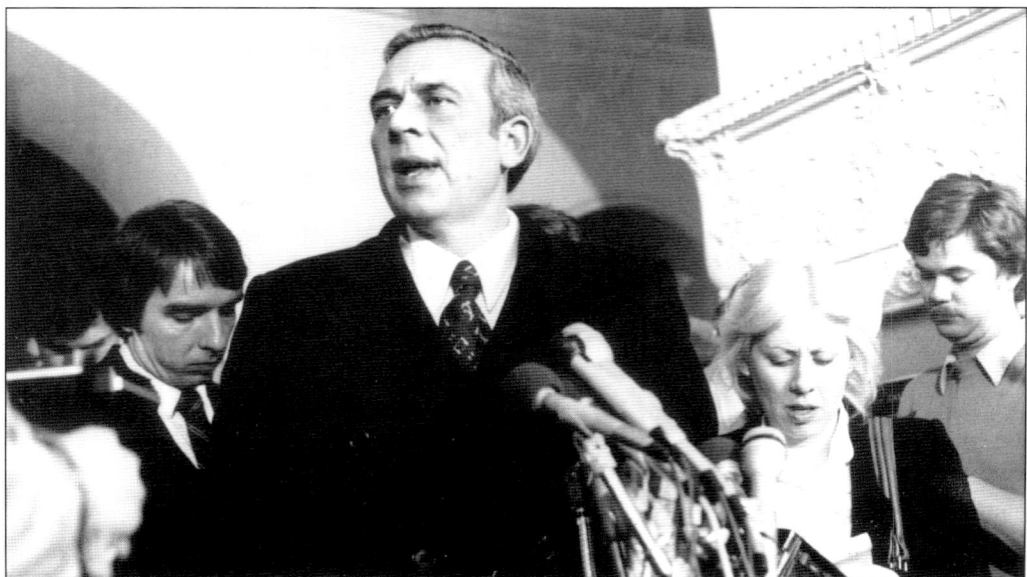

Four

PUTTING TIME OFF TO GOOD USE

"It was a simpler time. Children had time to play, unorganized, just for fun," Elizabeth Holdermann Frank recalled of her childhood days in Winamac, dating back to 1915. "So what did we do for entertainment? We provided our own, beginning with conversation."

Home entertainment ranged from board games, checkers, and cards to playing and singing around the piano with the latest popular sheet music. Schools, churches, clubs, and lodges gave programs and organized social events. They also addressed political and community issues. Street and county fairs showcased local talents. Summer band concerts on the courthouse square inspired some toe tapping on the redbrick streets. The Isis Theater showed many of the best silent films from actors like Mary Pickford and Rudolph Valentino. Local merchants fielded baseball teams in the summer. Stores were closed on Sundays.

"Summertime fun consisted of picnics and swimming, always with a freezer of homemade ice cream," recalled Lucille Degner Roth of growing up in the 1920s in the Star City and Pulaski areas. "The trains stopped in Star City and Winamac several times a day, and it was much more convenient than a crowded air terminal in Chicago, Indianapolis or South Bend. There were no warnings to fasten your seat belt or take it off, no citing of emergency oxygen masks."

During the Great Depression, Frank remembered that the railroad offered cheaper fares on Sunday excursions to Chicago. "That way many people were able to see the Century of Progress, Chicago's World Fair." Sometimes the trains provided entertainment simply by watching to see who got on and who got off.

In the big band era, the young (and those who imagined they were still young) could drive just out of the county to the dance pavilions at Bass Lake, Bruce Lake, Lake Manitou, or Lake Shafer. Bill Starr preferred the latter. "They had an excellent floor and good bands. On Sunday night girls got in free and men were charged 50 cents to dance all evening. Those were the days."

And, of course, one could always go fishing in the Tippecanoe River.

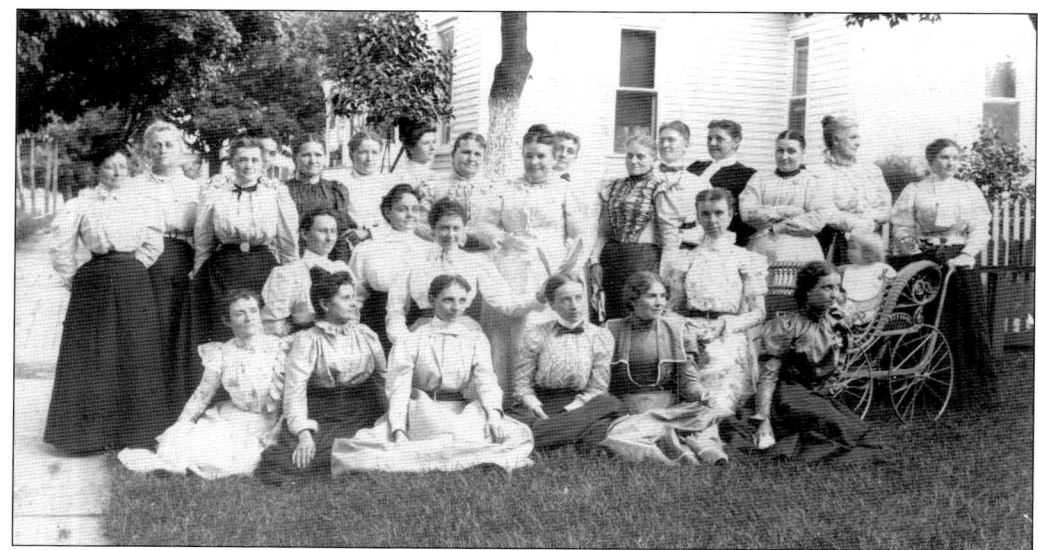

Aside from ladies' church societies, the Thimble Club was the first women's organization in Winamac. Formed in 1897, it was later known as the Embroidery Club. This picture was taken about two years later at the home of Jennie Anstis. Those present included Lydia Bennett, Melinda Burson, Martha Busick, Martha Steis, Nettie Keller, Mollie Thompson, Salle Morrow, Mary Weaver, Carrie Conner, Sarah Smith, Sophia Burgel, Louise Hoffman, Martha Moss, Jane Vurpillat, Dora Dukes, Mrs. W. D. Deford, Mollie Spangler, Jennie Gorrell, Katherine Huddleston, Fannie Weeks, and Jennie Anstis. (PCHS Museum.)

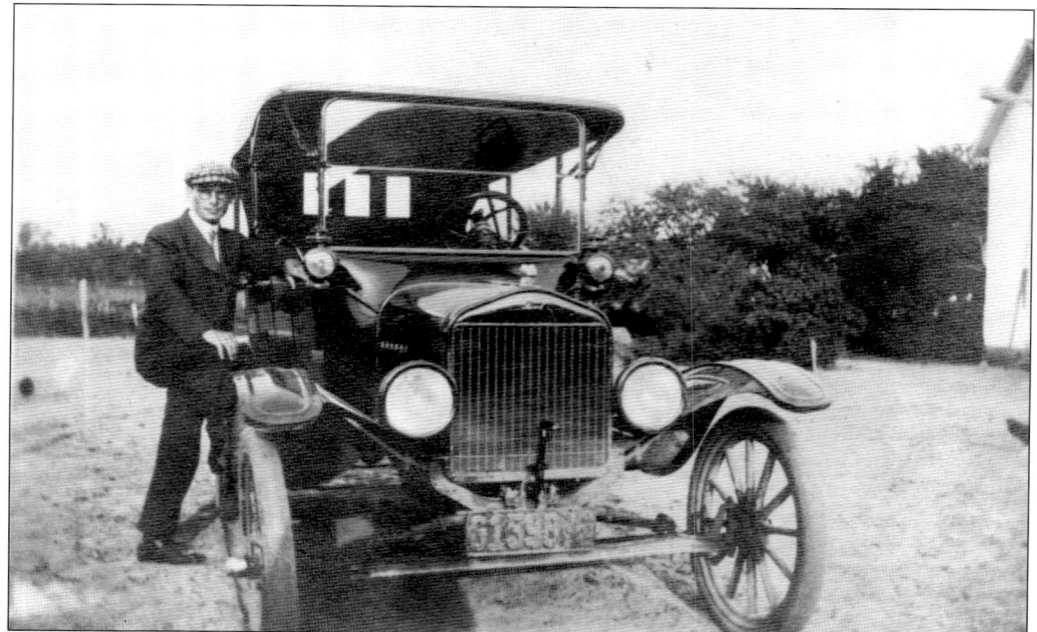

Sam Busch, age 21, of rural Francesville shows off his new Ford Model T in September 1917. He married Lola Westphal in 1919 and worked in the fertilizer business with his father. He also became an early-day motivational speaker in the neighborhood, visiting with neighbors and speaking at churches to lift spirits and morale. (Shirley Cords Busch.)

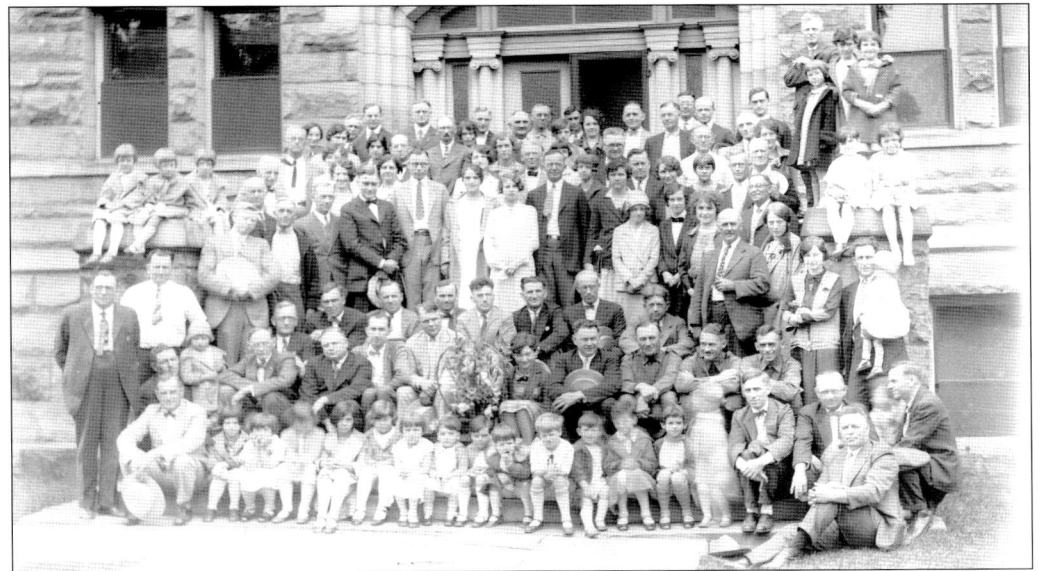

The Winamac Kiwanis Club was chartered in 1921, and most of its community service projects center around programs to benefit children. It has sponsored the local Boy Scout troop, scholarships, Riley Children's Hospital in Indianapolis, and clothing for needy children at Christmas. Daughter's Day, as shown in this undated picture at the courthouse, is a longtime tradition. Women were first admitted into the club in the late 1980s, and this event became Sons and Daughters Day. (PCHS Museum.)

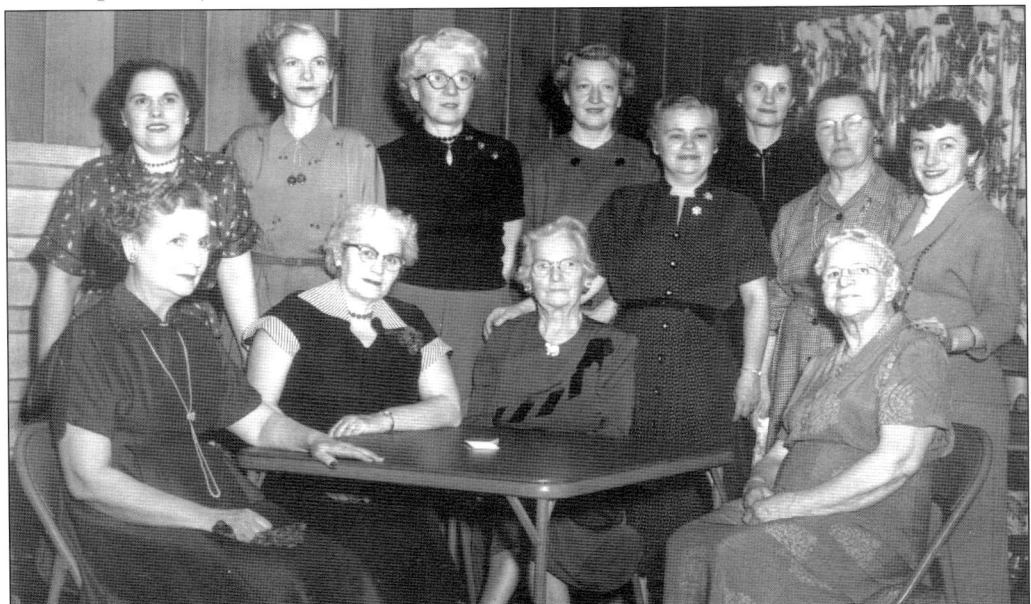

The ladies of the Golden Hour Bridge Club of Medaryville are pictured at one of their meetings in 1954. Members from left to right are (first row) Gladys Shortz, Alice Madaus, Mame Bremer, and Laura Hackley; (second row) Olive White, Beulah Faris, Margarite Wacknitz, Augusta Wacknitz, Zera Howe, Francis Duggleby, Mae McKibben, and Bessie Mayhew. (Medaryville History Museum.)

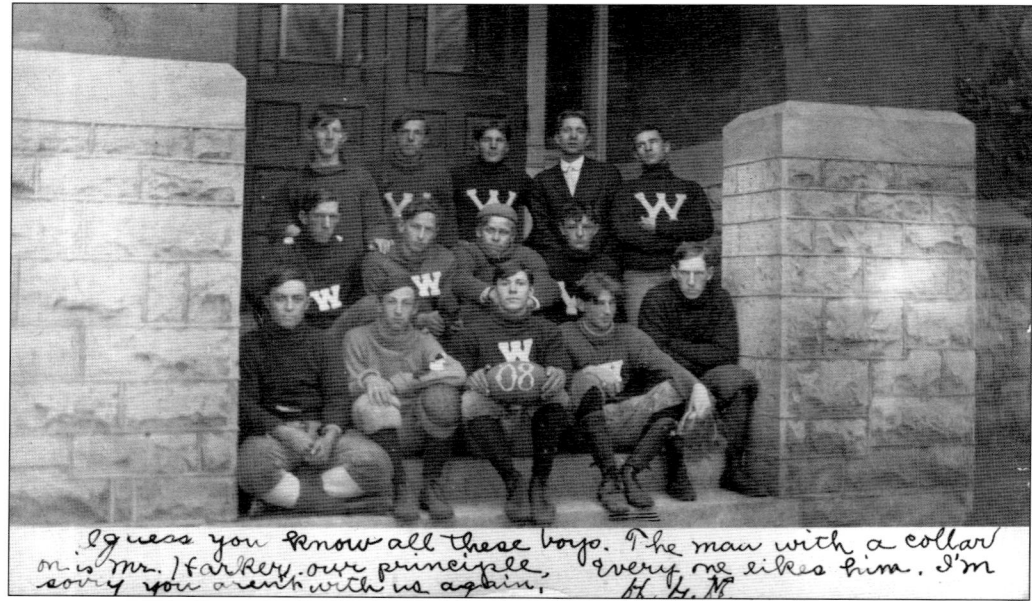

The 1908 Winamac High School football team poses for this photograph on the school steps. The picture later appeared on a postcard that was mailed by a lad who signed it as "Homer G. M." He mailed it to a Nellie Morgan in Chicago and wrote, "The man with the collar on is Mr. Harkler our principal. Every one likes him. We are feeling pretty good because we have only lost one game this season and played five." (Sara Slaven.)

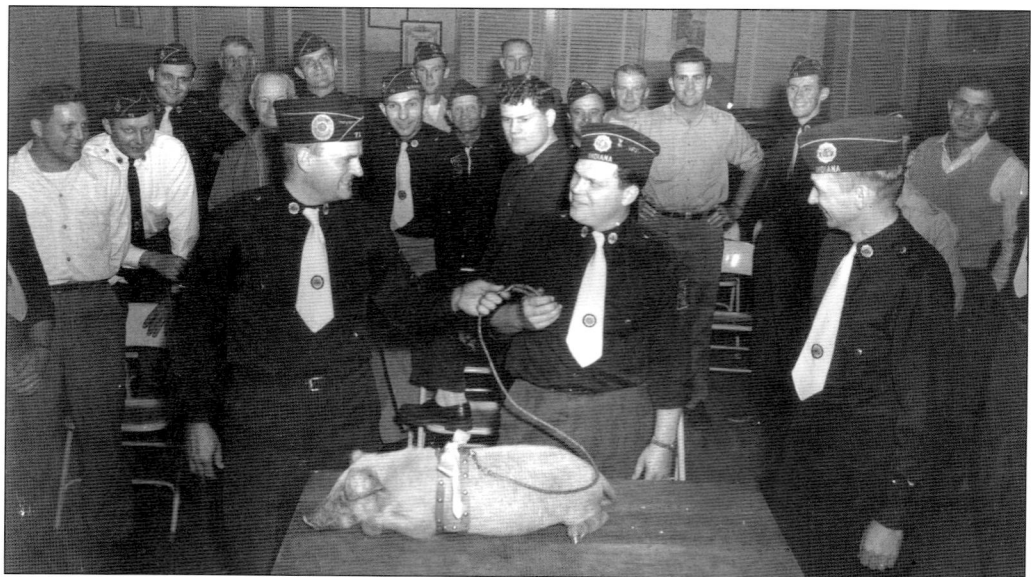

The leash for Buford the pig is passed from John Kruger to Stanley Henry as Lester Wilson looks on (front right). The porky friend was used by the Winamac American Legion in conjunction with a membership drive in 1949 and 1950. Others in the background include Lorwin Henry, Jim McClung, Roy Hollenburg, Harry Snyder, William Mohr, Everett Roller, "Doc" Swafford, Harold Budd, ? Shriner, Don Boulden, Gerald "Pete" Lebo, Keith Sayers, Jacob Nice, Harold Murphy, Richard Dickensheets, and Byron Henry. (Winamac American Legion Post No. 71.)

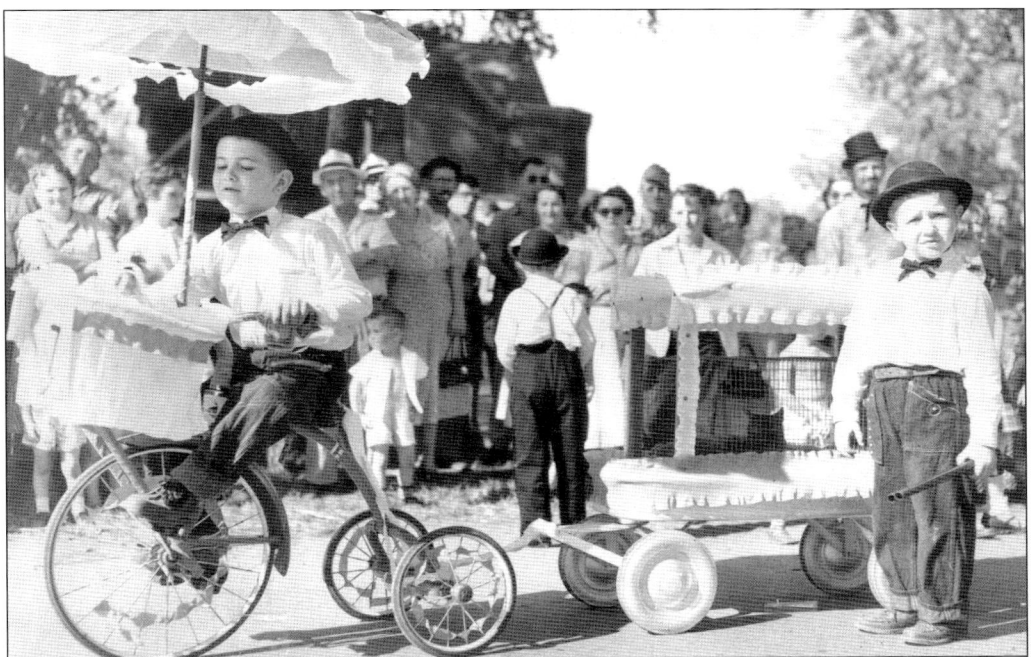

Roy McIlvain (on tricycle) keeps an eye on the chicken in his basket, while his brother Ronnie guards the caged cat in his wagon as they proceed along the children's pet and hobby parade route during the 1953 Medaryville centennial celebration. (Medaryville History Museum.)

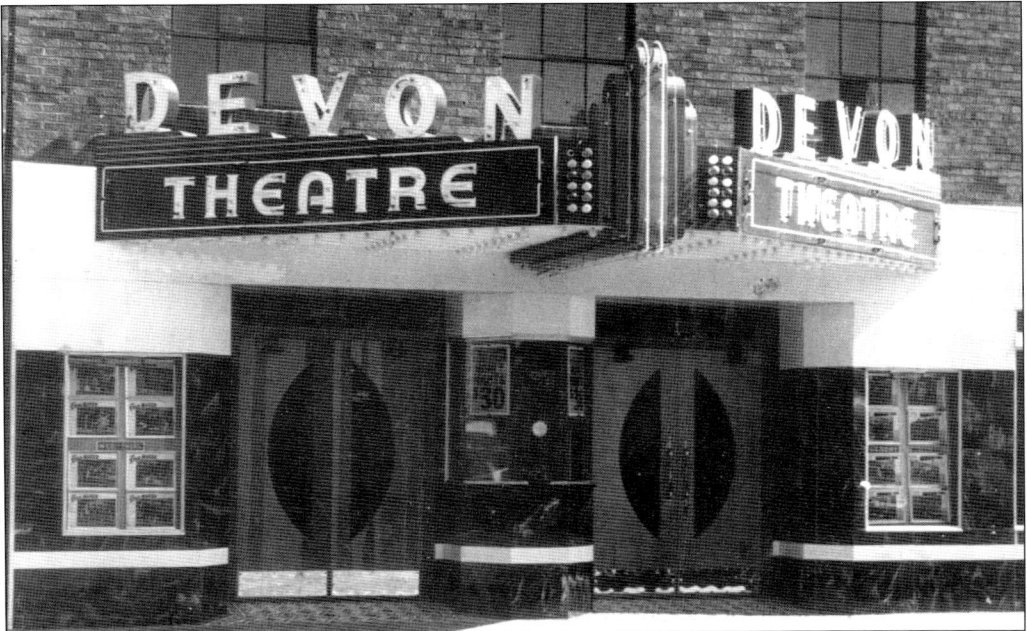

The Devon Theatre in Francesville was built in 1938 on a vacant lot on Bill Street. It was owned by Ernest and Sylvia Smith. The movie house was known as a family theater, and the first picture shown was *Only Angels Have Wings*. The business was sold in 1971 but failed to be successful. The theater was later torn down, and the property is used as a parking lot. (Francesville Tribune.)

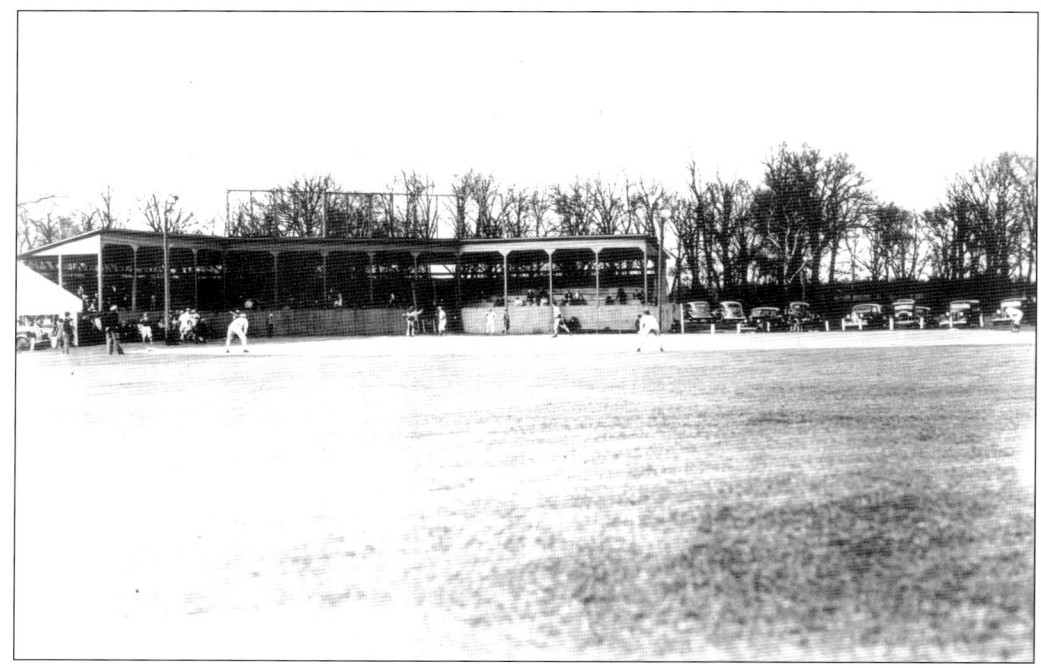

The ball diamonds that have always existed in the Winamac park reflect America's passion for baseball. This undated photograph shows a game in progress in the old park stadium. This facility was used to stage the county's 1939 centennial historical pageant. (PCHS Museum.)

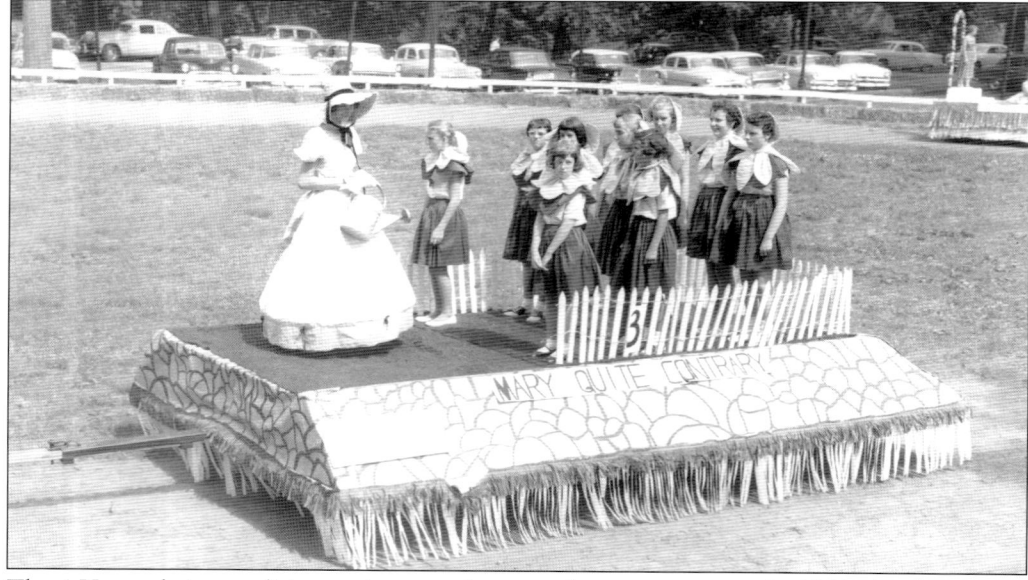

The 4-H parade is a tradition at the annual county fair every summer. In 1956, this float, Mary Quite Contrary, was entered by the Busy Beaverettes 4-H club from Beaver Township. Mary is Barb Markin. The other girls from left to right are (first row) Sharon Fisher and Paula Smidler; (second row) Marilyn Hoffman, Sue Lawson, Judy Huffman, and Dorothy Worley; (third row) Nancy Finnegan, Carol Hahn, Sherry Thompson, and Lorna Fitz. Cletha Kestle was the club leader. (Pulaski County Purdue Extension Office.)

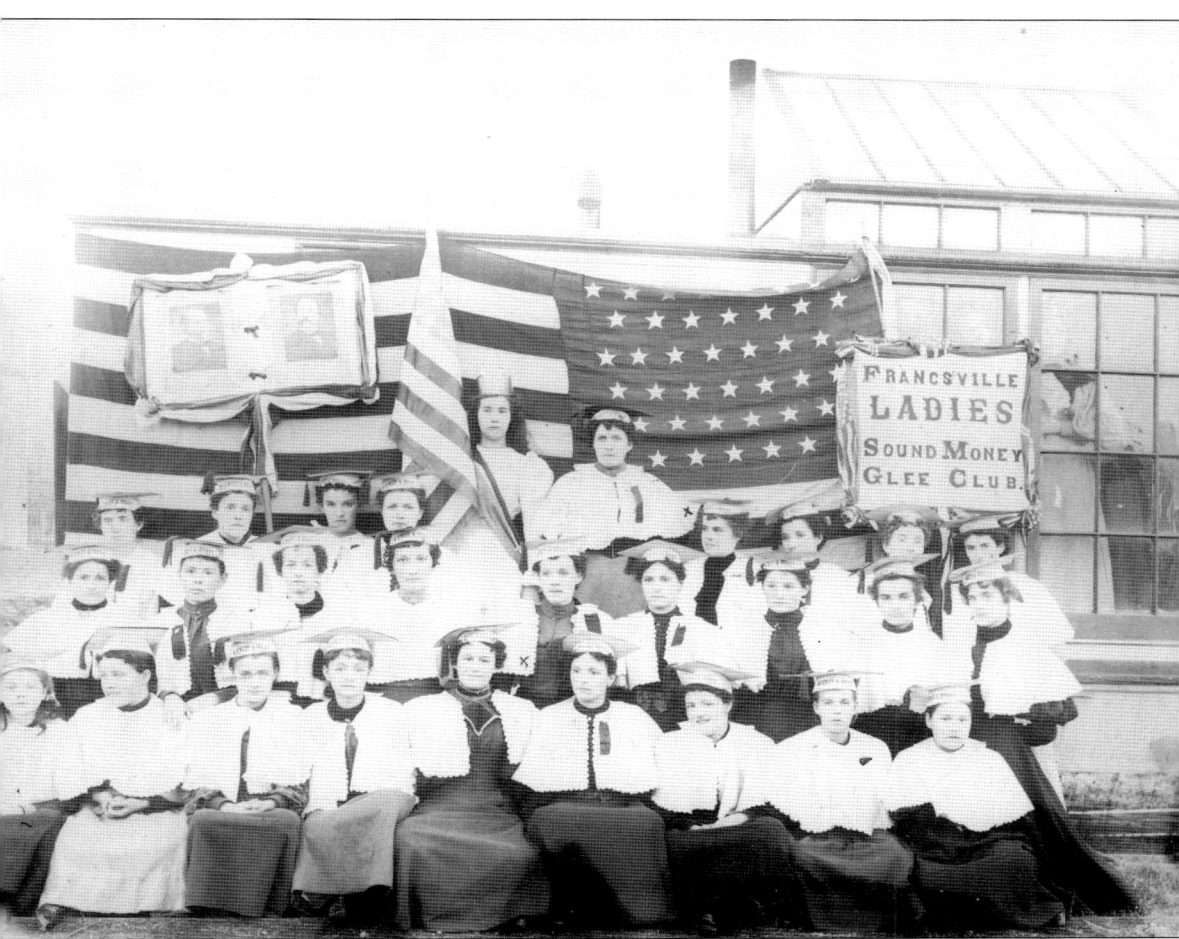

During the 1896 U.S. presidential election, Republican William McKinley and his running mate, Garrett Hobart, ran on a platform of "sound money," a pledge to stand firm on the gold standard and high, protective tariffs. McKinley's opponent, William Jennings Bryan ran on a "free silver" platform, a demand for free and unlimited coinage of silver, popular with the nation's farmers. Across the country, several women's organizations, known as Sound Money Clubs, formed in support of McKinley's platform. One such club existed in Francesville. The photographs on the placard held by the women are of McKinley and Hobart, who won the election. Ironically, these women could not vote in 1896, but McKinley reportedly believed women were important to court because they could influence their husbands. The women in this photograph include, in the first row from left to right, five unidentified, Zora Burget, unidentified, Delia Nelson, and Bess Tomlinson. The second row includes May Myers, Tillie Overmon, Gertie Myers Thrasher, Zena Hubbard, Alice Hill, and Cora Garrigues. The third row is all unidentified. In the fourth row are Emma Nelson (left) and Maude Hubbard. (Alyce Onken.)

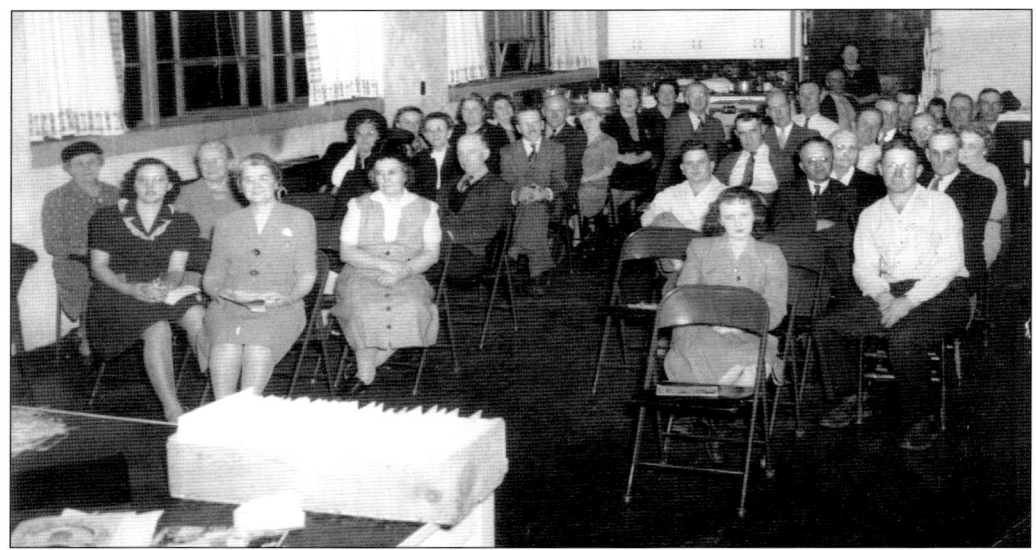

In January 1947, this group gathered for a Pulaski County Farm Bureau meeting in Star City where Leah Bishop was the speaker. Those in the picture include Fayetta Abbott, Beulah Reed, Lois Bishop, Mary Galbreath, Maud Wirick, Opal Knebel, Neal Hiatt, Anna Gross, George Gross, Jim Abbott, Ralph Bishop, Harvey Hiatt, Hazel Haselby, Eva Hiatt, Ross Cain, Firman Haselby, Effie Geier, Esther Moyer, Luella Drach, Nellie Winters, Cosmos Winters, Floyd Knebel, Bill Guff, Clark Reed, Chessie Newman, Esther Abbott, Frank Stephens, Don Newman, Bob Galbreath, Nathan Abbott, Ethel Stephens, Mary Blinn, Tom Densborn, Hy Allen, and Clint Drach. (Lois Bishop Heater.)

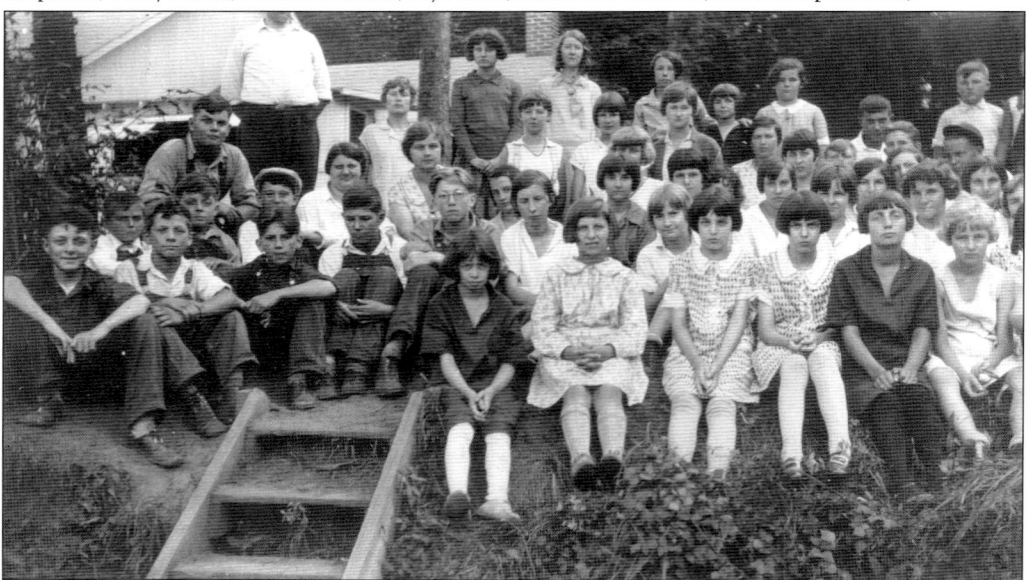

Pulaski County had an early start in 4-H youth programs. A couple of neighboring counties organized youth Corn Clubs in the early 1900s. In 1909, the superintendent of Pulaski County schools went a step further and formed Corn, Poultry, and Butter Clubs in the county. The 4-H Club provided an important social and education link for rural youth. In this late 1920s photograph, county 4-H youngsters attend an outing at Camp Paxton on the Tippecanoe River. (Mary Thompson Powers.)

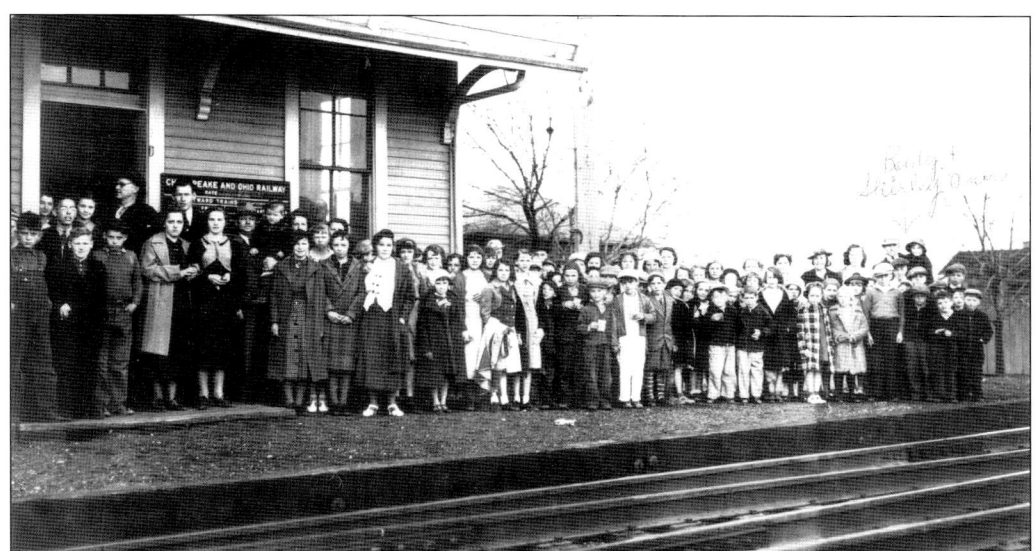

Students at Beardstown and Ripley schools north of Winamac await the Chesapeake and Ohio Railroad passenger train at Beardstown station in 1936 where most of the pupils were treated to their first-ever train ride. Franklin Township trustee C. G. Mays organized the trip to North Judson, less than 15 miles away. The railway company added an extra coach to the afternoon train, and when it pulled into the station, 93 passengers awaited, including teachers Rex Good and Elizabeth Weaver of Beardstown, Rudolph Cords of Ripley, Mays, and county school superintendent Donald Crise. (Shirley Cords Busch.)

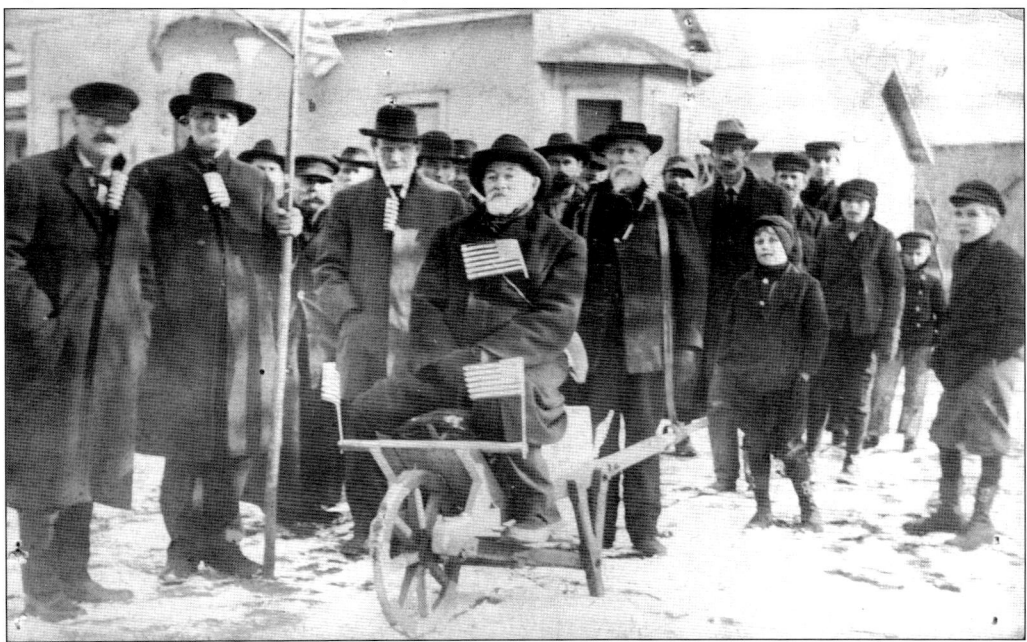

Josiah (Joe) Moyer had to push Tom Carey around Star City in a wheelbarrow in November 1908 to pay off an election bet. The three men at left are Captain Burson, Bill Moyer, and Mr. Warfield. The bet was on the outcome of the presidential election in which Republican William Howard Taft won over Democrat William Jennings Bryan. (Lois Bishop Heater.)

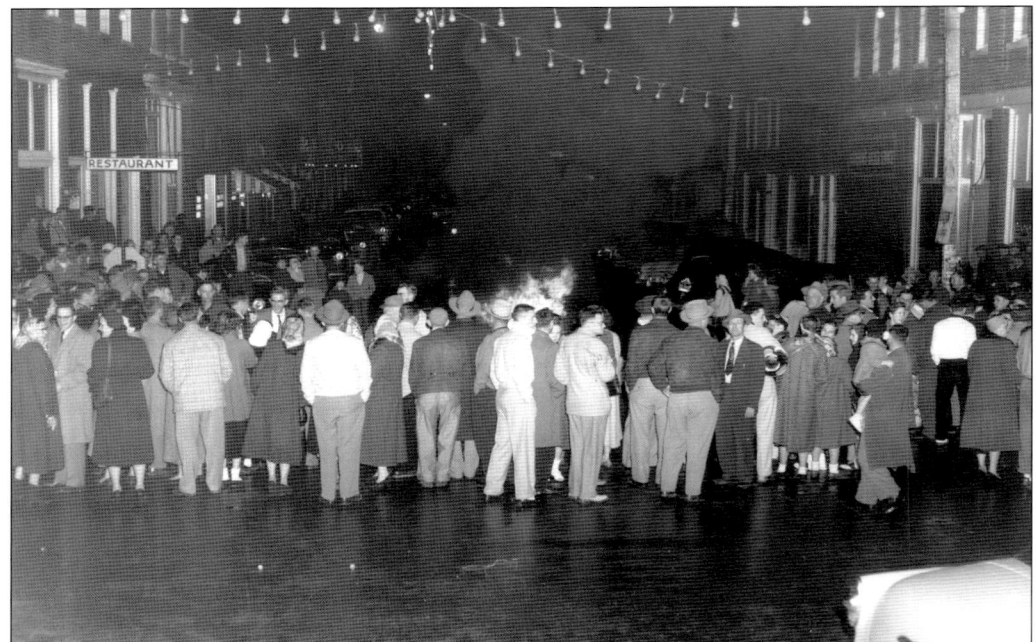

Ecstatic fans celebrate the 1955 basketball sectional championship won by the Francesville High School Zebras with a bonfire in the downtown streets following the game. (Francesville Tribune, photograph by Olive White.)

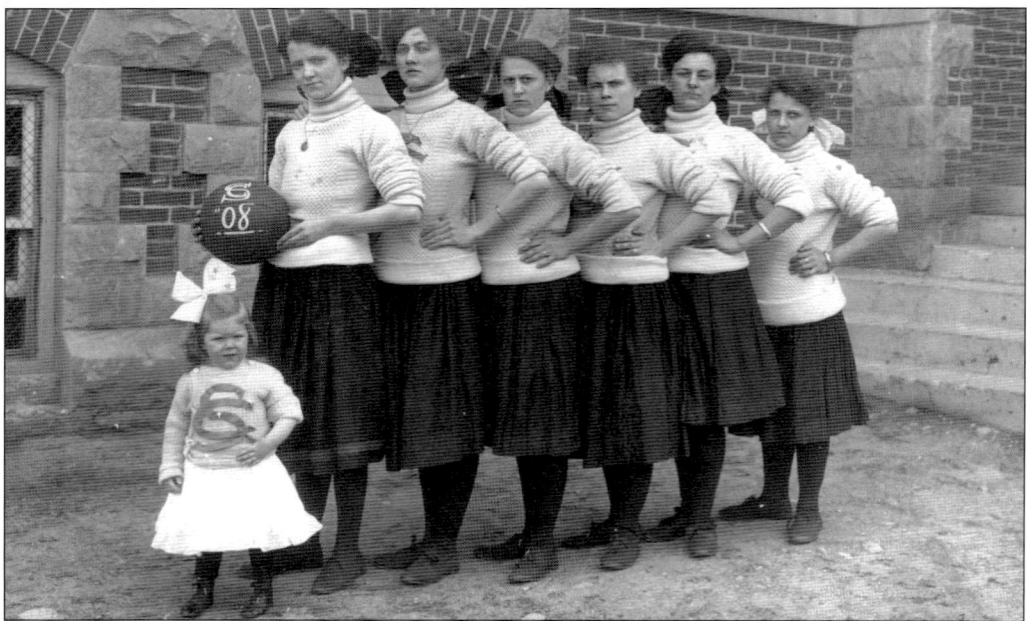

The uniforms may have been cumbersome, but in the early days of girls' basketball, there were six members on a team, and they only played half-court. These are the members of the 1908 Star City High School girls' basketball team. The little girl is Dorothy Washburn. Edna Stephens is holding the ball. The others from left to right are Ethel Davis, Myrtle Hamilton, Zella Stewart, Pearl Geyer, and Rose Washburn. (Lois Bishop Heater.)

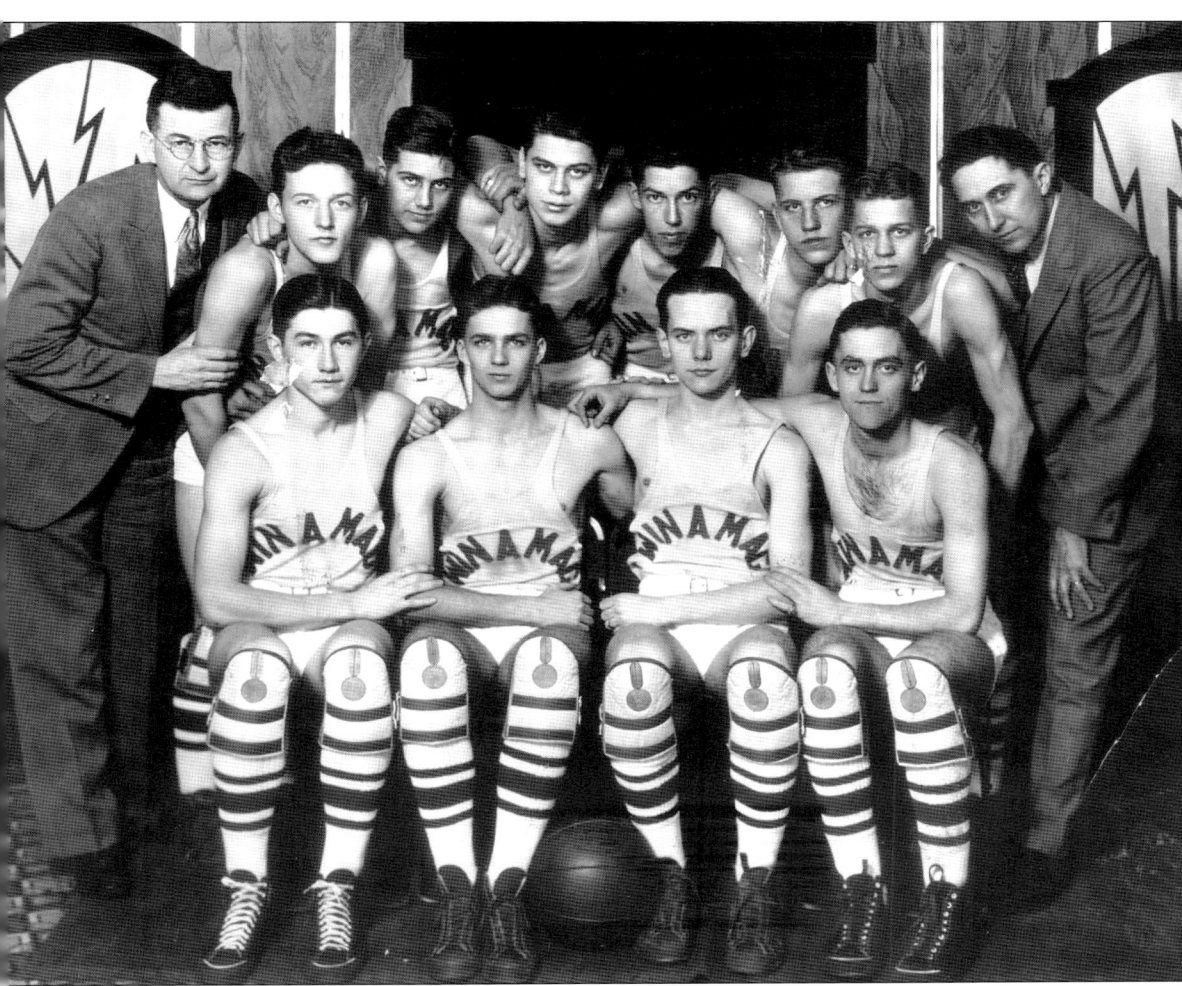

It was during the depths of the Great Depression that the most legendary basketball team in Pulaski County's history emerged as state championship runners-up in the 1932 Indiana basketball tournament. The 1931–1932 Winamac High School Indians beat Pulaski 28-11, Francesville 48-12, North Judson 35-12, and Star City 38-7 to win the sectional; and Nappanee 37-27 and Rochester 23-12 to win the Mishawaka regional. The sweet 16 teams met in Indianapolis the following weekend for the state tournament with games beginning Friday morning. Winamac beat Bluffton 48-30 on Friday afternoon, Lebanon 34-31 on Saturday morning, and Evansville Bosse 27-23 on Saturday afternoon before falling to Newcastle 24-17 in the championship game Saturday night. Team members from left to right are (first row) Merrill Wilson, Lester Stout, Harry Pearson, and Charles Miller; (second row) coach Earl D. Roudebush, Lewis Hood, Charles Holmes, Howard Reder, Carl Shank, Henry Kopkey, Marvin Stout, and principal Herman Stalker. Roudebush was inducted into the Indiana Basketball Hall of Fame in 1967. Also making headlines in the local paper in March 1932 was the kidnapping of the Lindberg baby, the Herbert Hoover versus Franklin D. Roosevelt presidential election, and a raid by federal prohibition agents from South Bend on a still in eastern Pulaski County. (Jay Kopkey.)

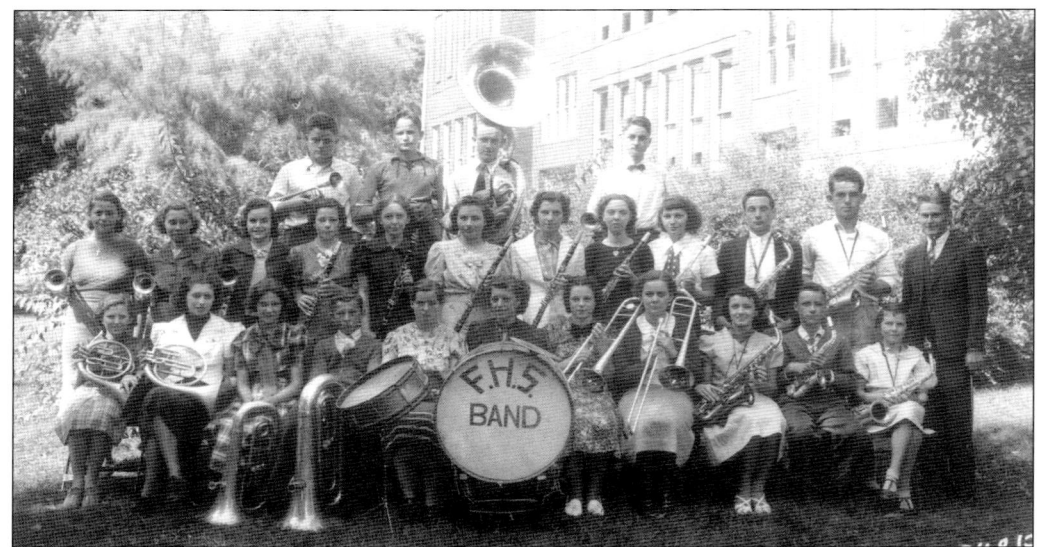

The Francesville High School band gathered outside the school for this photograph during the 1937–1938 school year. Members from left to right are (first row) Betty Getz, Mary Fitzpatrick, Donna Getz, Bill Ringger, Ruth Alkire, Ruth Weaver, Elizabeth Wuethrich, Ila Reish, Janice Burget, Wain Westfall, and Elizabeth Myers; (second row) Melba Long, Evelyn Ellis, Eileen Pelsy, Glendoris Wuethrich, Eleanor Tizlaff, June Culp, Nancy Wuethrich, Gertrude Myers, Rosemary Byrd, Fred Howat, Richard Overmyer, and director Glyndon Shull; (third row) Eugene Nelson, Eugene VonTobel, Paul Graves, and Marion Port. (Francesville Tribune.)

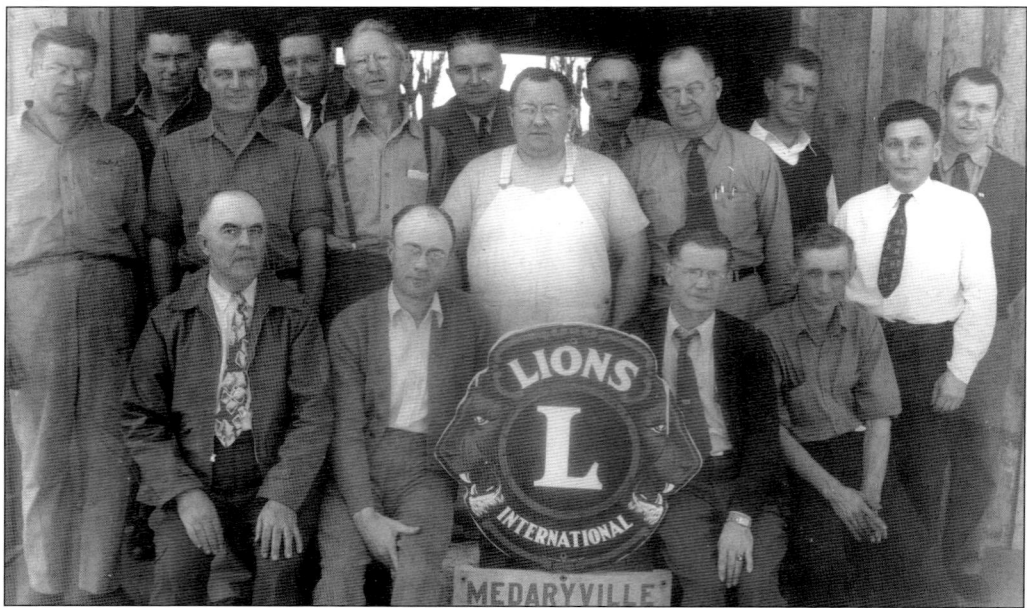

The Medaryville Lions Club gathered for this photograph at the town park shelter house on March 28, 1946. Members from left to right are (first row) Albert Egly, Harry Querry, Harvey Van Deman, and Ira Lewis; (second row) Homer Steele, Glen Howe, William Cupka, James Ahler, Ralph Kroft, and Theodore Rosenberg, (third row) Lowell Odom, Elwin Smith, Ralph Harris, Ernest Cords, Perry Cohen, and Harold "Casey" Rowe. (Medaryville History Museum.)

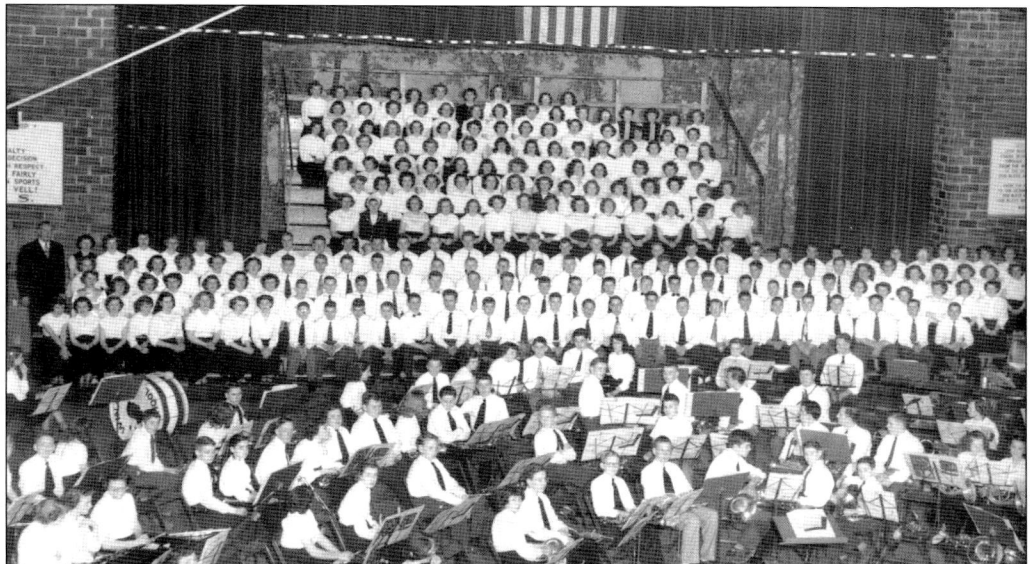

The first county music festival was held in 1949 in the Winamac High School gymnasium. It featured the combined bands and choirs of the county's six high schools in Monterey, Medaryville, Francesville, Pulaski, Star City, and Winamac. Guest conductors from Indiana University and the Jordan College of Music in Indianapolis directed the group. The students rehearsed all day, and a free public concert followed that evening. This picture is believed to be from the 1950 festival. (Emily Russell.)

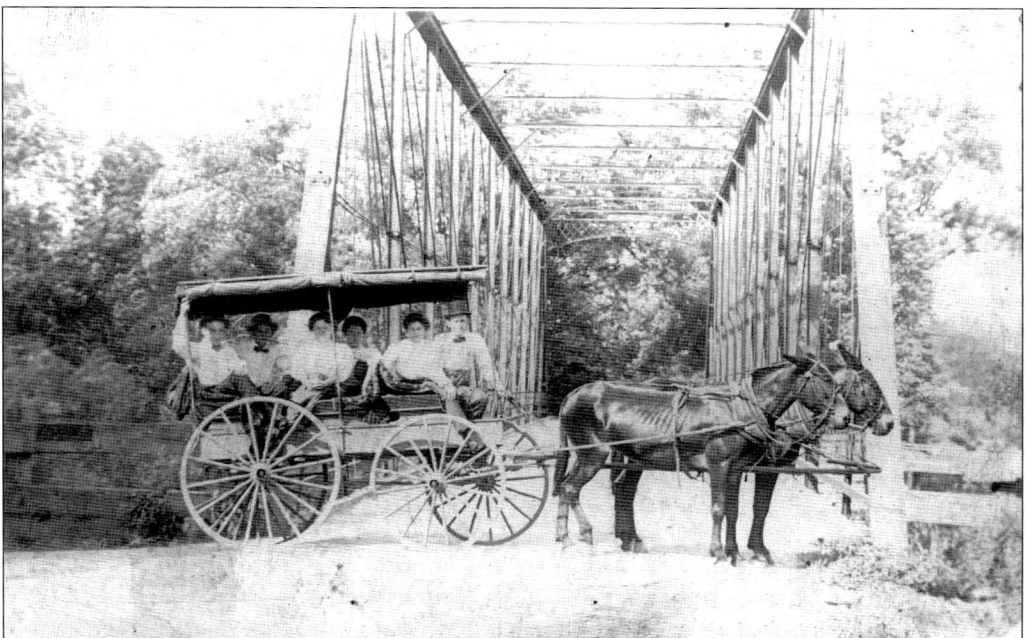

Little is known about this photograph, which is simply labeled, "Out for a Sunday drive, 1890s style." The passengers in the surrey-style, mule-pulled wagon are not identified. The picture appears to have been taken at the Washington Street bridge over the Tippecanoe River in Winamac. (PCHS Museum, donated by Lee Seidel.)

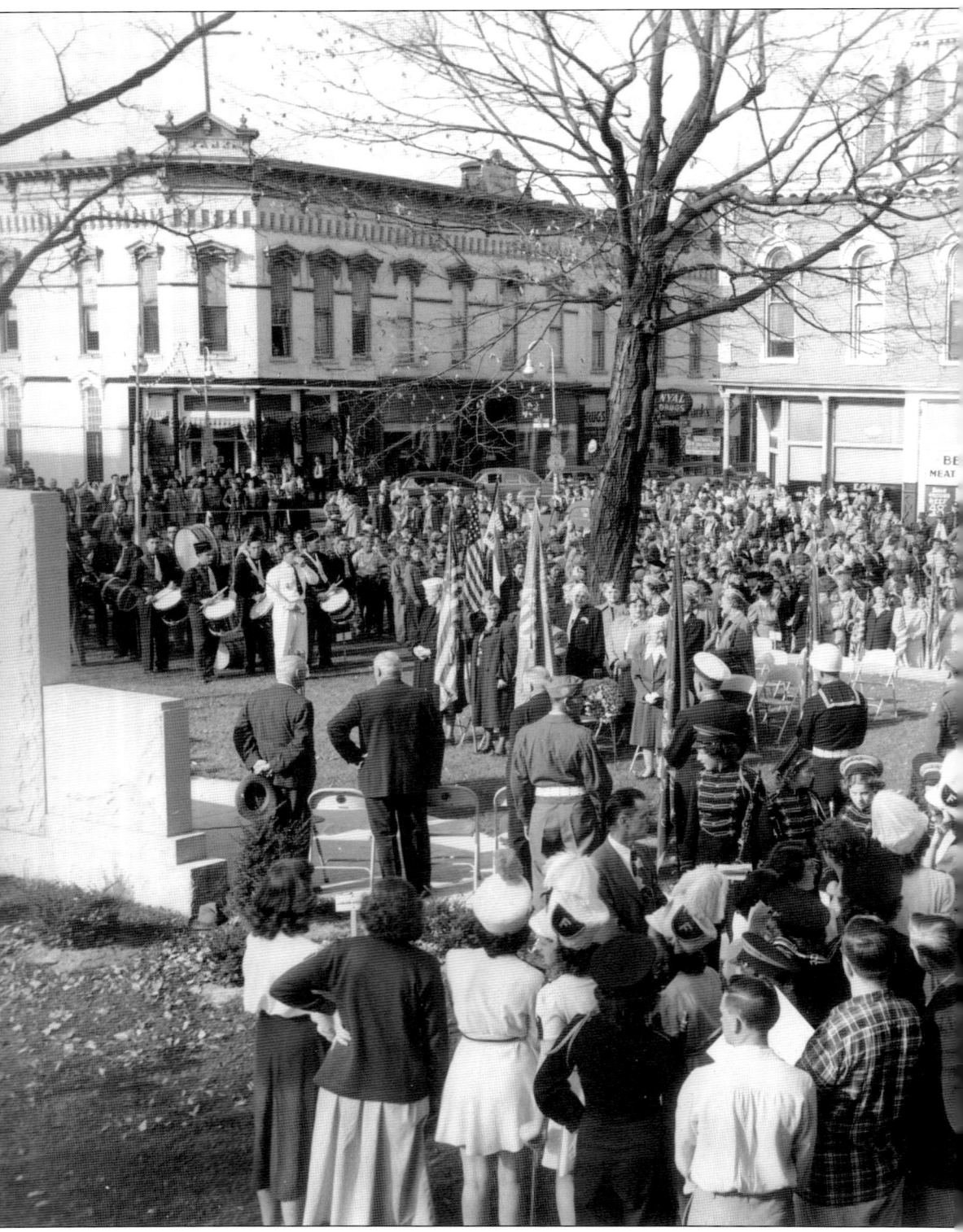

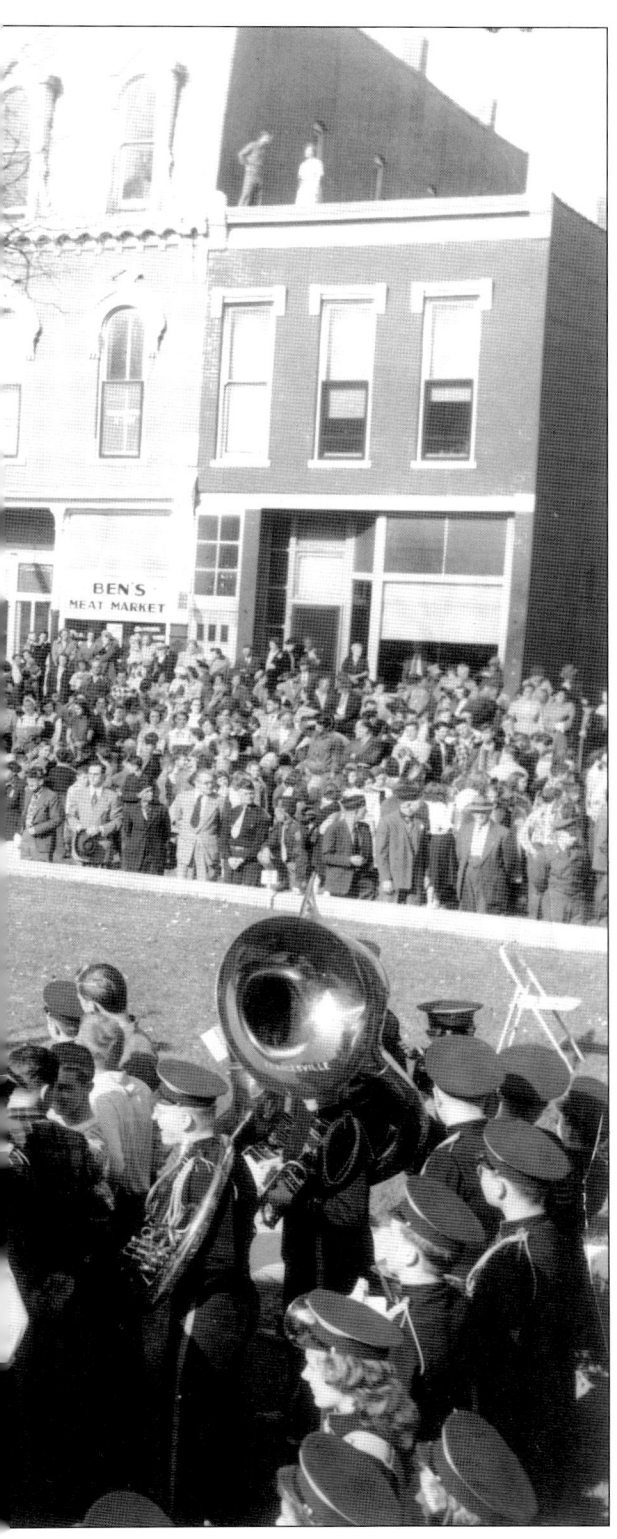

The war memorial on the courthouse square was dedicated during this November 11, 1949, Armistice Day observance, which attracted residents from across the county. World War II veteran R. Marshall Fritz was master of ceremonies. The Francesville High School band and chorus appear in the foreground. The Winamac Boy Scouts and the newly formed American Legion Drum and Bugle Corps are at the middle-left side of the picture. A similar service is conducted every Memorial Day and Veteran's Day when Pulaski County's military men and women are honored for their service. (Winamac American Legion Post No. 71.)

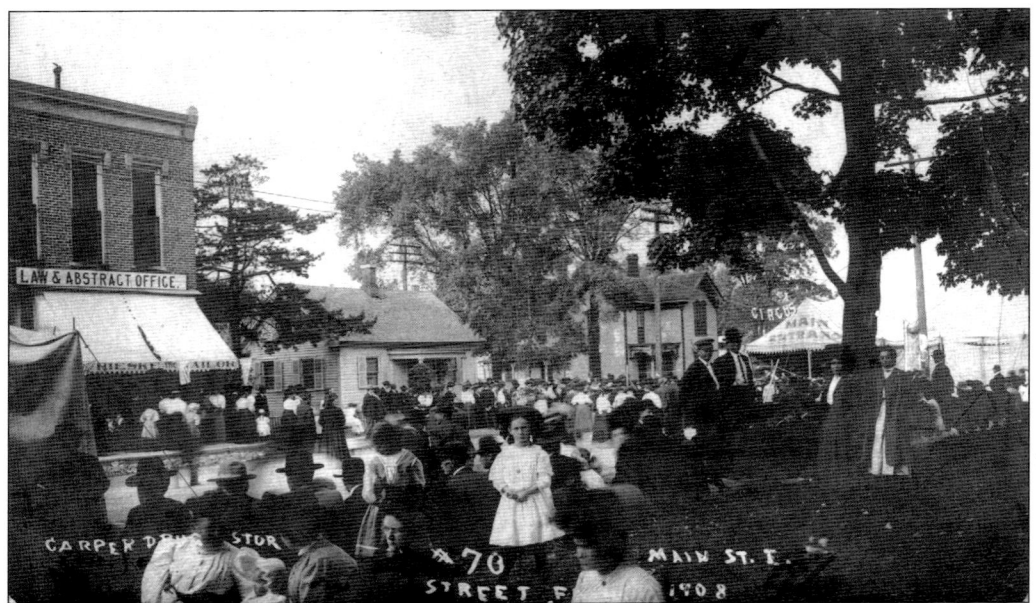

Advertisements for a four-day street fair in October 1908 in Winamac promised, "thrilling free attractions, a stock show, and all kinds of amusements." This picture postcard, sold by Carper's Drug Store, shows two of the fair tents pitched along Main Street and visitors milling around the courthouse square. The two-story house at the back of the photograph was known as the sheriff's house. (PCHS Museum.)

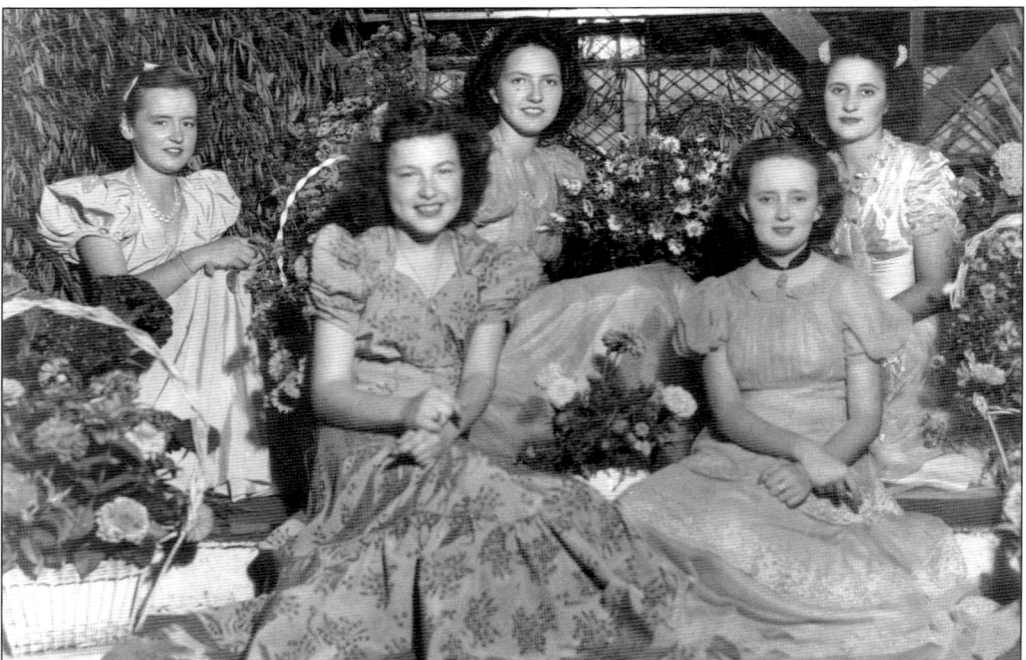

A flower show was held in Star City in September 1945. Posing with some of the displays, from left to right, are (first row) Virginia Lee Brown and Lois Ann Bishop; (second row) Yvonne Fisher, Margaret Ann Bonnell, and Doris Kistler. (Lois Bishop Heater.)

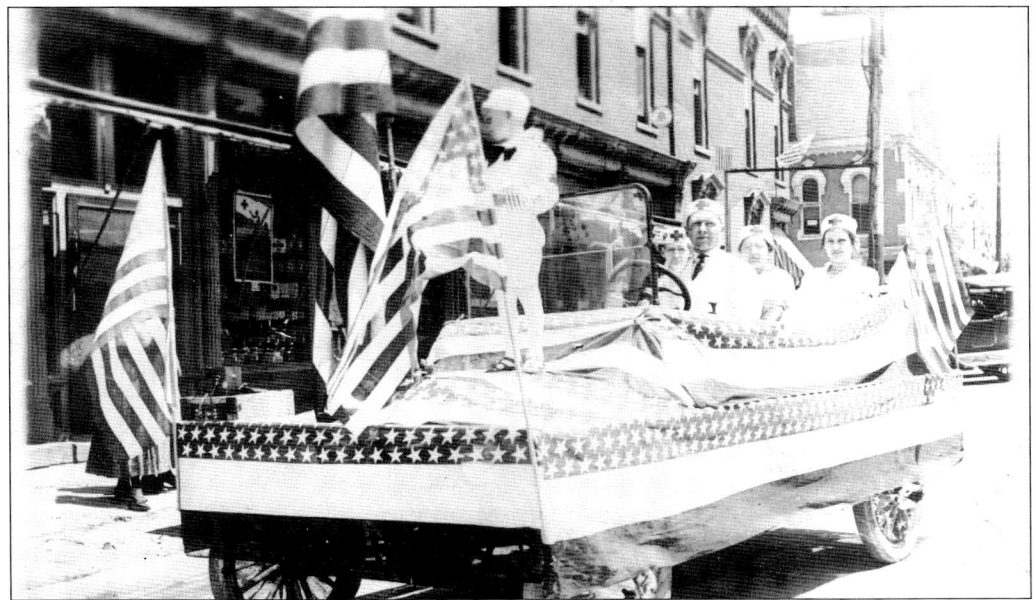

J. Earl Foreman drives what appears to be a Red Cross float in a 1918 parade in Winamac. This unit is proceeding west on Main Street past the Keller Block. There were two parades in Winamac that year, one for Decoration Day in May and the second in September for the annual Old Settlers picnic. The Red Cross was very active in 1918 during World War I. It ran a successful concession stand at the Old Settlers event. (PCHS Museum.)

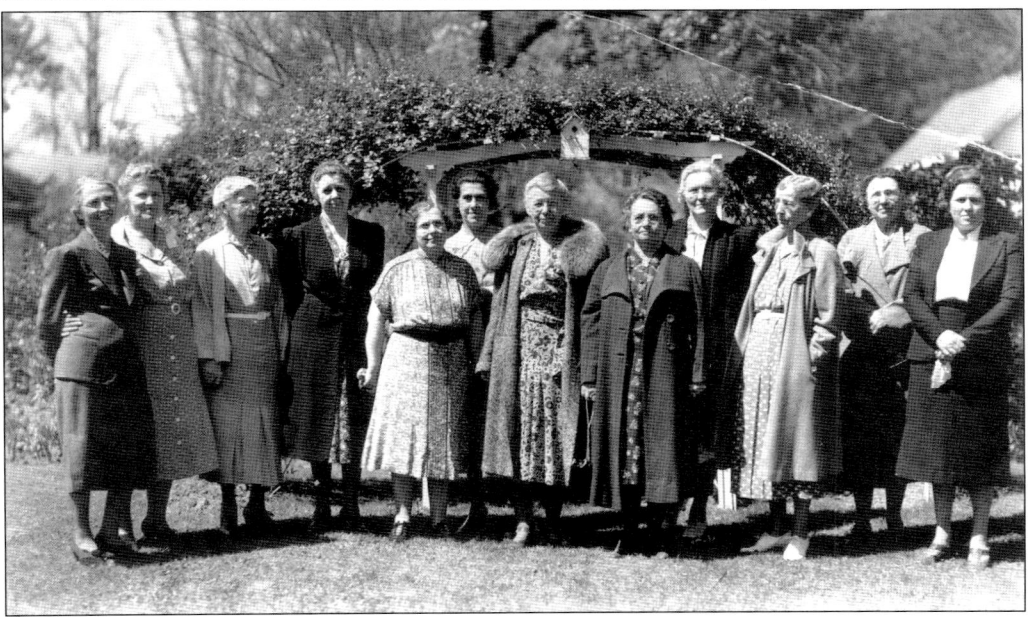

The Iris Elm Garden Club was founded in 1930 in Winamac. Club members gathered on May 12, 1939, for this breakfast at Mabel Hedge's home. From left to right are Ethel Shill, Mabel Hedges, Bessie Thompson, Cora Keller, Mamie Kocher (guest), Florence McCaskey, Stella McDowell, Pauline Gorrell, June Saidla, Kathryn Huddleston, Elnora Jackson, and Bernice Halleck. (PCHS Museum.)

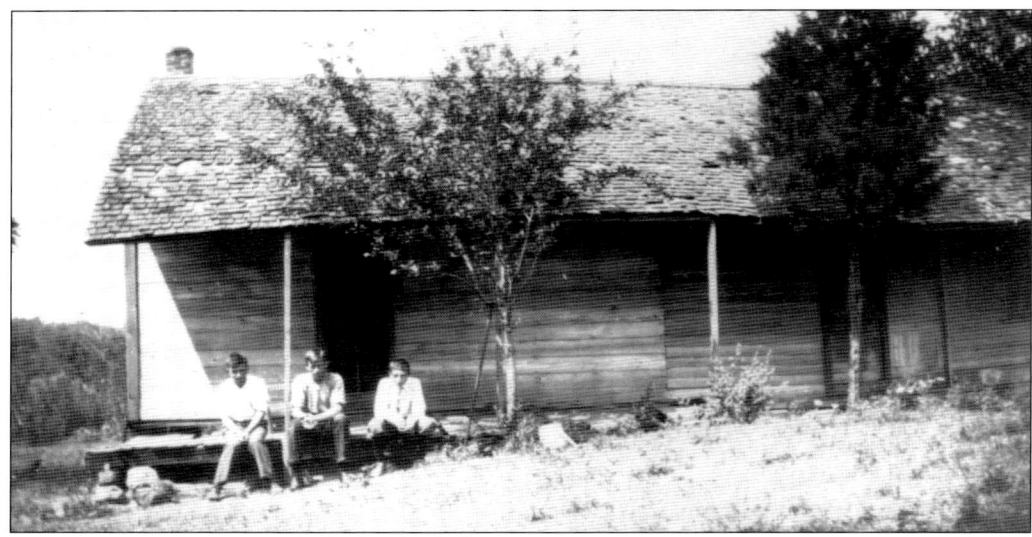

In the summer of 1911, these three young men appear to be whiling away some time on the porch of this rustic home in the Star City area. Two of them are Maurice Kahler and Walter Robinson. After graduation from Star City High School, Kahler earned a medical degree from Indiana University. He was a physician in Indianapolis for 60 years and then returned to Star City to practice from 1979 to 1982. (Neal Hiatt.)

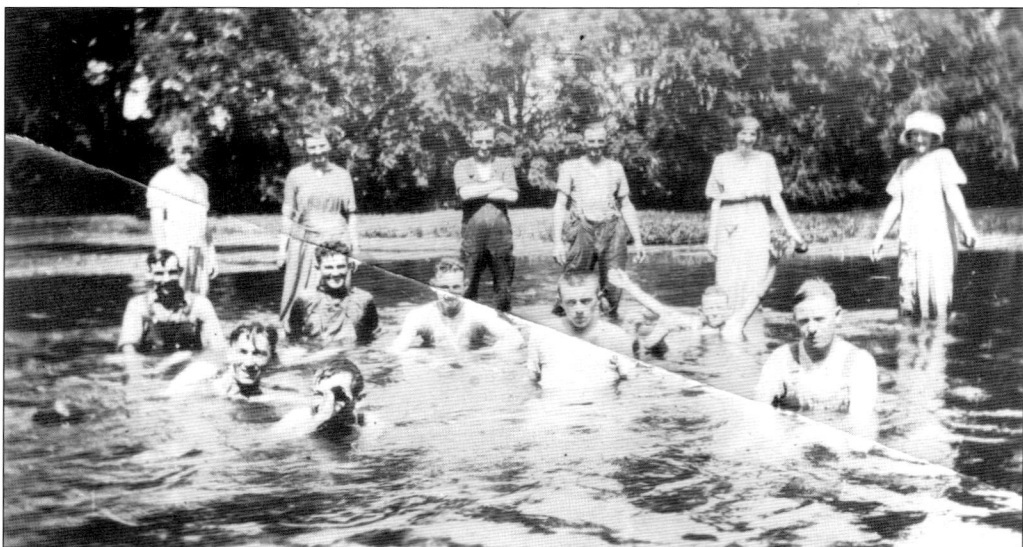

St. James Church of rural Francesville held this Sunday school picnic at the river near Pulaski in about 1910. Among those in the photograph are Marie Kruger Westphal, Minnie Kruger Cords, Herman Kruger, William Cords, Lola Westphal Busch, Ludwig Kruger, Charles Westphal, Ernest Cords, Fred Cords, Rudy Cords, Carl Cords, Everett Kruger, and Sam Busch. The St. James congregation was founded in the early 1860s by German immigrants to Beaver Township. German-language services were cut back to twice a month in 1919 and discontinued in 1925. (Shirley Cords Busch.)

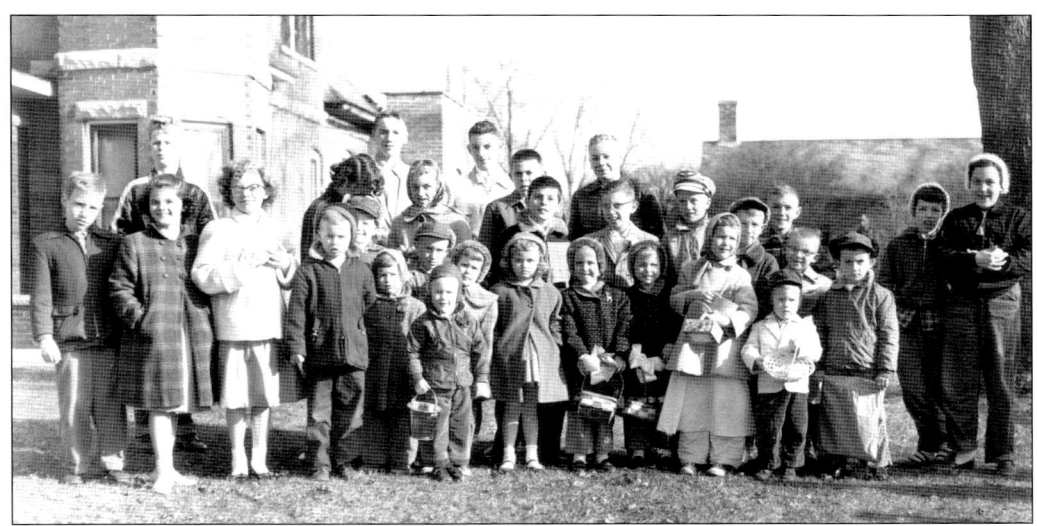

Community children look pleased with their discoveries following an Easter egg hunt at the Methodist church in Medaryville. The date is about 1957. The children from left to right are (first row) Bill Budd, unidentified, Jackie Runk, Rick Wappel, unidentified, Patrice Wappel, Denny Schultz, unidentified, Nancy Coburn, unidentified, Karon Sue and Linda Lou Risner (twins), Carol Rayonec, Bob White, and Gary Coburn; (second row) Don Wappel, unidentified, Carol Sue Sanders, unidentified, unidentified, John Wappel, Bob Schultz, Steven Fry, Mark Haring, Sandy Schultz, and unidentified; (third row) Wayne Mayhew, Raymond Conley, John Runk, and Robert Heath. (Olive White.)

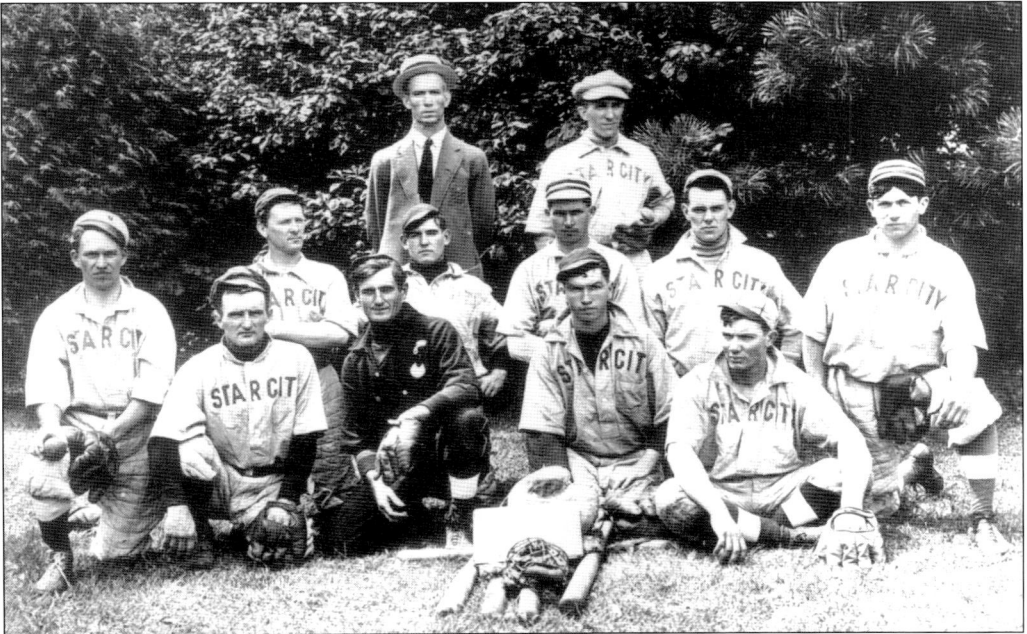

Star City fielded this baseball team in what was probably the 1920s. Team members are, from left to right, (first row) Tommy Heward, Newt Brown, Fon Gilsinger, Hale Fahler, and Merle Bowers; (second row) Harry Baker, Jimmy Witz, Cliff Baggerly, Neil Bott, and Vic Martin; (third row) Perry Calvin and Albert Yount. (PCHS Museum.)

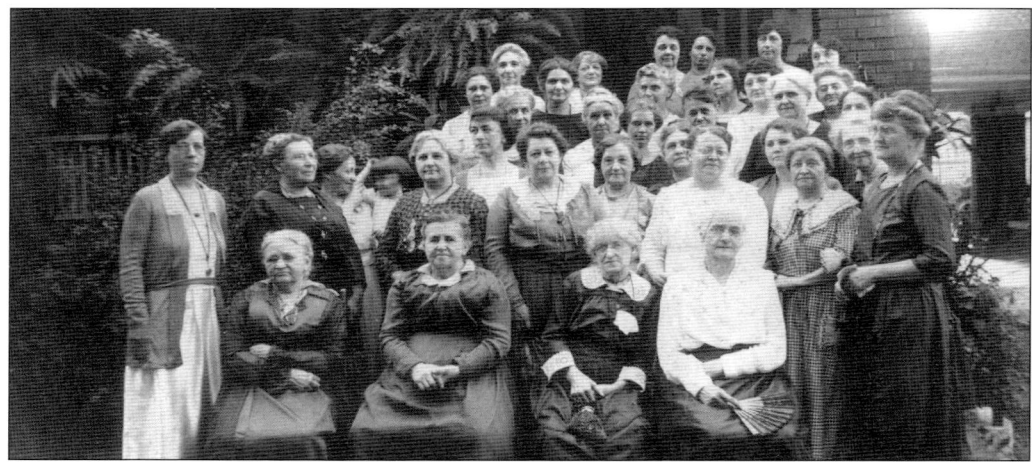

The Embroidery Club of Winamac observed its 25th anniversary at the home of Dora Keller on October 5, 1922. Those attending are, from left to right, (first row) unidentified, Mary Weaver, unidentified, and Ruth Manders; (second row) Belle Huddleston, Amanda Dilts, unidentified, unidentified, Dora Dukes, unidentified, Dora Keller, unidentified, and Elsie Hathaway; (third row) Viva Blinn holding Janet Gorrell and three unidentified; (fourth row) Katherine Cushing, Emily Benson, unidentified, Stella McDowell, Myrtle Starr, and unidentified; (fifth row) unidentified, Ina Terry, Bessie Thompson, Nettie Smith, unidentified, and Celia Haas; (sixth row) Emma Brown, unidentified, Cora Keller, Pauline Gorrell, Mayme Horner, and unidentified. (PCHS Museum, donated by William Starr.)

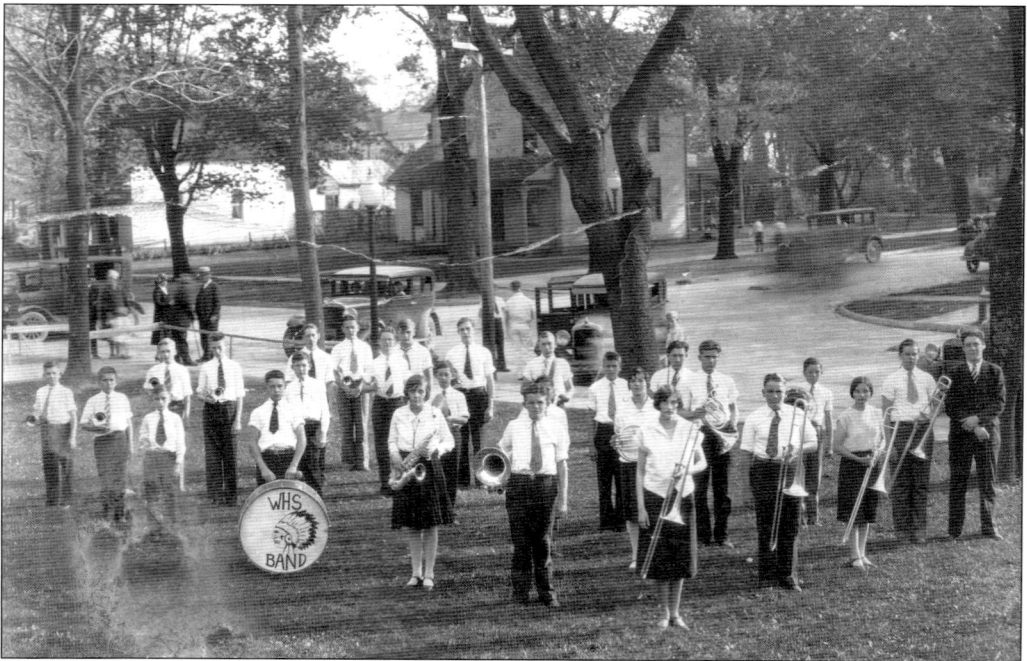

The Winamac High School band lines up on the lawn in front of the high school on Front Street in Winamac. The date is believed to be 1936. Russ H. Hughes was the band director. (Emily Russell.)

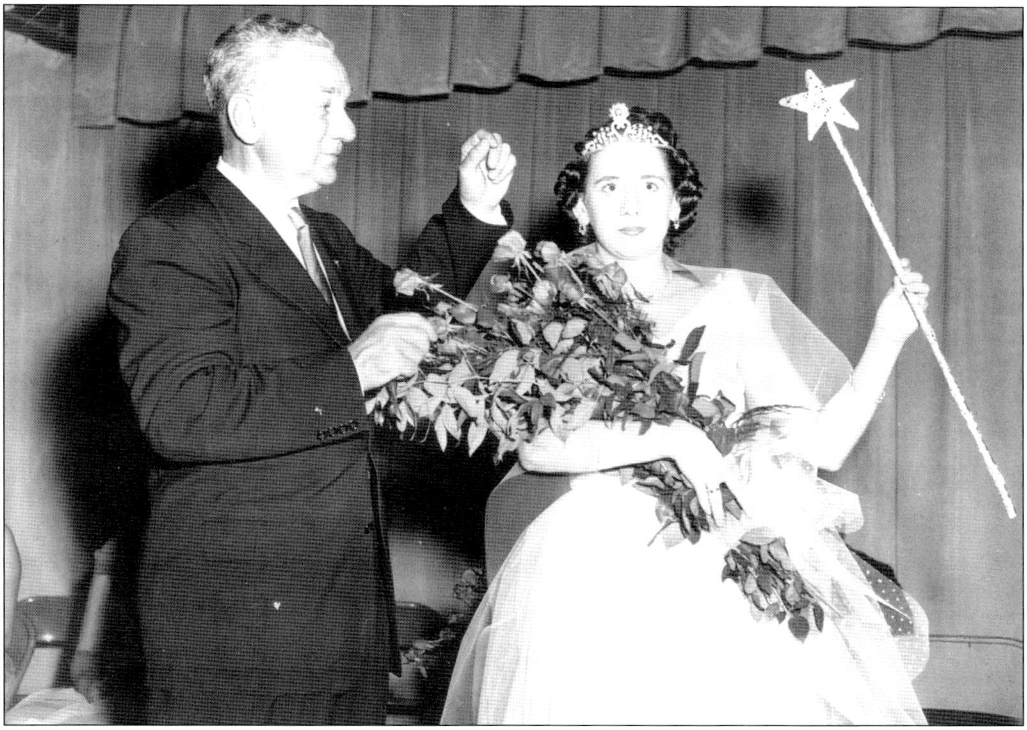

Shirley McCool was crowned queen of the Medaryville centennial in 1953. She is congratulated by Congressman Charles A. Halleck. (Olive White, photograph by O. H. White.)

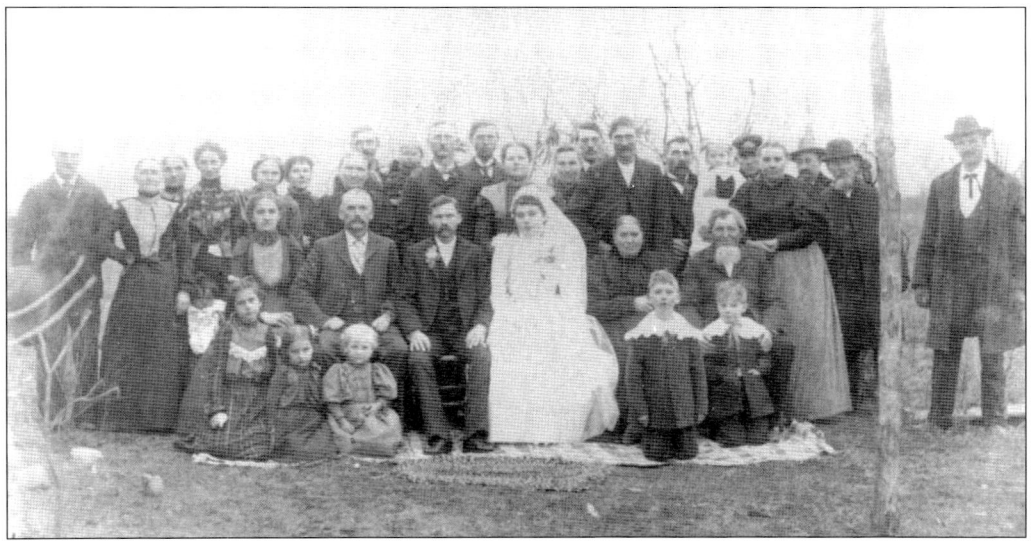

Lewis Edward Hertzberg and Marie Wilhelmina Schutterow were married at St. John's Church of Medaryville on December 3, 1899. The St. John congregation was established in Cass Township in 1862 and was then known as the German Evangelical Lutheran St. John Church. All the Schutterow family members changed their name to Shedrow except for the Christian Frederick Schutterow descendants who took the silent *e* out and made it Schuttrow. (Patrick Schuttrow, obtained from Linda Shedrow.)

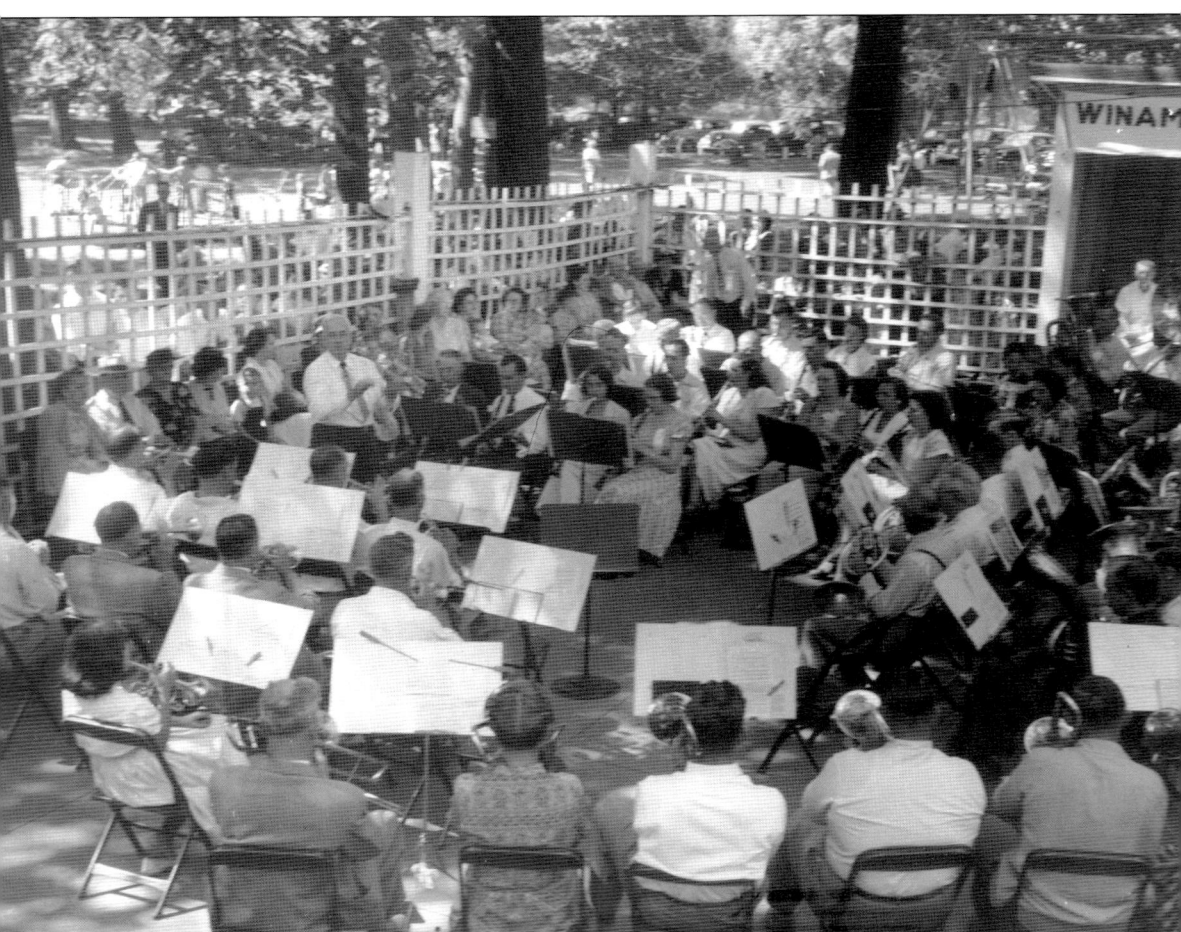

Old-timers speak nostalgically of the town band concerts that were held every Thursday night in summer on the courthouse square from 1916 through 1934. The band members were mostly from Winamac and included businessmen and college and high school students. During the last years, there were over 100 players in the band. While adults listened to the music, children played on the courthouse lawn and ate popcorn and peanuts sold at the newsstand for 5¢ a bag. Sometimes there was dancing, but it was difficult on the rough, brick street. In 1936, the first band reunion concert was held in conjunction with Old Settlers Day in the town park. It was such a huge success that the reunion concerts continued annually until 1965. The concerts usually began with a patriotic march, such as "Stars and Stripes Forever," then proceeded to old favorites like "Love's Old Sweet Song," "Little Brown Jug," or "Pop Goes the Weasel," and concluded with "Auld Lang Syne." This undated photograph shows one of the reunion concerts at the bandstand in the park. (PCHS Museum.)

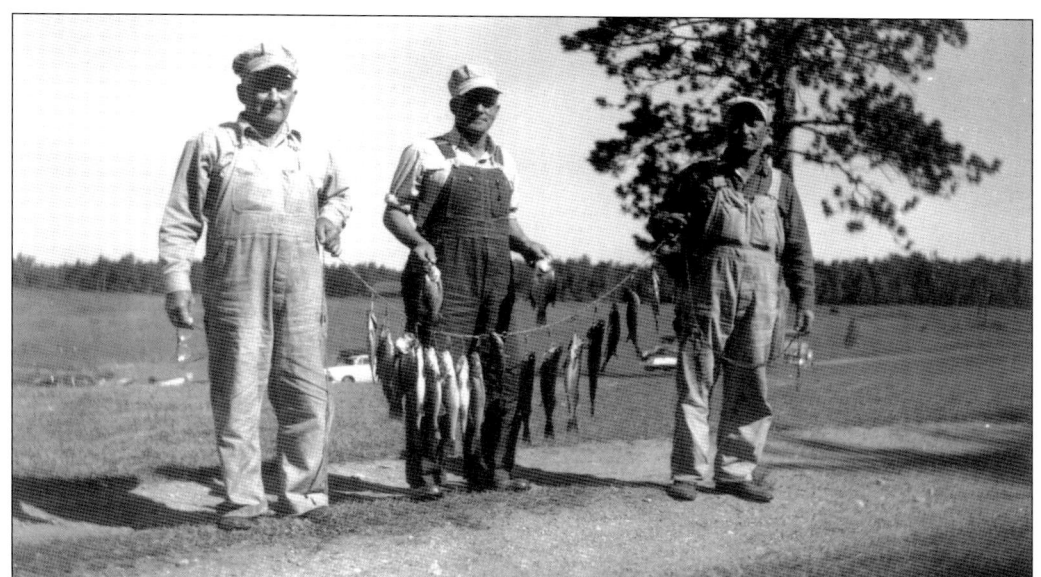

Blacksmith Lloyd Agnew and his companions return from a successful fishing trip in the Tippecanoe River, as evidenced in this 1940s photograph. (Donna Mohr Gates.)

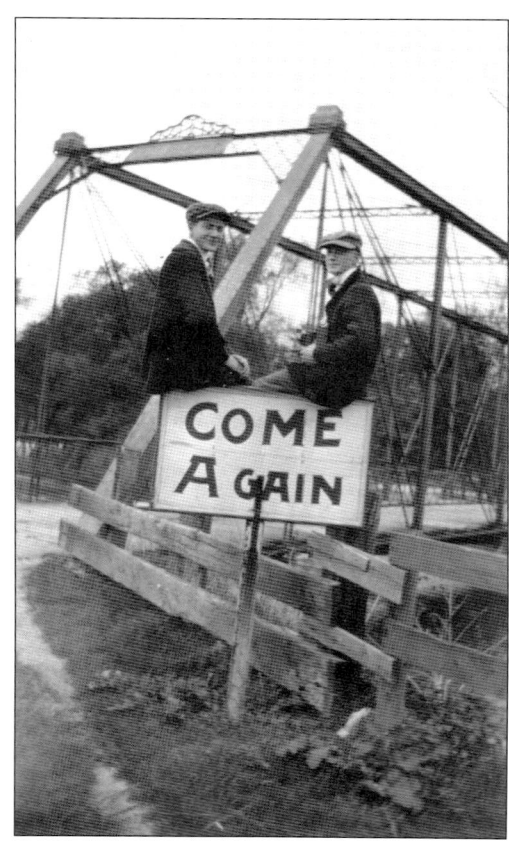

Joe Wentzel (left) and Fred Bauer perch in front of Monterey's original iron bridge over the Tippecanoe River and invite visitors to "come again." (Monterey-Tippecanoe Township Library.)

Across America, People are Discovering Something Wonderful. Their Heritage.

Arcadia Publishing is the leading local history publisher in the United States. With more than 3,000 titles in print and hundreds of new titles released every year, Arcadia has extensive specialized experience chronicling the history of communities and celebrating America's hidden stories, bringing to life the people, places, and events from the past. To discover the history of other communities across the nation, please visit:

www.arcadiapublishing.com

Customized search tools allow you to find regional history books about the town where you grew up, the cities where your friends and family live, the town where your parents met, or even that retirement spot you've been dreaming about.

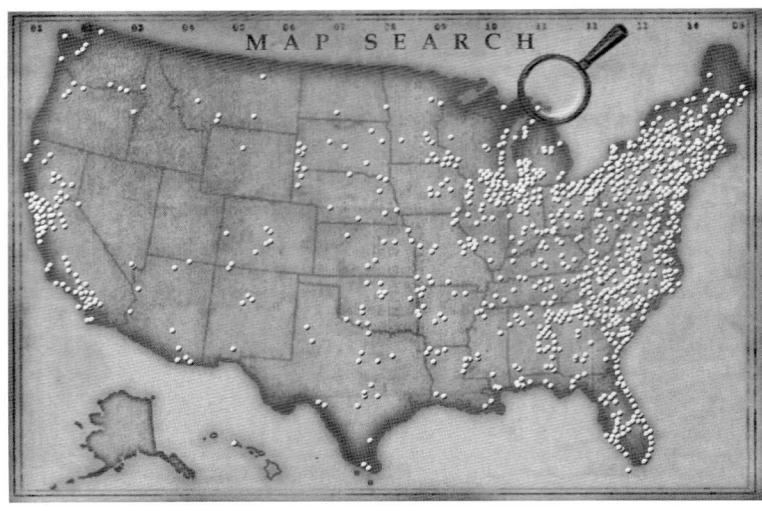